With warmest personal regards —
and the sincere hope you enjoy the book!

John Fricke

Inver Hills
Community College —

JUDY
GARLAND

A PORTRAIT IN ART & ANECDOTE

JOHN FRICKE

FOREWORD by LORNA LUFT

ART DIRECTION & DESIGN
RANSE RANSONE

BULFINCH PRESS
AOL TIME WARNER BOOK GROUP
BOSTON   NEW YORK   LONDON

For my sister, Patty,
for my brother, Michael,
and my sister-in-law, Linda,
and for my three nieces Erin, Noel, and Haley,
all of whom have been inundated with Judy Garland
and all of whom appreciate and enjoy that fact.

First Edition
ISBN 0-8212-2836-6
Library of Congress Control Number 2003103443

Bulfinch Press is a division of
AOL Time Warner Book Group.

PRINTED IN SINGAPORE

Page 1: *Judy Garland in a
rotogravure publicity pose, 1941.*

Pages 2–3: *At CBS Television City in
Los Angeles during the taping of* The
Judy Garland Show *TV series, 1963.*

This page: *M-G-M fashion
publicity still, circa 1944.*

Opposite: *January 1962, between
takes of the opening numbers for
her 1962 special (taped at NBC
in Burbank but televised on CBS).*

Foreword

There has been a lot written about my mother's life—some of it with informative heart, and some of it with only the author's personal agenda . . . for fiction! In this book, everyone has a chance to celebrate her talent, her artistry, her love of audiences, and the love that so many have felt for her in return, whether they were friends, coworkers, family, or fans.

There were a lot of things about my mother that I was too young to understand until I was an adult myself. When I was a child, it scarcely occurred to me how important and extraordinary "Judy Garland" was to the world. I'd be there in all her audiences, and everyone around me was going crazy: she was everybody's idol, everybody's icon. But she was my *mother*. And I was always looking forward to what would happen *after* the show: "Mama, can you please get off the stage, and can we go someplace?" (My daughter Vanessa reacts the same way when she comes to hear me; her attitude is always, "Could you hurry up and sing a little faster, so we can go out?") So she wasn't "Judy Garland" to me—she was Mama . . . and that was the kind of reality she brought to our lives.

As a parent, she was the best parent she knew how to be. And she always seemed to me to be ahead of her time, because we always knew how much she cared about us—my brother Joe, my sister Liza, and me. No matter what happened to her, no matter how difficult some moments might be or how angry she might be about something in her life, she always made it clear that those moments were not about us. We *always* knew we were loved.

She was also a great one for believing in personal, human values; that's what she taught us—both by her example and by her instruction. We were told: Be kind to people not as fortunate as you are. Don't brag. Always sign the autograph.

And always, *always* say "please" and "thank you." We were shown that it was very important to try to be kind and good human beings—because that's what *she* was.

There have been so many legends about the professionally "difficult" Judy Garland. As much as she had that reputation among some people, that wasn't what I ever saw as her daughter—whether in the midst of our incredibly fun times or in her really low moments. Those stories always seemed exaggerated to me . . . especially now when I hear about moments when I was there, and I *know* the events didn't happen as they're sometimes "remembered" by others. And if she was difficult at times, well—no wonder, given the pressures of always having to work, and raising three kids, and everything that went along with being "Judy Garland."

I first appeared with my mother on television, and then in summer stock and on Broadway at the Palace. On the stock tour, I picked my own songs—this was 1967, and I was doing some Petula Clark things—but first I brought the records to her to play for her approval. (I also did her own song, "In Between" from *Love Finds Andy Hardy*, just because I'd always loved it, and because it was written by Roger Edens, a wonderful man who had been part of her life since she was a little girl.) She would watch me when I worked, but she didn't coach or direct—she just stressed how important it was to be professional, to show up on time, and to *always* do the best you could. Again, I realize that goes against some of the legends about her, but I think it's very important to say that the only times she didn't show up or was late were those times when physically and mentally she just couldn't help herself; she was just worn out. And when you realize the body of work she achieved, during every decade of her life, you come to realize that very few people could accomplish what she did.

I was thrilled when John asked me to participate in this project. He has always presented my mother's legacy in a proper and loving way; her work in film, television, recordings, and concerts deserves no less. But his devotion to keeping her achievements in the public eye has been second to none, and this book is a beautiful example of that.

I have always told my children—both Vanessa and her brother Jesse—that, before Whitney, Britney, Barbra, Tina, or Madonna, there was Judy. She set the standards for all of entertainment. This book provides happy evidence of that, as well as of her humor, her heart, and her courage, just by letting her speak for herself and letting those who knew her best remember her as they do.

And as I do.

—*Lorna Luft*

Opposite: *At home in Los Angeles with baby Lorna, 1953.*

Right: *With Lorna (age seven) and her brother Joe (age five) in London, 1960.*

*W*hen she sang, God spoke."
— *W*hoopi *G*oldberg

Introduction

In June 1998, New York's Carnegie Hall paid tribute to the music of Judy Garland in two special concert performances. Veteran actor Robert Stack served as cohost for those sold-out evenings; he'd first met Judy in 1935, prior to the onset of either of their feature film careers, and their friendship continued for many years.

To kick off the Carnegie Hall event, Stack offered a thought-provoking and ultimately riveting perspective attendant to Garland's place in the entertainment pantheon. Judy Garland, he noted, would today be a show business legend if she had only played Dorothy in the 1939 film classic, *The Wizard of Oz*. Or if she had only performed as the preeminent female musical motion picture star of the 1940s and early 1950s in such vehicles as *Meet Me in St. Louis*, *Easter Parade*, and *A Star Is Born*. Or if she had only achieved her stage and concert career at the Palace Theatre, the Metropolitan Opera House, and Carnegie Hall in New York; the Palladium in London; and the Hollywood Bowl in Los Angeles. Or if she had only appeared on her celebrated television specials and TV series for CBS, or on her many recordings for the Decca and Capitol labels.

But, as Stack concluded, in a career that spanned nearly forty-five of her forty-seven years, Judy Garland did all of that and much more.

A prodigious amount of rapturously acclaimed multimedia accomplishment is, of course, not unique to Judy Garland. The preservation and presentation of visual and vocal ability was first made possible by the technical discoveries of the late-nineteenth and twentieth centuries. Since then, there have been a number of other entertainers—among the very best in their fields—who have left a remarkable legacy in a varied body of work or who continue to enrich their already exemplary professional reputations.

However, only a very few of those performers have flourished across seven decades, their powers oblivious to changing tastes in entertainment and music. Arguably, the most transcendent of all of them is Judy Garland. Her penchant for professional "comebacks" during the last two decades of her life was something the press never failed to exploit (and which she herself never failed to self-deprecatingly mock: "I'm the Queen of the Comebacks!"). But even given the inherent hyperbole and show business overkill of Garland's sobriquets, there was very little verbal or media challenge when she was described and billed during her lifetime as "a living legend" and the "world's greatest entertainer."

What is further unique to Judy Garland is the frequency and level of rediscovery continually inspired by her talent. Since her death in 1969, her abilities not only have been repeatedly remembered and embraced but have proved to be powerfully, emotionally timeless and, as they were during her career, cross-generational in appeal. Some of the ongoing praise for Garland comes from her peers, her contemporary critics, and the fans who grew up with (or at least watching) her. But an equal amount of jubilation now rises as well from the much younger but maturing reviewers and audiences of today. Millions have come to Judy in the decades since her passing; their initial, unforgettable encounter invariably occurred with Dorothy Gale from Kansas, but—in the new millennium world of cable and satellite transmission, home video, compact disc reissue, and the Internet—they can more quickly than ever discover that the Yellow Brick Road led to an overwhelming series of triumphs for the four-foot-eleven-inch girl from Grand Rapids, Minnesota.

Those who experienced her live theater work correctly argue that one needed to see Judy Garland perform in person to experience the full impact of her charisma. Such magnetism stemmed from an uncommon, singular amalgam of ability coupled with what a Garland coworker once appreciatively described as "a force field around her that was so powerful, it would reach the back of the house." Yet that potency—both during her lifetime and since—remains remarkably undiluted as well in its ability to impact even through the "cold" media of film, video, disc, and audiotape. As a recorded image, Garland continues to explode: an unsurpassed presence and a deeply felt emotional experience.

As such, she still reaches even the most stringently critical audiences. In autumn 2000, a Manhattan inner-city high school teacher showed Garland's rendition of "Battle Hymn of the Republic" to a United States history class immersed in studies of the Civil War. The performance had double relevance; as the teacher explained, Judy had performed it on a January 1964 episode of her CBS-TV series in unspoken tribute to President John F. Kennedy, who had been assassinated the previous November.

Raised in the quick-edit, lip-synched era of MTV, the students were initially disconcerted but ultimately electrified at the sight of someone standing and singing so passionately, alive and unencumbered. They knew Dorothy Gale; they were unprepared for Judy Garland. When she finished, there was an almost religious hush in the sometimes rowdy room. Then one student quietly ventured, "Is she dead?" A classmate rhetorically and almost omnisciently answered, "Who could sing like that and live?"

Judy Garland sang with richness, purity, and power. Her acting possessed equal sincerity, which made her real and believable in even the most lightweight of musical comedy scripts. She danced with such flair that critic Judith Crist once defined Garland as the only partner of Fred Astaire and Gene Kelly who was capable of drawing audience attention away from those extraordinary men.

Opposite: The joy of Judy Garland was seldom better manifested than in the penultimate moments and notes of "Hello, Bluebird," here being sung onstage at the London Palladium in May 1962. This particular performance would provide one of the highlights of her final film, I Could Go On Singing, *released the following spring.*

Her intelligence, ebullient personality, and comic timing made her even more entertaining onstage or on television than she was in the context of a film role.

Though motion pictures provided her worldwide fame, Garland had her heart and heritage firmly rooted in stage work. Excerpts from three contemporary critiques of her theatrical performances provide both a time capsule of that aspect of her career and a fair approximation of the professional reverberation her appearance could elicit—even during an era when professional critics were very seldom given to overstatement:

She sang in a way that produced in the audience sensations that haven't been equalled in years. She has the divine instinct to be herself on the stage, along with a talent for singing, a trick of rocking the spectators with rhythms, and a capacity for putting emotion into her performance that suggests what Sarah Bernhardt must have been . . . simple, sincere feeling that reaches the heart.

Her sense of rhythm and projection is simply amazing. Hundreds of people fought their way down the aisles to get a nearer look. After the last number had been repeated, and the entire audience seemed to move forward as in a gigantic ocean wave, the lights were finally lowered to an accompaniment of quasi-hysterical cries and shrieks.

We found her last evening to be an enchanting entertainer, an exquisite artist. . . . Her distinctive personality was intact, her mode of delivery strong and glowing, her personal charm indisputable. Her voice was bright with infectious vitality—it struck sparks. All the spectators arose and cheered; people streamed down the side aisles to applaud as near to the star as possible. She had a great triumph.

Perhaps even someone reasonably familiar with Judy Garland's history would consider the foregoing reviews as accompaniment to such a signal success as her first Broadway stage triumph in 1951 or her concert resurgence in 1961. True, Garland's working career covered five decades: the 1920s, 1930s, 1940s, 1950s, and 1960s. And there was indeed an almost laughably frequent Mount Everest-like range of performing pinnacles throughout many of those years. But 1951 and 1961 are generally conceded to be apex moments.

Remarkably, those three critical estimations are drawn from three different decades and span nearly thirty-five years of journalism. The first, excerpted from the appreciation of a Los Angeles journalist, describes his exposure to the twelve-year-old pre-Metro-Goldwyn-Mayer Garland in 1934. The second encompasses quotes from the Philadelphia critics, reviewing Judy at age twenty-one in her very first concert appearance, held at the outdoor Robin Hood Dell (where 15,000 people crowded into an amphitheater meant to hold 5,000, and 15,000 more were turned away). The final comments summarize the reactions of critics in Denmark, preconditioned by years of adverse publicity, who were, on the evening in question, getting their first glimpse of "Judy Garland live." She was forty-six; that Copenhagen performance in 1969 would be the final concert of her career.

Naurally, there are thousands of similar quotes from professional journalists—and perhaps a like amount from the hundreds of coworkers, friends, and family members who knew Judy Garland personally and professionally. Such opinions create an extraordinary portrait of her capacity to care and share, as well as an understanding of her inability to hold anything back, onstage or off.

Of course, the sensitivity that was paramount among Garland's personal and professional hallmarks could sometimes distance her from those viewers or listeners who were unable to deal with the authenticity and actuality of that kind of emotion. Additionally, the vulnerability that made her an original as both performer and human being left her infinitely more susceptible to the pressures of life in show business—even while such stress was readily absorbed by many of the more impervious souls around her. Regrettably (if understandably), Judy's emotional fragility would lose the battle again and again when pitted against the manipulative, sometimes abusive, and overwhelmingly commercial world of entertainment.

As a result, the decades of Garland's accomplishments have often been overshadowed by the media's disproportionate concentration on her consequent personal travail. Illnesses and hospitalizations, overwork and battles with prescription medication, canceled concerts and aborted film roles, multiple marriages and premature death were all described in detail as they happened. Since her passing, Garland's reputation has been further dragged through the muck by a score of biographies and documentaries, many grossly inaccurate and lacking in perspective.

But if these have been read and watched, they have also to some extent been dismissed. In this more informed era, the public can bring its own perspective to the family dysfunction, financial mismanagement, and substance abuse to which Garland fell prey. (They would also support the rationale put forth by one of Judy's wiser biographers, who pointedly told an interviewer in 1969 that there are many people who marry more than once, have emotional problems, and die young . . . and contribute nothing else to the world.) Given the pleasure Garland's work continues to provide—and as more and more accurate information becomes available about the reasons behind Garland's problems—her audiences, young and old, are ever more able to draw their own conclusions about both the human being and the performer, well beyond any media muckraking.

During her lifetime, Garland made monumental efforts to rise above and carry on despite any problems or rumors. (As early as 1959, she sagely dismissed a lot of conjecture with the blithe observance "So much hooey about me has been published . . . ") While she would at times privately rant and rail about the vicissitudes of her day-to-day life, she seldom offered any public complaint. Judy was more likely to burlesque that aspect of her public image, kidding about herself in the third person as she impersonated an imaginary friend: "Judy? Oh, she's *marvelous*. A *marvelous* lady. Poor girl. What's she doing now? I feel so *sorry* for her. I can't wait to see her again. . . . I hope she doesn't fall down."

For Garland, saving emotional grace often came in the presence of her three children; Judy was always acknowledged by family and friends as someone who did the best she could to support her children with love. She was more successful at some moments than others, but she was also a working—and often single—

Opposite: *Rotogravure portraits like this one, taken in 1940, served to hype the ever-increasing Garland product. Between that year and the next, she starred in six motion pictures (four of them with Mickey Rooney), made regular radio appearances (including a stint as the weekly vocalist and comic foil for Bob Hope on* The Pepsodent Show*), and cut discs for Decca Records (including the chart-riding "I'm Nobody's Baby").*

mother, long before society would generally comprehend the difficulties of such a role. Despite the sometime hell of their experiences together, all three of Garland's children are on public and private record with respect to the unwavering affection and laughter they shared with her. As daughter Lorna Luft has definitely pronounced in recent years, "Yes, tragic things happened to my mother. But *she* was not a tragedy."

Whatever the misbegotten media image of "poor Judy" over the past decades, Garland's talent and truth in performance have never failed to re-establish her. In 2001, journalist Matt Roush accurately summarized Garland as "the mercurial entertainer whose personal, financial, and physical calamities always threatened to eclipse her reputation . . . until she sang." In the past fifteen years, Judy's prestige has been additionally well served by the work of archivists and historians and their discovery of hours of Garland audio and visual rarities, unheard or unseen for decades. Such findings have included many of the original prerecordings for her films, covering material from the 1930s to the 1960s; home movies of her live performances from the 1950s and 1960s; and the master tapes (including outtakes) from her 1963–64 television series. Ironically, but happily, the vast majority of this material gives the lie to any negative Garland legend or temperamental behavior. The very few comparatively minor flashes of frustration are self-directed; what is again and again apparent is the work ethic she possessed and Garland's quiet determination to better herself and her performance. As one producer noted with satisfaction, such findings "belie the Hollywood mythology that surrounds her career. . . . What we hear is a consummate professional, having a great time and connecting with her innate, brilliant musicianship."

The litany of Judy Garland's professional achievement is traced in the ensuing pages, but it should be noted in brief that:

From age two until age thirteen (even before going to M-G-M) she performed in hundreds of vaudeville and radio shows with her two older sisters.

She appeared in thirty-two feature films, did voice-over work for two more, and was featured in at least a half-dozen short subjects. (For her screen work, she received a special Academy Award and was nominated for two others.)

She starred in thirty of her own television shows—Garland and those programs garnering ten Emmy nominations—and she guest-starred on nearly thirty others.

She fulfilled more than 1,100 theater, nightclub, and concert appearances between 1951 and 1969, and won a special Tony Award for the first of three record-breaking engagements at the Palace Theatre in New York.

She recorded nearly a hundred singles and more than a dozen record albums. One of these, *Judy at Carnegie Hall*, received an unprecedented five Grammys in 1962 (including Album of the Year) and was on the charts for more than ninety weeks—thirteen of those weeks as the number one bestselling record in the nation.

She appeared on nearly 300 different radio broadcasts and sang at countless benefits and in personal appearances for the military before, during, and after World War II. In 1967–68, she toured military hospitals in Boston, Washington, D.C., and Chicago to bolster those who had served in Vietnam.

At the height of Garland's 1961 career revival, *Show Business Illustrated* magazine offered a similar recap of her life (if only to that date) and opined that "one would have to be a very strong elf to survive it all." There were eight more years of equally hard work yet to come for Judy Garland, but—throughout past, present, and future—there was one principal, personal quality that sustained the "very strong elf." Even Mike Wallace, in a somewhat dour *60 Minutes* television remembrance of Garland in 1975, had to concede that Judy had "a terrific sense of humor. Everyone we talked to said that."

Today, Garland's humor and laughter remain a favorite memory of those who spent years in her company. "Nobody could laugh, *nobody* could laugh like Judy," offers comedian Alan King. "She had a laugh like a horse . . . a roar!" Coming from a different but equally valid point of view, composer Hugh Martin wonderingly asks, "Has there ever been a more beautiful laugh? To me, it was like a beautiful waterfall sound, a cascade. . . . It's like a song, it's a musical number, it really is. You feel it's had an orchestration and everything!" Scenarist Leonard Gershe confirms both perspectives: "She could roar with laughter and then laugh in a melodic way. Her speaking voice was mellifluous: it tinkled, like ice in a glass; it went up and down. And her laugh was like that."

In addition to her own joy in laughter, to this day Garland sustains a reputation as one of the wittiest women in show business. In 1977 Lucille Ball remembered Judy as "the funniest woman in Hollywood" and—whether in impromptu one-liner or full-blown anecdote—Garland repeatedly substantiated the claim. In the depths of her problems, she could shrug and grinningly offer, "Behind every cloud . . . there's another cloud." When she agreed to leave her footprints in a slab of wet concrete for a town wall of fame in Manchester, England, Garland was asked to prepare by first washing her feet in olive oil; in the process, she looked up and muttered to no one in particular, "Now I know what a salad feels like." When she finally stepped into the cement mixture, it began to settle faster than anticipated, and she was quick to leap out, later offering, "I could just see myself, stuck there forever, with people wandering by and commenting, 'There's Judy Garland, plastered as usual.'"

Judy's own career anecdotes date back to her earliest credits. One of the "little people" cast as a Munchkin in *The Wizard of Oz* (per Garland: "a gentleman who was about forty") repeatedly approached her for a date. The sixteen-year-old Dorothy Gale politely demurred, but he persisted, finally backing her into a corner to candidly declare, "Judy, I want to make love to you." She looked down at the diminutive man and riposted, "Well, if you do, and I ever find out about it . . . !"

Some twenty-eight years later, *Oz* was still a talking point as Judy wryly told Barbara Walters about the repercussions of having a famous—if apparently not quite famous enough—theme song from that film:

I [engaged] a lawyer recently . . . and he was married to a German countess. And he was very *aware* of his wife being a German countess. And I met her, finally, at my house, and she kept requesting me to sing "*Unter* de Rainbow"! Now I wanted to stay in good with my lawyer, but his wife kept asking me to sing "*Unter* de Rainbow." So I finally had to say, "Agnes, it's '*Over* the Rainbow'!" And she said, "No, no! Sing '*Unter* de Rainbow.' Or 'Four Coins in de Fountain.'"

Even in the face of public embarrassment, Garland knew the value of both humor and class behavior. The Reverend Peter Delaney was one of her great good friends in England, and he remembers "being with her when a newspaper carried a most scathing article about her personal life. Her reaction was not one of anger; she simply picked up the phone, asked for the author, and in a quiet voice said, 'Before you printed this, why didn't you ask me? It could have been much funnier.'"

Judy once drily told daughter Liza Minnelli that she planned an autobiography to be titled *Ho-Hum: My Life*. But when a two-part Garland article actually appeared in *McCall's* magazine in 1964, it was headlined "There'll Always Be an Encore." Judy couldn't have realized it at the time, but the selected title was infinitely more accurate and prophetic. After she died, her "eternal fame" was heralded by the *National Observer*, which gave the cornerstone of her legend as *The Wizard of Oz*. It was a canny prediction; thanks to now nearly five decades of national telecasts, more than twenty years of home video, and the combined power of interpretation, story, and song, *Oz* has made it virtually impossible to find anyone in the United States over the age of two who doesn't recognize Judy as Dorothy.

Oz can also be perceived on a grander level as the happily symbolic echo of Garland's own life and times: the little girl from the Midwest, swept away by the tornadic forces of an incomparable talent to a fantasy land called Hollywood. Along the way, she shared herself with an unparalleled generosity; the towering achievement of Judy's subsequent success serves as a happy reminder that, if indeed only Judy Garland could have so unforgettably portrayed Dorothy, then only Judy Garland could transcend Dorothy a million times over as well.

One final comment from another Dorothy. Dorothy Gilmore Raye was an M-G-M contract dancer in the 1940s; her versatility and talent meant that she appeared with or observed every major musical star of that era. For her, they all paled by comparison to Garland, and with an immediate smile and happy (if equally immediate) tears in her eyes, she now adds swiftly, clearly, and concisely: "Judy Garland was a gift from heaven. And the world was the beneficiary of that gift."

Not coincidentally, it is also the stance taken by many of Garland's better-known collaborators. Bing Crosby, Noël Coward, Fred Astaire, Mickey Rooney, Frank Sinatra, and Tony Bennett have all gone on record with similar declarative statements about Judy Garland. Given their fervor and knowledgeability, given the facts of her career, given the contribution she made on a personal level to her friends and coworkers (and their appreciation), and given the laughter and the ongoing music she provides, the joy of Judy Garland deserves not only remembrance but emphasis, underscoring, and—at last—equal time.

Thus, this celebration.

In her first comeback, Garland played to rapturous crowds at New York's Palace Theatre for nineteen weeks during the 1951–52 Broadway season. The tramp costume was a holdover from her 1948 screen triumph, Easter Parade, in which she and Fred Astaire introduced the comic song and dance "A Couple of Swells." The number had been written by the redoubtable Irving Berlin and—whether with another random partner in her stage shows or as a solo on television in the 1960s—it became one of Judy's signature routines.

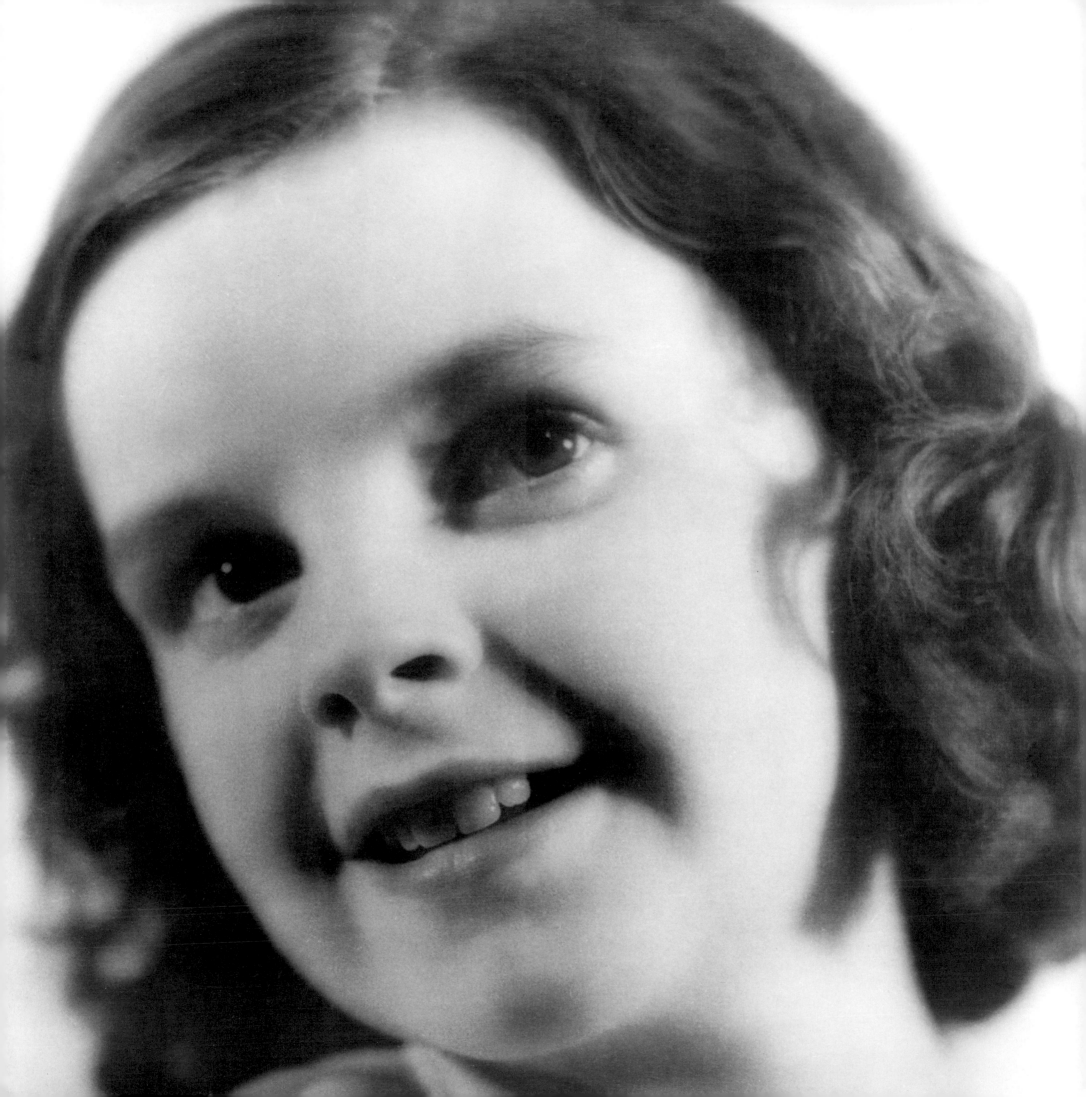

the 1920s

Judy Garland often included Noël Coward's "If Love Were All" in her latter-day concert and television repertoire. Not surprisingly, she brought especially telling emotion to that song's lyrical reflection on the "talent to amuse" possessed by an effective entertainer. It is a simple credo, but the phrase serves well as a succinct definition of Garland's own unique talent, born in and growing from the now almost-forgotten passion of vaudeville and music hall. A vigorous, live, "hot" entertainment that flourished early in the twentieth century, vaudeville created a new breed of popular performer. They were the artists who at best inspired, excited, and directly reached out to their audiences in a participatory program of superior ability and all-embracing, uplifting personality.

Eventually, vaudeville would be chilled, replaced, and virtually dismissed by the much cooler electronic media. But Judy carried the fervor of its communicative power into everything she did. Her versatility, her total lack of artifice, and the honesty and reality she brought to every song, role, and performing moment were contributing factors to the magic. Her style and approach, however, were part of her heritage, inherent from the very beginning: one worked for and to please an audience. When she died, more than forty-four years after her show business debut, her achievement was proudly summarized in one of many newspaper editorials: "Judy Garland dedicated her life to entertaining people. And in that she succeeded as few others have."

Garland's parents were small-time vaudevillians. After virtually singing his way through school in Tennessee, her father, Frank Gumm, took to the road in everything from minstrel shows to carnivals. He finally settled into theater work, alternating as a solo act and as the vocalist who led audience sing-a-longs between showings of silent motion pictures. Gumm's travels eventually led him to Superior, Wisconsin, where (after a sporadic courtship) he wed Ethel Milne, a transplanted Michigan pianist who accompanied whatever films and entertainers played the local show house.

Within weeks of their marriage in January 1914, the Gumms relocated to Grand Rapids, Minnesota, where Frank managed the New Grand Theater and Ethel played the pit piano. There was a brief attempt at wider, touring success as "Jack and Virginia Lee, Sweet Southern Singers," but the couple thereafter settled into a quiet family existence in the tiny North Country town. Daughter Mary Jane (later Suzanne or Susie) was born in 1915, and daughter Dorothy Virginia (later Jimmie) arrived in 1917. Frank and Ethel continued to entertain during movie intermissions at the theater, and both girls were logically, if informally, incorporated into their parents' occasional stage act.

On June 10, 1922, a third and final Gumm was born. Mother and father had planned on a boy to be named after Frank, but the tiny daughter was christened instead Frances Ethel and—from the onset—nicknamed Baby. By age two, the youngest Gumm was already singing in her sisters' backyard shows for neighborhood friends and clamoring for the chance to perform in the family act.

Finally, on December 26, 1924, The Gumm Sisters made their official debut as a trio at the New Grand, singing "When My Sugar Walks Down the Street." Baby was scheduled to cap the appearance in a one-verse-and-chorus solo rendition of "Jingle Bells." Instead, and to the delight of the hometown audience, the thirty-month-old gleefully refused to leave the stage. She went into reprise after reprise of her song, ringing a prop dinner bell and ultimately running in little circles in her excitement and reaction to the uproarious response from the crowd. Her grandmother finally had to stalk on from the wings and haul her off as Baby protested, "I wanna sing some *more!*"

Local residents remembered for decades afterward the already apparent vocal strength of the diminutive girl, and what was even then a God-given (if fledgling) charisma and sense of spontaneity. With Baby's success, the girls continued to perform together, both locally and in nearby towns; in the summer of 1926, the whole family took a West Coast vacation and, along the way, sang in more than a half-dozen minor venues across the northern United States. Frank and Ethel revived "Jack and Virginia Lee" on those occasions, after which the girls went on as a trio; Baby's Charleston dance was the highlight of their routine. (The proud father sent back periodic reports to the *Itasca County Independent*, a weekly local newspaper which on June 19 noted that the Gumms were "Progressing Toward the West: A card from Frank Gumm . . . located him and family at Shelby, Mont., where they had just appeared at a theater with gratifying results.")

Once on the Coast, Frank and Ethel were irresistibly drawn to the climate and burgeoning entertainment forums of southern California. Though they returned to Grand Rapids on schedule in July—and despite Frank's declaration to the *Independent* that home "after all, is the BEST place"—the Gumms were packed and gone for good by October. After five months' residency in and around Los Angeles, they relocated to Lancaster, California, three hours north of the city. Frank took over, renovated, and managed the Valley Theatre; Ethel again played piano, and the girls sang and danced.

The remainder of the decade played out with a continuation of that basic family pattern. But The Gumm Sisters were gradually becoming more and more active; apart from performances on their father's stage, there were local

---

Opposite: *Baby Gumm, circa 1929. More than forty years later, her Sunday school teacher Irma Story would describe the child even then as having "a sparkle to her." Another Lancaster resident recalled Baby's voice at the time: "Loud! It blasted out in that theater without a microphone . . . we loved it."*

parties, benefits, school shows, and cause-and-effect jobs out of town: one appearance led to another.

Life was an increasing dichotomy, especially for Baby: she disliked being torn from playtime with friends for auditions and rehearsals, but she loved the chance to sing to audiences who were genuinely receptive to a tiny child with a resonant voice and an undeniable appeal.

By September 1928, The Gumm Sisters were semi-absorbed into The Meglin Kiddies, an enormous group of aspiring professional children who trained at the Ethel Meglin Dance School. Even surrounded by dozens of others, however, Baby's ability stood out; when the troupe performed a week-long Christmas engagement at the Loew's State Theatre in Los Angeles, she was assigned a solo and dressed as Cupid to sing (as presumably only a six-year-old could) "I Can't Give You Anything but Love."

One of those December appearances was caught by famed vaudeville impresario Gus Edwards and, per legend, he either sought out the girl back-stage or arranged shortly thereafter to interview her and her sisters at Metro-Goldwyn-Mayer, where he was planning a series of musical shorts. At the meeting, Baby was suffering an infected lip, a stye in one eye, and the results of a disastrous home permanent: "I couldn't see, my eye was practically shut, my mouth was swollen with the cold sore, and my hair looked like Topsy's after a pillow fight. [But] Mr. Edwards told my mother that my sisters and I should resume our trio singing—'With her ear,' he said, 'nothing musical is beyond her.' I remember his exact words on account of how I thought he mentioned my ear because my ears were the only parts of me that were not disfigured!"

Edwards's recommendation led The Gumm Sisters to develop musical arrangements as a three-part-harmony group, providing a solid musical back-ground against which the junior member could shine. By 1929, the girls were enjoying their greatest opportunities to date: a semi-regular local radio slot; more—and better—stage appearances outside Lancaster; and, under the Ethel Meglin aegis, their motion picture debut.

The Big Revue was shot within days of Baby's seventh birthday, and The Gumm Sisters were afforded one of the film's few individual showcases amidst the en masse routines of the rest of The Meglin Kiddies. Seen today, the Gumms' rendition of "That's the Good Old Sunny South" remains entertaining only because of the presence of the future Judy Garland. Although Baby does little more than holler her vocal line, her stare-down-the-camera nonchalance and her intense ease in delivering the accompanying choreography befit the entertainer to whom performance would always seem an integral aspect of her persona.

By autumn 1929, the girls had left the Meglin group and joined Flynn O'Malley's Hollywood Starlets; Ethel was employed as accompanist and vocal coach for the entire unit of about twenty girls. In turn, O'Malley then sent mother and daughters to Roy Mack at Warner Bros., who put The Gumm Sisters into three additional musical film shorts between November and early January. Released by First National–Vitaphone Pictures, *A Holiday in Storyland*, *The Wedding of Jack and Jill*, and *Bubbles* afforded the girls the chance to appear as a trio in each scenario. But Baby's individual charm was once again recognized, and she was also given solo songs: "Blue Butterfly" in *A Holiday in Storyland* and the almost laughably prophetic "Hang On to a Rainbow" in *The Wedding of Jack and Jill*.

It was an auspicious professional finale for the decade, although the emotional and physical problems that would beset Garland for the rest of her life had also manifested themselves by the late 1920s. Her parents' marriage had long been a rocky one; Grand Rapids rumors about Frank's homosexual activities—and the corresponding displeasure of some of the local citizenry—were purportedly part of the reason for the family move to California in 1926. (Nine years later, similarly inspired public pressure brought about the loss of the lease of his theater in Lancaster.) Ethel had been aware of Frank's infidelities at least as early as her pregnancy with Baby; as a result, she didn't want a third child and, in late 1921, she and Frank sought medical advice in a tentative attempt to obtain an abortion. Family friend and medical student Marcus Rabwin talked them out of the idea.

Depending on which Garland biographer one trusts, Ethel's subsequent theatrical aspirations for her girls—particularly Baby—were bred either from an attempt to fulfill her own thwarted musical ambitions or from the desire to escape an unhappy home life and protect the children from rumors about Frank. Throughout the late 1920s and into the 1930s, Ethel and her daughters traveled and stayed away from home more and more. Whether she was or was not the quintessential stage mother, there is no question that she determinedly (and increasingly ceaselessly) sought work for the girls. There is also conjecture that it was she who—however innocently—started her children on a regimen of whatever stimulating or relaxing medication could then be legitimately obtained to keep them appropriately sparkling or rested for performances and interviews.

Whatever the troublesome underpinnings, there was (at least) one saving grace for Baby: the joy she found and provided in her singing. For the rest of her life, she glowingly remembered the best of those days when she first fell "hopelessly in love with audiences. The roar of the crowd—that wonderful, wonderful sound—is something I've been breathing in since I was two years old. Years later, coming off the stage to the applause and love of the audience is still a terribly thrilling thing, like all your dreams coming true at once.

"I still love them, and it has been a serious romance."

The whole family went to Hibbing [Minnesota] to provide special entertainment between shows at the local movie theater. As a schoolgirl helper, I had the happy treat to go along; I enjoyed being backstage waiting with Baby—she was two and a half then and dressed in a party dress. Mr. Gumm also came backstage, and when it was Baby's turn, she readily walked on. The audience kept applauding, and she walked past the center stage mark; evidently, she was spellbound. "She's going back to Grand Rapids!" Mr. Gumm said in a stage whisper. But she [finally] did stop and sing her song—"Jingle Bells"—and needless to say, she was a big hit.

Another time, a group of girls including Mary Jane and Virginia held a Neighborhood Garage Talent Show at a cost of one cent per person. Baby was the best talent. She did her part in a child's rocking chair, singing a song called "Baby Your Mother."

— Ethel Mills, Gumm family "hired girl"

Ethel was so vivacious: little, short, and kind of round. And she would run up and down stairs, singing all the time. Always active. She played bridge with a group of women who were also very active in Grand Rapids. And she played the piano in the pit of the theater.

Frank and one of my sisters did some duet work, operetta-style. He was a tenor, she was a soprano. And he was so gentle . . . a real sweet man. I was very little then, but he must have impressed me as being just very dear, because I do remember that.

When Judy came back to visit in 1938, I remember the high school band was on the stage playing "The Sweetheart of Sigma Chi," which was identified with her for a long time. And I remember how she was so dear and very, very shy. I don't remember her saying anything at all; her mother did all the talking!

Later on, whenever I saw Judy in movies, I was impressed with her artistry, but I also felt that she was somebody I would like to have known.

—Eleanor Downing, Grand Rapids resident

Above: *Frank Gumm, 1926.*

Right: *Ethel Gumm in one of her "Virginia Lee" stage costumes, circa 1925.*

*E*verything I remember about Grand Rapids has charm and gaiety . . . a beautiful, beautiful town.

I remember the first time I was singing when anyone took notice. My father was playing the piano, and I had a little girl-friend my age . . . she was so small, she couldn't have been more than two. And we had a piano at home, and [my father] played it and taught us to sing "My Country, 'Tis of Thee." And then he conned my mother and sisters into listening to me, and I was terribly proud because they said I was good: "Baby Gumm can sing!"

A little later that year, it was Christmas time; there was a show at my dad's theater. And I was sitting on my grandmother's lap in the audience. My two sisters were on stage; they were old pros by then—they'd been appearing in the theater for years. And my grandmother pushed me off her lap and said, "Go on! Get up on the stage!"

So I went to my mother, who was in the pit playing piano, and I asked her if I could sing. And she said, "Not tonight, but next week. . . ." Evidently, they had these [live shows] once a week. Anyway, we went home, and she made me this white dress. And they taught me "Jingle Bells" to sing on the stage.

And I remember going on stage and singing that song. And I'd run in a little circle. And everybody started to applaud [as if to] say it was good. And I just stayed there and stayed there, and I sang one chorus after another. My mother was howling with laughter, but she kept on playing, and my father was in the wings saying, "Come on! . . . Get off!" I guess I fell in love with the lights and the music and the whole thing. I must have sung about nine choruses; my father finally came out and got me over his shoulder . . . but I was still singing "Jingle Bells" into the wings. And I was a big hit! So then it became "The Gumm Sisters."

— *J*udy *G*arland

Baby Gumm in 1924—the year she began her singing career.

Left: *Jimmie, Baby, and Susie at home in Grand Rapids, circa 1925. By this point, their parents were preparing skits, songs, and dances for the girls to perform during intermissions at the New Grand. Locals acknowledged the talents possessed by the two older girls, but Baby was clearly the favorite of everyone. Seven decades later, her exceptional abilities and intelligence were still a topic of conversation among longtime residents.*

Below: *Advertisement for the family's two-night stand in Whitefish, Montana, June 18 and 19, 1926. Though advertised as three years old, "Baby Frances" had actually celebrated her fourth birthday on June 10.*

*F*rank and Ethel were good family people and adored their children. Frank was like a song-and-dance man; that was a holdover from his vaudeville days. He was dapper and liked to dress kind of flashy . . . a pretty good looking man. And Baby was the apple of his eye. Ethel was quite a different personality than Frank. I believe she was the decision maker in the home. She pushed the girls more into the show business than Frank did, but they both helped train them. And they were a singing family; they were always rehearsing and learning new songs. They didn't only perform at intermission at the theater. There were church [services] and lots of things that went on in Grand Rapids when they would perform for people. And they were well known and well liked; they played cards, and they had people in their house, and they'd go to other people's houses for parties.

Baby Frances was called "Baby" by everybody . . . so she hardly knew her name was Frances Ethel. Her mother made the best peach conserve I ever tasted—with a syrupy background, and chunks of peaches and English half-walnuts in it. This was Baby's favorite. Each night, before she went to bed, I would spread a large piece of bread with the peach conserve for her bedtime snack, and Judy would start from one end of the kitchen cabinets—balancing herself with one sticky hand and holding her slice of bread in the other—and walk clear across the tops of the cabinets, one to another, to the end of the kitchen.

My father came to take me home for the weekend one time, and Ethel asked if he would like to hear Baby sing. And he said he was so deaf, he couldn't. Ethel just said, "I'll fix that!" And she sat him on one end of the piano bench with Baby in the middle. And Ethel played, and Baby just sang her heart out for my dad; he just always remembered that. After she became famous, he was really proud of the fact that she had sung for him. He'd tell people all about it.

Even at the age of two or three, Baby could memorize complete songs; it wouldn't take her any length of time, and she never made a mistake on the words or tune. She had perfect pitch; nothing was too difficult. The audience couldn't really believe she could belt out a song like she could. I think Ethel knew Baby could be a star right from the start, before anyone else—and how to prepare her for stardom. And Baby knew she was good, [but] she wasn't spoiled at all; she just loved to sing. And she was a ham for sure; she didn't ever want to stop. She loved the applause and adoration of the audience.

*— W*ilma *C*asper, Gumm family nanny/housekeeper, Grand Rapids

After Mother and Father's act, she'd dash into the pit to play the piano, and he would dress us in our costumes backstage. I did those horrible Egyptian belly rolls in an Egyptian outfit with those big balloon pants and a lot of ankle bracelets and spangles. My sisters wore Spanish costumes, with those funny hats with little balls hanging all around the brims and toreador pants, and sang "In a Little Spanish Town."

While they were singing, Father was backstage trying to get me dressed. It was dark, and all he had was a flashlight. Can you imagine trying to dress a [four]-year old belly roller in the dark? Well, he usually managed to get both of my legs into one pant leg, so there would be a big, ballooning pant leg left over. Then he'd run to the wings and tell my sisters to do another chorus. No wonder they hated show business; they had to sing fifteen choruses of "In a Little Spanish Town" while I was getting dressed!

—Judy Garland

Poised to begin a new life on the West Coast, the Gumms spent the winter of 1926–27 in Los Angeles.

Left: *Mother and daughters in front of 3154 Glen Manor, the Los Angeles residence in which the family lived prior to settling in Lancaster in spring 1927.*

Below and opposite: *At home in Lancaster. In addition to their work at (what Frank renamed) the Valley Theatre, the Gumms were musically active at St. Paul's Episcopal Church: Frank played the organ, Ethel played the piano, and the girls sang in the choir. There were also appearances in school shows and local little theater, but vaudeville remained the primary training ground for The Gumm Sisters. Although taking her work reasonably seriously, Baby in performance was capable of random moments of mischief. Susie later grinned, "Judy stood in the middle where she could tickle our ribs while we were singing and not break up herself. She was always trying to break us up. But we loved it—and so did the audience. She was the biggest part of the act. Jimmie and I were just charming background."*

I started school in Lancaster, but I was never fond of it, really. The only teacher I felt attracted to was Miss DuVal—I never knew her first name; I don't suppose I even thought she had one! She taught the kindergarten, and she also managed all the school plays. She liked me and thought I was talented. When she put on Goldilocks and the Three Bears, she gave me the lead, which impressed me because my hair was neither golden nor curly. Shortly thereafter, the school board dismissed Miss DuVal—I still think it was because she had too much imagination!

—*Judy Garland*

Above: *A backyard snapshot of Baby in Lancaster, 1928.*

Left: *Baby (front and center) and Susie (second from right) with friends in Lancaster.*

Below: *Advertisement placed by Frank to announce the family's personal and professional arrival in town; from the Antelope Valley Ledger Gazette, May 20, 1927. (The weekly newspaper reviewed the show on its front page a week later; see quote, below left.)*

*G*UMM FAMILY WINS LANCASTER APPROVAL

   Frank and [Ethel] Gumm and family who have just purchased the Lancaster Theater from Ben Claman, made their first acquaintance with their new patrons on Sunday and Monday evenings with an offering of songs and dances in connection with the regular picture program at the theater. Mr. and Mrs. Gumm are accomplished musicians and gave two very pleasing songs, while the little daughters completely won the hearts of the audience with their songs and dances.

—*Antelope Valley Ledger Gazette, May 27, 1927*

Production still from The Wedding of Jack and Jill, one of four 1929 musical short subjects featuring The Gumm Sisters. The front-and-center marital couple are actors John Pirrone (later John Perri) and Peggy Ryan; Baby Gumm—in her balloon pants—stands just behind Pirrone's right shoulder. Nearly seventy years later, Grand Rapids resident Eleanor Downing exulted: "We all flocked to the theater to see the short [The Gumm Sisters] were in! There was lots of publicity about that. All three of them looked wonderful, and we could relate to them, because they looked like they did when they left—it had only been two or three years before." When Judy returned to Warner Bros. to make A Star Is Born (1954), assistant director Mecca Graham remembered her 1929 stint at the studio, even though she didn't: "I was only five [sic] then.... Besides, my film debut was rather inauspicious!" At Graham's suggestion, a couple of the shorts were located in the Warner vaults and screened for the star; per a press report, "Judy laughed at them (in the wrong places)" but Star director George Cukor enthused, "Judy had a big, appealing voice even then."

the 1930s

Given their Meglin association and screen credits, The Gumm Sisters coasted into the new decade with reasonable momentum. Initially, acclaim was sporadic and limited to the West Coast, but Ethel's determination resulted in several hundred stage and local radio appearances for the girls between 1930 and 1935. During that time, the act gradually evolved from a close harmony trio into a more specific showcase for Baby. The piping precocity of her voice was rapidly maturing into a powerful, soulful sound, and audiences and critics began to react in astonishment; the press would note again and again the showstopping caliber of her work and the demands for encores from her listeners. Even other young professionals were seemingly beyond jealousy when it came to Baby Gumm; she was an immediate favorite with fellow aspirants, whether during her association with the Maurice Kusell Theatrical Dance Studio or Lawlor's Hollywood Professional School.

In summer 1934, Ethel and the girls went east, although their professional luck was initially poor. An engagement at a gangster-run concession at the Chicago World's Fair ended badly when (as Judy recalled) "Mother tried to collect what they owed us, [and] they told her to shut up and stay healthy!" The trip was redeemed by a chance last-minute booking at the Oriental Theatre. It was there that emcee George Jessel provided the girls with a new stage name (taken from that of New York drama critic Robert Garland); Jessel's patronage and Baby's uproarious success in the show provoked a subsequent Midwestern tour for "The Garland Sisters."

The 1934–35 season in California proved even more exciting. There were more rave notices for Baby when the girls played up and down the Coast. Then Decca Records manifested genuine (if for the moment unfulfilled) interest, and—finally—the girls secured their first feature film contract when Universal signed them for its forthcoming *The Great Ziegfeld*. Unfortunately, the studio soon thereafter sold the property to Metro-Goldwyn-Mayer, which dropped the trio from the picture. By June 1935, however, The Garland Sisters were headlining at the Cal-Neva Lodge in Lake Tahoe. During that engagement, Sue found a fiancé and Baby found an agent; she also adopted the name "Judy" for herself from the title of a contemporary song.

With Sue's marriage, the trio dissolved, and Judy was trundled from studio to studio as a solo act by new agent Al Rosen. Everyone everywhere was ecstatic over her talent, but no one knew what to do with her. (In 1943, when friends made a mockumentary recording, "The Life of Judy Garland," as her twenty-first birthday gift, one of their character re-creations was that of a bedeviled Hollywood executive circa 1935 who declaimed, "We don't want a little girl with a great big voice; we want a great *big* girl with a little voice!")

M-G-M manifested the most interest—however inconsistent—in Judy, who gave at least three auditions on the Culver City lot. (Two of these predated Rosen's representation.) The first, in December 1934, derived from the coalescent efforts of studio executive secretary Ida Koverman, producer Joseph Mankiewicz, and test director George Sidney, all of whom saw Judy at the Wilshire Ebell Theatre. (Sidney later recalled that The Garland Sisters were still a unit at that point and that Metro was only interested in the twelve-year-old.) When the girls played the Paramount Theatre in spring 1935, composer Burton Lane was responsible for arranging another visit to the lot for Judy. Finally, Al Rosen took notice of an August 28, 1935, *Variety* feature ("Metro Rounding Up Tuner Talent for Grooming to Bolster Stock Company") and wangled a further interview on September 13.

It was a spontaneous appointment and, with Ethel away in Pasadena for the day, Frank Gumm took Judy out to Culver City. M-G-M staff pianist Roger Edens was called in to play for her; he later remembered: "Here was this chunky kid in a navy middy blouse and skirt, nervous—her palms were wringing wet—her large eyes filled with love and hunger. [Then she] opened her mouth and out came 'Zing! Went the Strings of My Heart.' And I mean *zing*. It was a moment to remember. Even at twelve [sic], she had that rare vocal quality of breaking hearts. That bunch of hardened show business pros [sitting in on the audition] suddenly found themselves in tears."

Within days, Judy had signed a seven-year contract with the most prestigious of all Hollywood studios. (Her starting weekly salary of $100 would increase incrementally at the onset of each of seven option periods—if M-G-M didn't decide to drop her first.) But the joy of such achievement was decimated a few weeks later by the death of Frank Gumm, who was felled by a fast-acting case of meningitis in November 1935. Judy would ever after cling to the memory of their association and gratefully recall his presence at her Metro audition: "It was the first time he had ever personally entered into any business arrangement; he always left any bookings for us girls to Mother. I'm so glad he did come, because I like to feel he brought me luck. . . . I know he watched and helped me get my screen start."

Judy found her first months at Metro disappointingly slow. It was an era when film stars were either moppets or fully grown adults, and as Garland herself later summarized: "They wanted you either five years old or eighteen, with nothing in between. Well, I was in between and so was little Deanna Durbin, and they didn't know what to do with us. So we just went to school every day and wandered around the lot. Whenever the important stars had

---

Opposite: *Judy, 1935. Years later, critic Judith Crist summarized Garland's unique appeal: "The Hollywood star system, some experts hold, came a cropper when the studio publicists started turning stars into the folks next door. But when the girl next door becomes a Hollywood star—ah, well."*

at an exhibitors' conference in spring 1936 that the two girls were paired for a legitimate short subject, *Every Sunday*, recorded and filmed in June and July 1936.

By that time, however, Deanna's M-G-M contract option had been allowed to lapse, and she was signed for *Three Smart Girls* at Universal (which first wanted Judy for the picture). Meanwhile, 20th Century Fox was simultaneously preparing a sturdy showcase for Garland in the musical comedy football feature, *Pigskin Parade*. M-G-M loaned Judy to Fox, and when her fellow actors heard her in full action for the first time, they spoiled the take with their uncontrollable applause and cheers. The film, its songs, sports, and inherent irreverence made for a solid popular hit; Judy won special accolades, and *Pigskin Parade* was the beginning of a growing public awareness and a genuine fan base for the girl.

The real turning point came in February 1937, when Garland was selected to provide entertainment at an on-set birthday party for Clark Gable, male superstar of the M-G-M lot. Taking a musical routine that he'd originally prepared for Judy to sing on the radio to orchestra leader Ben Bernie, Roger Edens constructed the number as a fan letter and interlaced it with intratrade humor: his "Dear Mr. Gable" then led into the 1913 song standard "You Made Me Love You." Both studio chieftain Louis B. Mayer and Gable's girlfriend, actress Carole Lombard, approved the pointed lyric, and West Coast head of publicity Howard Strickling never forgot the moment: "Judy sang with knees shaking and a bashful quaver in her throat, which was all the song needed to bring a lump to the throat of everyone on the set."

The studio had already slotted Garland for *Broadway Melody of 1937* (which was in preproduction so long that it had to be retitled *Broadway Melody of 1938*). When the on-the-lot success of the Gable number was then surpassed by its reception during Judy's appearances at trade conferences and local benefits, the routine was added to the new picture as well. (By this time, Edens had considerably modified the original lyric and patter, making it less "inside" and more accessible to a general audience.)

Judy played Sophie Tucker's daughter in *Broadway Melody of 1938*; the veteran vaudevillian both publicly bequeathed her own legendary billing to the girl and trumpeted the teen's potential: "Judy will be America's next Red Hot Mama!" Reviewed as Garland's "best opportunity to date," *Broadway Melody of 1938* also won her a long-term Decca recording contract, immediately drawn up by the corporate president on the night he saw the picture previewed.

By autumn 1937, M-G-M's plans for Judy had begun to almost overwhelmingly overlap. She assumed semi-regular status on the studio's network radio show *Good News* after spending nearly five months on the air in the spring as the much-acclaimed vocalist of the *Oakie College* program. Such was her professional reputation at this juncture that David O. Selznick wanted to test her for the role of Scarlett O'Hara's youngest sister, Careen, in *Gone With the Wind*. But Metro was finally ready to place into production several of its own properties that had already been in the works for Judy for a year or more.

Between August 1937 and September 1938, she had starring roles in four films: *Thoroughbreds Don't Cry*, *Everybody Sing*, *Love Finds Andy Hardy*, and *Listen, Darling*. The first and third of these were notable in that they marked her initial onscreen associations with Mickey Rooney, a compatriot of the days at the Lawlor School. Ever after, Judy credited him with her screen acumen: "Mickey took me in hand and showed me the ropes. He was tough, generous, gifted, loyal." When she was written into the Judge Hardy Family series,

parties, though, they called the casting office and said, 'Bring those two kids!' We would be taken over, and we would wait with the servants until they called us into the drawing room, where we would perform." She added wryly, "We never got [paid]. . . . We got a dish of ice cream—and it would always be melted!"

Judy received her first national radio exposure under the Metro aegis, but the rapturous response only underscored the frustration she felt at her general inactivity. Finally, a test reel of her and Deanna together proved such palatable entertainment

Garland was given further, succinct acting advice by Rooney, already well established as the precocious teenage son of those hugely popular films: "Honey, you gotta believe [this]. Live it—say those words like they're yours."

While plans were elsewhere under way at M-G-M for her most prestigious vehicle to date, Garland made the stopgap *Listen, Darling* in late summer 1938. It was typical of her screen fare during that era: commercially appealing film-making that seldom ranked as classic cinema but provided audiences with often glorious pleasure. If critically categorized by the higher-brows as "a feeble fable," *Listen, Darling* could be (equally) accurately heralded by *Box Office*: "By means of its unpretentious but utterly captivating romantic charm, this adolescent comedy with its splendid vocal interludes by Judy Garland is sure to register as solid entertainment."

Garland capped the decade with *The Wizard of Oz* and *Babes in Arms*. Released in October 1939, the latter coupled her again with Rooney, this time in a full-fledged musical comedy. (Its runaway success all but swamped them in public affection as a new and favorite performing team.) The remarkable *Oz* was one of the most ambitious and expensive productions in M-G-M history and, beyond its initial raves and accolades, achieved rank in succeeding decades as the most widely seen, best-loved motion picture in history. The screen role and songs of Dorothy Gale were written to emphasize Judy's communicative power and capacities; it was one of the most stellar showcases that could be envisioned, and the Garland talent was singularly, uniquely equipped for that challenge.

In August 1939, Judy and Mickey were sent east to ballyhoo *Oz* and *Babes in Arms*. They wound up on Broadway for a two week engagement at the Capitol Theatre that defied all media attempts to convey the scope of the crowds, clamor, and public passion for the two. On her return to Los Angeles in September (and while waiting for her next screen assignment to begin preproduction), Garland segued into virtually weekly radio work for the season as special guest singer on Bob Hope's *Pepsodent Show*. In October, she was invited to join several dozen screen immortals by putting her hand- and footprints in cement at Grauman's Chinese Theatre.

From "Hang On to a Rainbow" to "Over the Rainbow," it had taken just a decade; seventeen-year-old Baby Gumm was one of the nation's top ten box office attractions for 1939.

Opposite: Every happily promotable event in the life of a star provided an opportunity for publicity. Judy was just about to celebrate her fifteenth birthday in June 1937 when she was posed to brandish a diploma, signifying graduation from Bancroft Junior High. Though primarily tutored at M-G-M, she enjoyed the chance to attend classes with nonprofessionals when her schedule allowed.

Right: Artwork for the cover of La Presse, *a French-Canadian rotogravure (November 25, 1939). Judy was seventeen and glowingly described by the magazine's editors as "the incomparable young ingenue of* The Wizard of Oz."

The first time I ever saw Judy, she was walking down Broadway (in Los Angeles) to [Maurice] Kusell's. I'd been studying dance there for some time; I was around Jimmie's age then. But there were the three girls and an older woman behind them—the mother. And I thought [Judy] looked funny: she had long legs and a little short fur coat . . . a little white rabbit fur coat, and her hair was way out and all frizzy. She was cute, but she looked like a little girl who didn't have anything and was still trying to look her best. Which we all did at that time.

And as soon as I saw her work, I realized how talented she was. She and her sisters carried the show [Stars of Tomorrow]. She had a way of singing . . . she did something with her throat that was very clever; it was like a little voice break, and the way she timed it in the song was very, very clever. She didn't act like a child; she was very old for her age. She was very much to herself. . . . But there was no doubt about the audience reaction. Judy was outstanding. She was little, and she had a powerful voice, and she just took over everything. You knew right away when you saw her that "There's somebody that's gonna go someplace." Well, I knew—and I was only fourteen. I knew it.

Ethel was definitely a stage mother. Absolutely. What she said, went— whether they liked it or not. I think she and Maurice got very close; I'm not sure, but I think so! And she took over [his] studio in regard to teaching people to sing, making them rehearse. She was like the owner of the studio.

—*Dona Massin,*
Kusell Student

The Gumm Sisters in 1930.
The next year, they began training in
Los Angeles at the performing academy of
director/choreographer Maurice Kusell.

Below, clockwise from top left: *A 1934 advertisement for the trio's appearance in Bellingham, Washington—proof positive of the many (usually unfortunate) variations to which the family name was inadvertently subjected. On July 19, 1934, Baby was a sensation at Children's Day at the Chicago World's Fair. She was selected as guest of honor, rode in an open motorcar during a parade, and served (as shown) as featured soloist for an afternoon concert, a radio audition contest, and a one-act play. The Gumms' seven weeks in Chicago were highlighted by an unexpected engagement at the Oriental Theatre, where headliner George Jessel was bowled over by the little girl "who already sang like a woman—a woman who had been hurt."*

Above: *A hoydenish Baby Gumm, circa 1931. That year brought her and her sisters increasing professional notice. In their first performances under the aegis of Maurice Kusell during the week of July 10, 1931, the* Los Angeles Examiner *offered "special praise . . . to The Gumm Sisters in harmony songs." The* Hollywood Filmograph *was even more exultant in its suggestion that Baby's duet and dance with fellow pupil Betty Jean Allen in the finale "should make the Duncan Sisters, the Boswell Sisters, and any other sister team in the whole wide world watch out . . . they are just 'IT.'" That appearance led to Baby's first agency contract; the office changed her name to Frances Gayne and sent her in August to a Universal casting call for the Zasu Pitts/Slim Summerville feature film* The Unexpected Father. *Baby made it to the final audition and was then eliminated in favor of Cora Sue Collins; she returned— as Frances Gumm—to Kusell recitals and local work in and around Lancaster. (The* Ledger Gazette *testified on October 9 that, under any name, she was still a hit: "Four encores testified to the charm of her performance" at an Easter Star benefit in Tehacapi.) In Kusell's final booking for the year, Baby was chosen over thirty-five other acts to headline the All-Star Kiddie Revue at Warner's Hollywood Theatre. The show ran from December 24–30, and the* Examiner *noted that Baby's "singing and dancing literally stopped the show."*

In spring 1934, Judy enrolled at Lawlor's Professional School. At that time, she was eleven-year-old Frances Gumm, a frail child with a backstage pallor and enormous brown eyes. She was wearing a dress that was two inches too long, and the black grosgrain-ribbon bows with which her tap shoes were tied were wilted and worn.

Viola F. Lawlor, the rawboned, middle-aged New England matron who owned and operated the school . . . led this forlorn-looking child to the piano. I felt [this] was needlessly thoughtless and cruel. Obviously, the Gumm girl was not a real professional at all, but the amateur product of some tacky, small-town dancing school. Why expose her to shame? Why put the poor girl through this ordeal?

Every student in this room, from kindergarten age to high school—dancer, singer, actor, musician— was a seasoned professional. Most of us had been performing on stage or before a camera since we were toddlers. However, I saw Mrs. Gumm, in true stage mother fashion, was already rippling her fingers over the keys. Frances perched her small frame on the grand piano and crossed her legs, while the rest of us braced ourselves for the worst.

"Blue moon . . . You saw me standing alone. . . ." The students' respectful silence became a profound hush, as an emotionally charged and utterly mature voice flooded the hall. Everyone was stunned. Among fifty performing veterans, not one of us could match this little girl's surprisingly powerful and dramatic delivery of a song. When she finished, there was a thunderclap of spontaneous applause, the heartfelt approval of kids who—of all people—knew a show business winner when they heard one.

Far from being jealous of Judy, everyone at Lawlor's supported and loved her. It was we who insisted she be given the next-to-closing spot on the bill of our annual Christmas Show, staged at the Wilshire Ebell Theatre. Mickey [Rooney] was always the emcee, Judy the star who invariably stopped the show, giving encore after encore until 2 a.m.

—Diana Serra Cary,
"Baby Peggy" of silent films

Posing in Chicago in 1934, Baby offers "Bill," the signature song of Show Boat *star Helen Morgan. This musical impression was the highlight of the girls' act during that season.*

*W*hen we were in Chicago in 1934 at the end of the World's Fair, we met three girls who had a trio; their mother played piano for them. They were the only friends we ever made in those early days. They were staying at the same hotel . . . they had worked [the Old Mexico Café] at the fair, and they didn't get paid for the last week, so they were on their way back to California.

One day, they came knocking at the door [when] we were rehearsing. One of the sisters was a chubby little girl about twelve years old. They wanted us to sing a song for them, which we did. Then they said, "We're a girls' trio," and we said, "Can you sing for us?" Their mother wasn't there to play for them, but the little girl said, "I want to sing for you." So LaVerne helped lift her up and put her on the piano, and she sang "My Bill." LaVerne played for her, and we stood there with tears in our eyes, she was so great, so wonderful.

We were finishing a week with Georgie Jessel at the Oriental Theatre, and we knew that we were being booted out for the second week. He came to us and said, "Do you know of another girls' trio?" and we thought of the kids at the hotel. I got ahold of the little one and said, "Baby, tell your mother to take you over to see Georgie Jessel first thing in the morning."

—*M*axene *A*ndrews,
The Andrews Sisters

*T*here was a fellow called Jerry Wills, who was a sheriff of Crystal Bay: a great, big, lusty guy. One night he came over, and he was so excited: "There's a show at Cal-Neva! Cal-Neva!" I said, "Yeah, fine. I know Cal-Neva." But he insisted, "There's this little girl. She's just so good. She's wonderful. . . . She's twelve years old." Well, being sixteen, I was not really in love with the idea of going out with a twelve-year-old girl. But Jerry said, "No, you've got to come and listen to this girl. There are three of them: The Gumm Sisters." So we went, and sure enough: there were The Gumm Sisters. And this little one—the one in the middle, her name was Frances—was cute. Loud! She sang "Zing! Went the Strings of My Heart" right through her nose; you'd hear her across Lake Tahoe! She blew me right across the lake!

She was kind of like a small Ethel Merman . . . but with a good voice! She had bobbie socks and little short skirts, and she was cute as a bug . . . and that, of course, was a precursor of Judy Garland. And she had it then. Even I picked up on her special mix of joy and poignancy. Nobody knew who she was, but she had that thing that grabbed them.

—*R*obert *S*tack

Above: La Fiesta de Santa Barbara *was a Louis Lewyn short subject, filmed in August 1935 and released by M-G-M the following spring. The Garland Sisters' rendition of* "La Cucaracha" *marked their final formal performance as a trio; their somewhat inattentive listeners here are the porcine Paul Porcasi and the flirtatious Concha Frandinho.*

Right: *On August 8, 1935—about a month before the Metro audition that would seal her fate—the beaming movie-hopeful went to court to gain contract approval for her association with Al Rosen. Judy was still a minor, so such a procedure was essential; Rosen's representation required the agreement of Frank and Ethel Gumm as well.*

Far right: *Within hours of Judy's September 1935 M-G-M audition, the studio offered her a seven-year contract, effective October 1 and with a weekly stipend of $100, guaranteed for the following twenty weeks. (As her father proudly wrote to friends in Lancaster: "The salary advances every six months; a very attractive deal. Of course . . . she has to make good, or they have the privilege of letting her go at the end of every [option] period.")*

*W*hen I heard her at the Paramount, she had the voice of a person who had been singing for fifty years. What she did was so natural to her, and that's what struck me the first time I saw her on stage: her gestures, her poise, her total manner when she was singing was that of someone who had many, many years of experience. Her phrasing, the intelligence that she put into her songs was wonderful. No matter what she did, it was true, and when she sang a song, every song she sang came true. And I was so struck by her that I went out in the lobby of the theater to find a phone, and I called the head of the Music Department of M-G-M and told them I had seen someone who was just electrifying.

And I went backstage and I met Judy's father; within a few days, they came up to my office at M-G-M. I played for her audition. And when the head of the Music Department heard her, he called L. B. Mayer, who was the head of the studio: "Mr. Mayer, you've got to hear this kid. She's simply wonderful." And when Mr. Mayer heard her, he looked up, and he said, "I want every producer . . . every director . . . every writer who is around on the lot to hear her."

And that was her audition. We started at around nine in the morning, and it wasn't until 7:30 that evening that everyone who was supposed to hear her heard her. And I was the piano player. She did "Zing! Went the Strings of My Heart" and a Hebrew song which had become rather popular in vaudeville in those days, "Eli, Eli."

She had a wonderful feeling when she sang. You can't teach that; it's just there. It's immediate. And she instinctively knew the right thing to do; it came naturally to her. She had great respect for every song she sang. And the world loved her singing; they responded to the naturalness of her presentation—it was almost as if everything that she sang was written for her.

—*B*urton *L*ane, Composer

Judy's first M-G-M portrait sitting in November 1935 occurred just days after the death of her father. Devastated by the loss, the girl was nonetheless required to fulfill her duties at the studio, where (initially, at least) there was much jubilation over her abilities. "We have just signed a Baby Nora Bayes" was the gleefully awed cry of Metro executives, who compared the magic of Judy's voice with that possessed by one of the great women of early-twentieth-century vaudeville. Both Maurice Kusell and Al Rosen later claimed partial credit for Garland's poignant vocal wail; each man offered that he'd arranged for her to be coached by a Los Angeles area cantor, feeling that such training would enhance the girl's already-recognized and inherent soulful sound.

Left: *A holiday is declared for the students under contract to M-G-M in December 1935. The contemporary Metro caption for this publicity photograph reads: "CHRISTMAS VACATION IS HERE— the Metro-Goldwyn-Mayer studio school for juvenile players recesses until after the holidays. Closing with a Christmas party during which presents were exchanged, carols sung, and a good time had by all— Miss Mary MacDonald, the teacher, wished her pupils a happy vacation. Shown left to right: Garett Joplin, Mickey Rooney, Judy Garland, Robert McClurg, June Wilkins, and Miss MacDonald." Apart from Mickey—and to use the phrase Judy herself would later proffer to wistfully (if pointedly) comment upon the career of child actress Juanita Quigley—most of her fellow classmates "never made it."*

Right: *A Gumm family reunion, circa spring 1936. Top row, from left: Judy, Frank's brother Robert Emmett Gumm, Ethel, Susie. Bottom row, from left: Jimmie, Mrs. Robert Gumm, Lee Kahn (Susie's first husband), Richard Gumm (Robert's son; cousin to the Gumm Sisters). The Robert Gumm family was living in Seattle when Frank died the preceding November. They relocated to southern California, and Robert took over the management of the Lomita theater—Frank's last entrepreneurial effort.*

Opposite: *A Garland rotogravure pose, circa 1936.*

*W*allace Beery was the emcee for a radio variety show; we had worked together a number of times, and I was invited to be there. And he had this little thirteen-year-old girl as guest—about eight or nine months older than I. She sang "Broadway Rhythm." Now I was an aspiring musician at the time, but I couldn't believe what I was hearing: the energy she put into this material, the range in her voice, the maturity of her voice at that age.

Then her mother and my mother got together: "Oh, the kids want to see each other; let's have them over to the house and have dinner, Judy has records . . . they might enjoy it." That was our first date. Judy had gotten some of the very newest Benny Goodman records; it was a big evening for us.

And I wasn't old enough to get a driver's license yet, so my mother hired a driver! And if Judy and I had a date to go to an afternoon movie or an early dinner, the driver would wait for us; we started holding hands . . . and we were kind of like "going steady." Until she met Billy Halop—I couldn't compete with a guy two years older than me!

Judy and I and those that hung around us considered Deanna's singing pretty corny—all that opera kind of music. Very square. (I don't know if we used that expression in those days, but that's what we meant!)

—*Jackie Cooper*

Above: *Edna Mae (soon to be Deanna) Durbin, Jackie Cooper, and Judy in a spring 1936 attempt by the publicity department to emphasize the all-American habits and interests of the average teenage movie player.*

Left: *It was expected that even a thirteen-year-old "contract player" would realize her obligations to studio and industry and make appearances at suitable and noteworthy public functions. Here, Judy and child actors Freddie Bartholomew, Mickey Rooney, and Edith Fellows gather in December 1935 to honor the great character actress May Robson.*

Opposite: *Although they would more quietly date on occasion, the innocent dalliance of Cooper and Garland was too promotable to be kept private at all times, and the duo was happily photographed on numerous outings in early 1936.*

A lot of people first saw her in Pigskin Parade and had this wonderful preview of this brilliant talent. We went to Grauman's Chinese (my mother and myself) to see it; Jack Haley [who was the star of the film] was a friend of our family's. And when we walked out, all anybody talked about was Judy Garland—"the kid"... how wonderful she was, this young girl. How she just broke up everybody in the picture and stole the picture. And I started crying; "She's the best singer I ever heard in my life. I want to be like her."

—*Margaret Whiting*

Left: *A color cover portrait from the 1940 Spanish magazine ¿Quién Soy Yo?, derived from a 1936 publicity portrait of Judy as Sairy Dodd in Pigskin Parade. Costar Patsy Kelly later noted that she "loved that [movie] because of Judy. She was [fourteen], something like that, and if you remember the picture, she used to want to sing all the way through it, and we were pushing her aside. And the whole place fell in love with her ... and of course the public did, too, very quickly."*

Below: *A November 1936 cartoon from a Kansas City newspaper, extolling the male lead and four of the female principals of Pigskin Parade. An effervescent "B" picture, the film became a huge popular favorite due to clever scripting, catchy songs, expert performances, and—as per the Kansas City critic— "Judy Garland! Judy Garland!! Judy Garland!!!"*

Opposite: *Judy and Deanna Durbin between takes of* Every Sunday, *M-G-M, July 1936. Judy would later humorously (if appreciatively) note that—after a dozen or so years of movie work— Deanna renounced the world of entertainment and moved, married and a mother, to France: "She got rich, and she lives in a lovely château outside of Paris. I talked to her one time, and she said, 'Why don't you get out of that business, you dumbbell!?!'... She likes to get fat and have babies and sing if she wants to and buy vegetables and [do] all kinds of things that are absolutely abnormal!"*

SO IT'S "RAH! RAH! TEXAS S-T-A-T-E!" AND HOW MUCH FUN!

JUDY GARLAND

BETTY GRABLE

DIXIE DUNBAR

STUART ERWIN

ARLINE JUDGE

Judy Garland, Betty Grable, Dixie Dunbar, Arline Judge and Stuart Erwin are only five of the many principals in "Pigskin Parade," the football film at the Mainstreet. Girls, boys, songs, dances, comedy and exciting gridiron scenes are included in the picture. You'll have a great time seeing it.

Below: *In January 1937, Judy enjoyed such success as a guest on the CBS radio series* Jack Oakie's College *that she was invited to join the regular cast for the rest of the season. Set on the campus of a fictitious university, the sixty-minute program afforded her the chance to build a listening following; each episode showcased her in at least one (if not two) special arrangements prepared for her by M-G-M's stellar vocal coach, Roger Edens. Oakie, a veteran stage and screen comic, can be seen upstage in mock professorial garb in keeping with his radio characterization. The casual clothes of the others on stage suggests that the photograph might have been taken at a rehearsal.*

Above: *Judy's work with Oakie and her autumn screen success in* Broadway Melody of 1938 *ensured the fact that M-G-M would assign her to its own radio program for the 1937–38 season,* New Faces of 1938. *She is shown here on November 3, 1937, in rehearsal for the next day's premiere broadcast of the series; the title of the show would become* Good News of 1938. *Her musical director appears to be young Meredith Willson, later acclaimed as composer/lyricist of such Broadway shows as* The Music Man *and* The Unsinkable Molly Brown.

Roger Edens had arranged "Drums in My Heart" for Ethel Merman; I was wild to sing it. "You're too young, Judy," he said. "That song is for a woman, not a girl. I'll write you a special song all of your own. If you don't like it better than the Merman number, you can sing 'Drums In My Heart.'" I came back from lunch, and Mr. Edens had "Dear Mr. Gable." That song gave me my great opportunity for the screen.

—Judy Garland

His birthday party was held on the set of Parnell, the picture Mr. Gable was making at the time. All the big stars were there with Mr. Mayer. Robert Taylor, Walter Pidgeon. John Barrymore with his brother, Lionel. Joan Crawford. Jean Harlow. And I said, "Ladies and gentlemen, my name is Mickey Rooney, and I'd like for you all to hear the finest voice in the world . . . the world's most wonderful personality . . . Judy Garland."

—Mickey Rooney

Judy's rendition of "You Made Me Love You" to "Dear Mr. Gable" made an intratrade, screen, radio, and recording sensation. Another benefit she gained from the song was the charm bracelet she models here; it was given to her by Gable himself, "created" for the occasion by the studio press corps. The charms included a Grand Rapids city seal; another for Murfreesboro (birthplace of Frank Gumm); a theatrical trunk; three little girls with pearl heads (representing The Gumm Sisters); a gold package of gum bound with a garland of flowers and the name George Jessel; two wedding rings (both Susie and Jimmie were married by this time); a replica of M-G-M studios; a microphone; a contract scroll; and a miniature book including Gable's photo and the inscription "To Judy, my favorite actress [a paraphrase of the last line of patter from the song], Sincerely, Clark Gable."

I first saw Judy and her two sisters at one of the [Wilshire Ebell] Sunday night benefits. I never forgot her: this charming youngster at one point in the act climbed on top of a piano and did the greatest imitation of Helen Morgan that I had ever seen. The scarf she used was bigger than she was. This cute, bright-eyed, wonderful little girl turned out to be one of the greatest stars of all time . . . the greatest all-around talent ever in show business.

She couldn't have been more than twelve or thirteen years old when I met her; Billy Grady, the M-G-M casting director, brought her into the dance studio at Metro, and we became close friends. I used to call her "Grandma," a nickname she seemed to take to. We would try to make up some new steps with a generous assist from Roger Edens, who would dream up new rhythms and tunes.

Broadway Melody of 1938 was the film that made Judy a star. All of us who watched her perform on the set knew immediately that she had that extra something . . . that magnificent quality. Her voice could make you laugh or cry almost at the same time. There was never anyone like her.

She soon passed Deanna Durbin and everyone else along the way. . . . She could do anything, and she did it in a way that was just—Judy.

—*George Murphy*

Opposite: *The finale set for* Broadway Melody of 1938 *(1937). Garland is already eminently worthy of the all-star company presented here (from left): Charles Igor Gorin, Sophie Tucker, George Murphy, Eleanor Powell, Robert Taylor, and Buddy Ebsen. Unfortunately, her powerhouse solo ("Your Broadway and My Broadway") was cut from the penultimate moments of the picture; the surviving audio track remains an awe-inspiring accomplishment—especially for a fourteen-year-old.*

Above: *Only months before, Judy had wept for joy at the chance to see Sophie Tucker in person in a café. The chance to work with "La Tuck" overwhelmed the girl.*

Right: *Contemporary advertising herald.*

Front cover of the campaign press and publicity book for Garland's second 1937 release; such lavish handouts were prepared for theater owners and included feature stories and promotable information, reproductions of poster art, designs for newspaper advertisements, and suggestions for attention-garnering gimmicks to help "sell" a picture. One of Thoroughbreds' selling points was the reunion of Judy with Sophie Tucker. They'd been stage mother and daughter in Broadway Melody of 1938; here, they were aunt and niece—and Tucker ran a boarding-house for jockeys (including Mickey Rooney). Sophie's veteran showmanship had been of earlier inspiration to Garland; she would later acknowledge that Tucker "gave up her lunch hours to coach me," teaching the young singer the various tricks of the vaudeville trade she'd learned in thirty years of show business. Their friendship extended to the social when Tucker threw open her home to the studio youngsters: "My Sunday luncheons were mostly for children—Judy and Freddie Bartholomew would bring their friends, and the gang would have a swell time in the pool." In the 1950s, Sophie would champion Judy at the world premiere of A Star Is Born and suggest Garland as the ideal entertainer to bring Tucker's story to the screen. Such a film was never made, but—during Steve Allen's guest stint on her TV series in 1963—Judy and he shared three of the songs he'd written earlier that year for the unsuccessful Broadway stage biography Sophie.

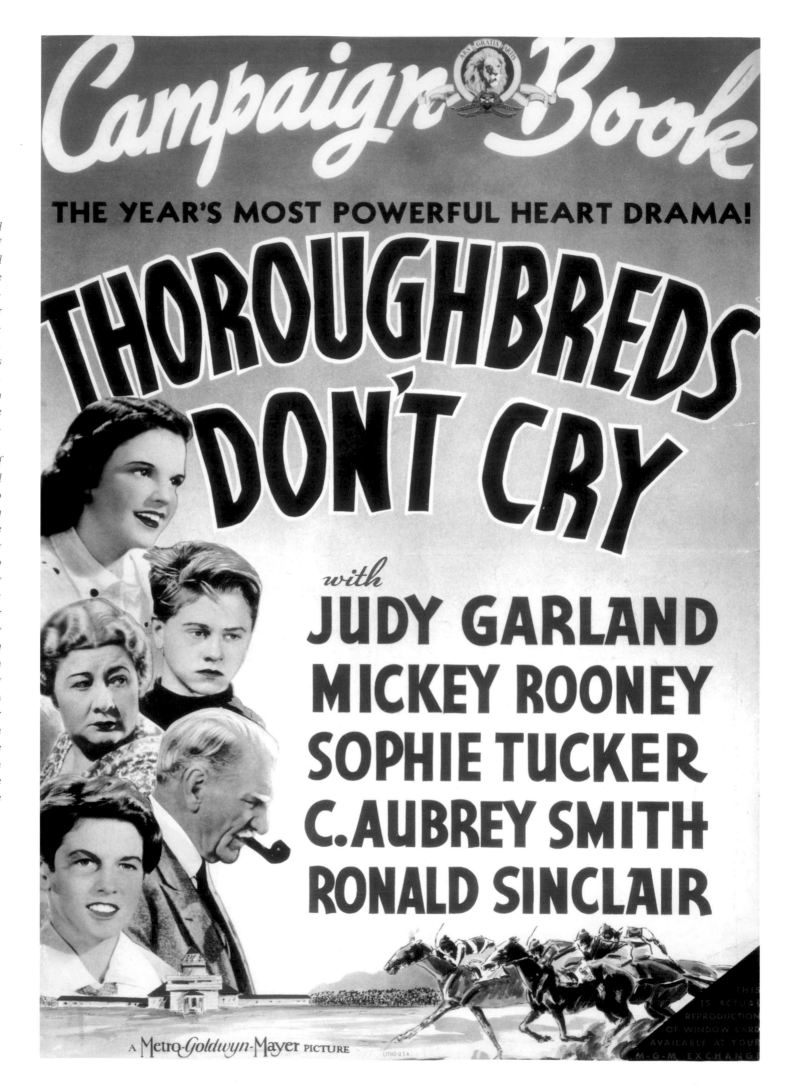

Above: *Mickey Rooney's seventeenth birthday is celebrated on the set of* Thoroughbreds Don't
Cry, *circa September 23, 1937. Joining Tucker and Garland to salute the diminutive Mick is New
Zealand actor Ronald Sinclair (right), who had replaced Freddie Bartholomew in the film. Judy would
later laughingly describe* Thoroughbreds Don't Cry *as an "inexcusable" picture, but it was actually
a pleasant programmer, cranked out on a low budget but with an exemplary cast and pace. The
plot insisted on coupling Garland with Sinclair but in this, her first of ten pictures with
Rooney, the real chemistry and interplay was already apparent between Judy and Mickey—
he brusque and full of bravado, she alternately championing and challenging him.*

Right: *Sheet music cover art for Garland's solo in the film. The song was actually a deleted tune
from the Arthur Freed/Nacio Herb Brown score for* Broadway Melody of 1938, *in which it was to
be delivered and danced by Eleanor Powell. In* Thoroughbreds Don't Cry, *Garland made the offhand
but happy little ditty into a memorable, catchy piece, aided (as ever) by an adroit vocal arrangement
written for her by Roger Edens. Her second number in the film was "Sun Showers," another Broadway
Melody/Freed/Brown castoff, where it was to have been operatically sung by Charles Igor Gorin.
Judy recorded and filmed a soulful rendition (which she delivered to cheer Sinclair at a low-ebb*
Thoroughbreds *plot point), but her version ended up on the cutting room floor as well.*

SCREEN JUVENILES

AUGUST 1937
25c

JUDY GARLAND
M-G-M sensation

Judy Garland Looks Back Over 10 Years in the Show Business
also features on **Deanna Durbin** · **Shirley Temple** · **The Mauch Twins**

Above: *By summer 1937, the M-G-M publicity department was suddenly in full swing in its attempts to capitalize on Garland's* Pigskin Parade *success the preceding autumn, the public response to her regular radio work that spring, and her forthcoming showcase in* Broadway Melody of 1938. *Judy would serve as a magazine "cover girl" on hundreds of occasions during her career, but August 1937 marked the first time she received such an honor. (That same month, she was similarly front-featured on* Modern Movies.)*

Right: *Mickey Rooney, Judy, and Jackie Cooper sail into the March 23, 1937, premiere of M-G-M's* Captains Courageous, *in which Rooney had a featured role. Garland's nautical garb may or may not be intentional; never underestimate the inspirational power of a press agent!*

951X93

Judy treasured pets over the decades. Here, her at-home 1937 companions are two Pekinese: Ming-Toy and Ming-Lin. Her passion for dogs led to random adventures over succeeding years. During Garland's 1945 summer honeymoon in New York with director Vincente Minnelli, their dog Gobo escaped from an open car; the combined New York police force answered Judy's SOS to trail, track, capture, and return the wandering hound. Dogs named Sam and Oliver were part of the family entourage in, respectively, the 1950s and early 1960s. When another named Skippy bounded up to greet Garland in 1965, she tripped over him and broke her arm. Brandy, the London Talk of the Town nightclub guard dog, was "appropriated" by Garland and husband Mickey Deans in 1969; Judy would admiringly refer to the dog's "Dirk Bogarde eyes," which—per her good friend Lorna Smith—was "intended as a mutual compliment."

Right: *An all-star M-G-M cast strolls between the Culver City soundstages for the still camera. Such a pose was typical for arm-in-arm prominent players in many Metro offerings during that era: the principals from* Everybody Sing *(1938) include, from left, Fanny Brice, Allan Jones, Billie Burke, Reginald Owen, Judy, Reginald Gardiner, and Lynne Carver. (The latter was an up-and-coming starlet—kind of a younger, bus-and-truck Norma Shearer.)*

Below: *A 24-sheet poster, designed for full-size outdoor billboards. Judy would work with most of this cast on future occasions as well. Billie Burke was the giddy and unflappable Glinda the Good in* The Wizard of Oz. *Owen was featured in* The Pirate, *and Brice, Jones, and Gardiner appeared with Garland on radio.*

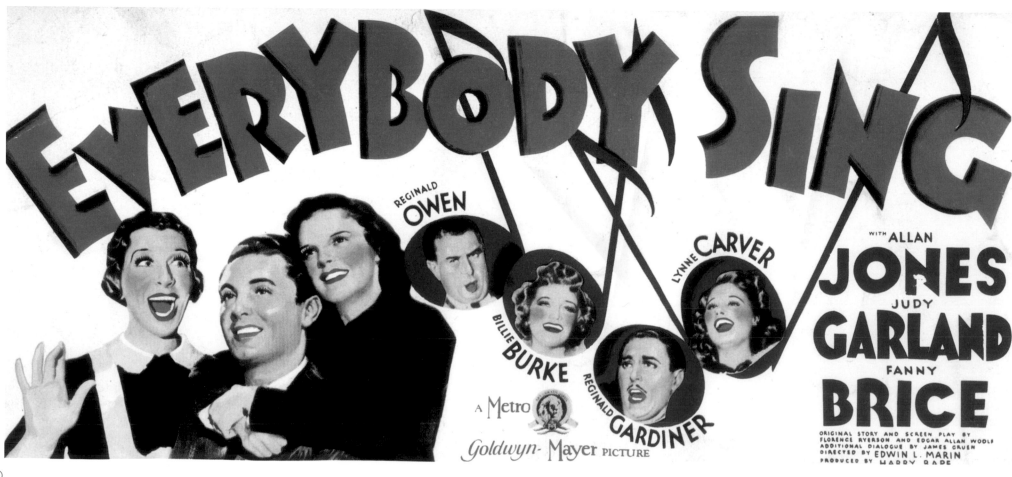

Above: *Title lobby card for* Everybody Sing *(1938); the film remains a quintessential example of the all-encompassing talent pool at Metro-Goldwyn-Mayer during Hollywood's halcyon era. Alternately billed second or third in publicity for the picture, Judy was nonetheless the focal point of the plot as a teenage singing sensation struggling for her own forum in a madcap and crazed theatrical family. If played for laughs,* Everybody Sing *also provided no few musical thrills; Garland demonstrated a singular ability to project on film as if in a live performance. Her powerhouse rendition of "Melody Farm" roused cinema audiences to cheers wherever the picture was screened.*

Left: *Two twentieth-century entertainment legends in their only onscreen encounter. Fanny Brice had created her Baby Snooks character during stage work earlier in the decade;* Everybody Sing *marked the Snooks film debut, although she was by then a radio star as well. Judy joins her here as Little Lord Fauntleroy in the nursery-room duet "Why? Because." Garland and Brice remained friends until the latter's death in 1951; Katharine Hepburn glowingly recalls all of them at the elegant dinner parties hosted by director George Cukor, "that Selznick-Brice-Judy-Spencer-Peck-Walpole-Maugham atmosphere." Garland herself credited Fanny for providing the encouraging tirade that propelled Judy into her London Palladium engagement thirteen years after* Everybody Sing*—and Brice's producer son-in-law Ray Stark initially proposed Garland for the title role in what eventually became* Funny Girl.

Above: *Ethel Gumm and Judy en route to Grand Rapids, March 1938. It was their only return visit to the girl's hometown and the final stop after a seven-week, seven-city promotional theater tour. Garland did four shows a day in between films in such locales as Chicago, New York, and Cleveland—all of them designed to herald the approaching* Everybody Sing. *(She also sang and appeared at that film's premiere in Miami.) It was a triumphant, if brief, return to the stage for Baby Gumm; she was a particular sensation in her first real Broadway performances at Loew's State, and Roger Edens was on hand to play for her. But even in Cleveland, her impact was such that it was singled out forty years later when local historians assembled a history of the venue in which she'd sung: "One can't always believe rumors, but some say there was a golden magic that she brought to the Ohio [Theatre] that day which never has tarnished."*

Right: *During their Windy City stint on the 1938 tour, Roger Edens arranged a portrait sitting for her at the Chicago studios of famed theatrical photographer Maurice Seymour.*

Opposite: *This unretouched publicity portrait of Judy was taken July 6, 1938. She had just finished playing a substantial role in* Love Finds Andy Hardy, *her second film with Mickey Rooney, and was about to begin preproduction for* Listen, Darling *opposite Freddie Bartholomew.*

Maurice Seymour
CHICAGO

*M*eeting Judy was a great moment for me. [Ethel] Merman was the first real pro singer in my life; the next was Judy. I came [to M-G-M] and Judy came to my life in another year. I worked with her exactly the way I worked with Ethel in New York.

Now, at that time, I would go East once or twice a year; I would always see Ethel. And I started telling her about Judy: "I've got this wonderful kid out there: the greatest, greatest singer that I've ever known. Wait'll you see her!" Well, Ethel was very cute because she was a tiny bit jealous: "Well, who is this? Who is this?" And I said, "Well, she's just a little kid, Ethel. . . ." "Well, what's she like? You're not showing her any of my tricks, are you?" So I had to [placate her:] "Awww, just forget about it."

The next year, Judy was fifteen. I took her to New York to appear at Loew's State; I played for her. Well, Ethel was there practically at the first matinee, and when I took Judy out to meet her, Ethel was just darling with her: "So, you took my man"—kidding about me—and Judy was [sheepish]: "Oh, yes."

Over a period of years, Ethel would come out here to make pictures, and finally, they got very friendly and very close. They saw quite a lot of each other. One night after dinner at my house, we started this real rivalry thing. They decided to see which could out-sing the other. It was the greatest thing I've ever known; they just died laughing at each other. Ethel would say, "Remember an old one I used to sing? He used to do it for me." And then she would sing. And then Judy said, "Well, he did an older one for me!" They finally ended up singing duets; it was one of the great, great evenings.

—Roger Edens,
M-G-M Arranger/Songwriter

Above: Love Finds Andy Hardy (1938) was the fourth of an increasingly popular series of M-G-M films that detailed the lives of a Small-Town America family. Judy played the visiting girl next door whose crush on the picture's title character remained unrequited in the face of competition from older (if muted) sirens Lana Turner and Ann Rutherford (above). Nonetheless, Garland's Betsy Booth manages to snag Mickey Rooney's Andy as a date for the local Christmas Eve dance—and her impromptu singing for the guests is rewarded by the chance to lead the evening's Grand March. The picture was simple but somehow enormously effective (and profitable) fun and provided further evidence of the Rooney/Garland chemistry.

Left: Insert poster for Love Finds Andy Hardy.

Opposite: In addition to her film assignments, mandatory schooling, homework, radio vocalizing, recording sessions, and personal appearances, Judy also spent countless hours participating in scores of photo shoots. These were designed to supply magazines and newspapers with the artwork best suited to promote an ever-more-popular teenage "featured player." Here she models a slightly more sophisticated ensemble than those in which she was at this point generally allowed to wear on-screen; Metro was determined to keep the girl a child as long as possible, even though she turned sixteen in June 1938.

Above: *Title lobby card for* Listen, Darling *(1938). Though at best a minor effort, the film was a typical M-G-M offering with a superlative cast. Amidst all the talent, there was also room for three songs and a reprise. Most noteworthy of the musical selections was Judy's "Zing! Went the Strings of My Heart," which she had performed again and again in 1935: at Lake Tahoe, at one of her M-G-M auditions, and on the radio on the evening of November 16—the night before her father died. (His doctor, Marcus Rabwin, phoned the girl to say that her father would be listening from the hospital; "I sang my heart out for him, but by morning, he was gone," she later remembered.) "Zing!" became one of her radio, record, and stage show staples.*

Right: *Strolling on the set with Charley Grapewin and Freddie Bartholomew; the latter ultimately left motion pictures and went into advertising in New York. ("He got smart!" Judy would jibe.) A much-respected stage and screen veteran, Grapewin announced his retirement after* Listen, Darling *but returned to M-G-M in February 1939 to play Garland's Uncle Henry in* The Wizard of Oz.

Left: *A Danish poster for* Listen, Darling. *Whether before, during, or after World War II, Hollywood product made an impression abroad wherever it was shown. Judy Garland generally delighted (and sometimes mystified) foreign audiences in her guise as the quintessential American girl. Even though her dialogue was dubbed, her songs remained in her voice and language. As a consequence, her stage appearances overseas in the 1950s and 1960s found a happy and anticipatory core audience.*

Below: *A costume test for* Listen, Darling.

I did love making The Wizard of Oz.
And I had a terrible crush on the director, Victor
Fleming—a lovely man, and a very fine director.

Ray Bolger was the Scarecrow. So right. So
convincing. And he never stopped dancing, on the
set or off. I'll bet he and Eleanor Powell are the
only people in the world who probably down lunch
in their tap shoes.

Jack was a dear, dear man. You know, I really
believed he was searching for a heart. He touched
me; I cried.

Frank Morgan nipped a bit, you know! I loved him,
but most of the time, I'm not sure he knew exactly
what he was doing. And he did it so damn well!

And Bert. So talented. So warm. And just so
funny as the Lion; it was hard for me to keep from
laughing what with all those whiskers and that tail.
(His tail was guided by a man up high with a fish
pole.) And I had to say, "You're a very mean lion!"
And he'd go "Ooooooh," and he had waterspouts
[built into his headpiece] so he could cry. And I
wasn't supposed to laugh!

Why is it God sometimes takes those who should
be able to stick around if they wanted to?

—*Judy Garland*

Apart from cartoon figures such as Mickey Mouse and
Bugs Bunny, are there any motion picture characters more
familiar to more people across more generations in more
places than these? From left, Ray Bolger as the Scarecrow,
Jack Haley as the Tin Woodman, Judy Garland as Dorothy
Gale ("from Kansas"), and Bert Lahr as the Cowardly Lion
in M-G-M's The Wizard of Oz (1939). This unique
Kodachrome photograph was seen only in a 1939 Life
magazine advertisement for Oz, where it was inadvertently
printed in mirror image. That error has been corrected here.

An unretouched Garland publicity portrait for The Wizard of Oz, printed from its original camera negative, November 5, 1938. The production had just begun reshooting the day before under its fourth director. Norman Taurog was first assigned to Oz the preceding May and perhaps oversaw some preliminary Technicolor tests in July and August. By September, however, he'd been replaced by Richard Thorpe, who filmed the first two weeks of the picture in October and was then dismissed by dissatisfied producer Mervyn LeRoy. George Cukor was next in line—if only as a stop-gap—and changed Garland's hair and makeup from a "fancy-schmancy" approach to the more natural appearance shown here. He also commandeered changes in her wardrobe and ruby slippers. Finally, Victor Fleming started filming the picture from scratch on November 4. He would complete most of Oz by mid-February 1939; when he left to similarly rescue a foundering Gone With the Wind, Oz was completed by King Vidor.

Left: *In the Emerald City Wash & Brush Up Co., Judy gets spruced up before her audience with the Great and Powerful Oz. The sequence was filmed in early winter 1939, and Judy would herein duet the bridge of "The Merry Old Land of Oz" with radio singer Lois January (in pigtails, at Garland's left).*

Below: *Judy and Terry, the female Cairn terrier who was her six-days-a-week companion throughout the nearly six-month schedule of Oz filming. One of Judy's regrets was that she wasn't able to purchase Terry at the conclusion of the picture; the dog was ultimately too valuable to owner/trainer Carl Spitz.*

I believe that Mervyn LeRoy lucked out in casting Judy. Shirley Temple as a child could not have sung or acted the role with the same maturity Judy brought to it as a teen. The whole project would have suffered, for the story would have lacked aesthetic weight. The audience took Judy seriously as she strove to get home to Kansas; it's the basis on which all the sentiment in the picture depended.

—Jack Haley

We all very much felt that Judy accepted all the little people as troupers—like herself. Although we felt that she was a very sophisticated young lady, and we all looked up to her with a lot of respect, she looked upon us as part of the gang. She was very congenial and talked with us in a very down-to-earth manner; she was very poised, but we never had any feeling that she was acting superior. Working with her was absolutely the high point of my career. All of the other people I've worked with did not measure up or compare in any way to Judy.

—Meinhardt Raabe, Munchkin Coroner

Below: *The famous four (plus Terry/Toto) pose with Frank Morgan as the Wizard.*

Right: *A rare production still taken on the Witch's Castle set in October 1938 when Richard Thorpe was still in charge as Oz director. Judy is in her blond, "Lolita Gale of Kansas" wig and makeup; even more noteworthy is the presence of originally cast Buddy Ebsen (left) as the Tin Woodman. His allergic reaction to the aluminum powder in his makeup (and ultimate replacement in the role) was one of the many problems that made Oz the most expensive M-G-M production since Ben-Hur in 1924. The $3.7 million final cost—including prints and advertising—was an investment that only Metro could or would have made.*

The choreographer, Bobby Connolly, called me to work on Oz around July 1938: Buddy Ebsen was going to do the Tin Man. And then all of a sudden I realized he was gone, and Jack Haley came in. I finally found out why: because of the [aluminum powder] makeup. When we first started on Oz, Judy was working on another picture. So she'd just come in and watch me do the routines as they were set: she looked at it and then just did it. I mean, she was talented. *She picked up things very quickly.*

— Dona Massin, *Oz Assistant Choreographer*

Above: *A technician tests lighting on the Oz set. Technicolor was a comparatively new process in 1938 and required intense, bright, hot light to effectively register on film.*

Right: *Another snafu in the works, as new Tin Woodman Jack Haley cavorts with Garland and Bolger in November 1938. Fleming shot for three days before anyone realized that the Ebsen costume (which had been cut down for the shorter Haley) was shiny and bright—and that the character in these scenes was supposed to be rusty and tarnished. Fleming had to junk all the Haley footage and begin the sequence again. (This was one of several times during the course of Oz production that Loew's, Inc., M-G-M's parent company in New York, threatened to cut its losses and abandon the picture entirely.)*

Opposite: *Although Il Mago di Oz (1947) didn't get to Italy until after World War II, the poster art designed and distributed there was overwhelmingly evocative and an ebullient reminder of the film's magic— and mainstay. Though Judy's champions at the studio (including Edens and Oz assistant producer Arthur Freed) had to first fight to get her the role and later fight to keep "Over the Rainbow" in the film, all efforts were justified.*

She was a typical high school girl, a typical teenager. She'd come on the set and call out, "Hi, gang, how are you?" And we felt so good because she recognized us; I think she got a bigger kick out of meeting us than we did out of meeting her.

But she was underage at the time, and any underage kids had their eight-hour day divided for them: four hours for shooting [a film], three hours for schooling, and one hour for recreation. So as soon as she was through with a scene, two people grabbed her and pushed her right into the classroom, because every minute counted. And she was a big star by then, so they needed her for everything: wardrobe, photos, interviews.

And she was just wonderful at everything. She was the all-American gal. If I were six feet tall, I'd want to marry her!

—Jerry Maren,
Lollipop Guild Munchkin

It was just before Christmas, and one morning when the Munchkins came on the set, the studio had a surprise for Judy. Off in a corner, they had prepared her own private [trailer] dressing room on wheels. It was wrapped all around in a big red bow. And when she walked in, they gave her the key and a scissors, and she cut this big red ribbon and opened the door; oh, she was so excited. She invited each Munchkin in to tour the dressing room, and then she gave every one an eight-by-ten autographed picture.

Then she said that she would like to give each of us a Christmas present, but with 124 of us, she couldn't afford it. So she bought a huge box of candy—I guess twenty-five pounds or more. (To me, it looked like a hundred pounds!) But she put it on the Yellow Brick Road, and she looked at all the Munchkins, and she said, "Merry Christmas. Sweets for the sweets." And we each had a piece of candy from Judy for Christmas.

—Margaret Pellegrini,
Flowerpot Dancing Munchkin

Grace Hayes and Charles Winninger do the promotional honors for Rooney and Garland to herald Babes in Arms (1939).

Left: *Garland and Rooney, plus their classical musical counterparts and costars, Douglas McPhail (left) and Betty Jaynes (fourth from right), veteran stage star Charles Winninger (third from left), and a cast of vaudeville old-timers. Babes in Arms was basically the story of a show business generation gap; in this publicity pose, Garland's impish sense of humor finds its outlet in her left hand.*

Below: *The title lobby card for the M-G-M hit, loosely based on a 1937 Richard Rodgers/Lorenz Hart Broadway musical. The film was produced by Arthur Freed as the first of his many vehicles for Garland; Judy returned the favor by introducing the Freed/Nacio Herb Brown song "Good Morning" (in duet with Rooney) and reprising Arthur's earlier ballad "I Cried for You." The rest of the score ranged from the title song and "Where or When" to "I'm Just Wild About Harry" and Arlen and Harburg's "God's Country." That latter paean to the American way included a winning (and Metro-promotional couplet): "We've got no Duce / We've got no Fuehrer / But we've got Garbo / And Norma Shearer!"*

I don't think I knew how good Judy was until I played opposite her. Her timing was like that of a chronometer. She could deliver a comic line with just the right comic touch, or say a poignant line slowly enough for the poignancy to hit hard but still stay short of schmaltz. She could turn on intensity, as I could turn on intensity, memorize great chunks of script, as I could, ad-lib, as I. Alone, she could take an ordinary scene and by sheer strength of talent, make it a scene that people everywhere remembered.

When I was acting with [an actress] who was struggling, I played everything straight. Clown, fiddle with timing, ad-lib, and you rattle a novice and ruin a scene. With Judy, it was the other way. We actually tried to rattle each other. Take a scene of tenderness, where the script called for me to whisper something sweet. With a novice, I really would whisper something sweet. With Judy, I might whisper, "Are you wearing a green garter belt today?" Then Judy, when it came time for her to whisper something to me, would hit back the same way.

None of the things we said rival the lines of George Bernard Shaw. We were a couple of teenage kids, proud of our talent and our poise, trying to make each other lose that poise on camera. I couldn't rattle Judy and she couldn't rattle me. God, we had fun.

— *Mickey Rooney*

*I*t was a news event, it wasn't just a comfortable social thing. It was run by the assistants of Howard Strickling, who was the head of the M-G-M publicity department. We went there, figuring, "Well, we'll all have fun . . . they're going to let us swim in the pool and everything." We never got to the sand on the beach. We never got away from being directed the entire time: "Put your suit on, come out here, do this, do that, jump in the pool, sit over here, you kids talk about this, talk about that." They took shots of us all over the place . . . all with Judy, of course. And when they had enough, they told us we could go home. But that's the way it was. You did what you were told, you appeared where you were told to appear—whether you liked it or not. You wore what you were supposed to wear. Judy lived that life so long; she was raised like that, [like] a young Nazi storm trooper!

—*Jackie Cooper*

Judy's seventeenth birthday at the Mayer beach compound, June 1939. From left: June Preisser, Sidney Miller, Mickey Rooney (at the piano), Jackie Cooper, Douglas McPhail, director W. S. Van Dyke, Betty Jaynes, Virginia Weidler, Busby Berkeley, Leni Lynn, Ann Rutherford, and Judy.

Right: Judy and Mickey running for a Los Angeles train, August 6, 1939. En route to one-day theater appearances in Washington, D.C., Bridgeport, New Haven, and Hartford, the duo would wind up on Broadway at the Capitol Theatre, performing between showings of The Wizard of Oz.

Below: In Bridgeport, August 10. The M-G-M publicity machine arranged gala arrival receptions for them everywhere—and quickly found out that America's first teen superstars were so much anticipated, adored, and about to be mobbed that the drumbeating was hardly necessary.

*W*e had thousands—literally thousands—of people waiting for us at the train in Grand Central Station when we got to town; they hustled us right off to the Waldorf Towers. And then we did five shows a day. Seven on weekends. They had to have police around the stage door to control the crowds.

— *Mickey Rooney*

*T*he Martins were Ralph Blane (who became my writing partner), myself, and two little girls from Frederick, Oklahoma, named Phyllis and Georgine Rogers—darling, sweet, wonderful, talented girls. We were hired to sing "back up" to Judy; we'd been engaged by Roger Edens to appear with her and Mickey Rooney, along with the opening of The Wizard of Oz at the Capitol Theatre.

I wasn't even aware of Judy Garland at that point, and when we came to rehearse, I was in the wings and listened to her sing "The Lamp Is Low." And we all stood there, riveted—everyone connected with the show . . . this glorious voice coming out of this little girl. We couldn't believe it; it was like a miracle. And there were a lot of tears—she really, absolutely pulverized us.

We didn't realize [that engagement] was going to be a legend until we looked out of our dressing room windows and saw all the way around the huge New York block, four abreast, people wanting to get in. Then it began to occur to us that something interesting was happening!

She also sang "Comes Love," which was from a current Broadway show. Mickey did his impressions; they danced together. And the audience reaction was staggering! I never saw anything like it.

—*H*ugh *M*artin,
Arranger / Songwriter

"Cutting a rug" at the Waldorf-Astoria, August 16. The invitational Rooney / Garland luncheon was attended by 150 teens from the Greater New York area; per Metro publicity, 200,000 had applied for the privilege.

*Judy was great in all departments,
from belting over a song to socking
over comedy lines. [That season] I
had thirteen writers on the payroll;
we even made jokes about it during
the show. Once I summoned all of
them to a script meeting; on the air,
Judy cracked, "It looks like Notre
Dame coming out for the second half."*

*The scripts had established that
Judy had a schoolgirl crush on me—
now is that so hard to imagine? I was
always talking about the beauty of
Madeleine Carroll, and I promised
that she would appear on the show.
Two or three weeks of buildup went
by, and finally Madeleine Carroll
appeared. I had been impressing on
the show's cast to be respectful to her.
Finally, I had to introduce her to Judy.*

*Judy immediately contemplated
Madeleine's blond locks and said,
"Hmmmmm . . . peroxide." I never
heard an audience laugh so long.*

—Bob Hope

Above: *Garland began a one-season stint
as the vocalist on Bob Hope's radio show
in September 1939. She was soon copping
awards as a new airwaves favorite and
here shares honors with her host.*

Right: *M-G-M publicity portrait, 1939.*

Left: *Judy joined (among others) vocalist Sylvia, Al Jolson, and Rudy Vallee on a special December 16, 1939, radio program that celebrated the opening of the Arrowhead Springs Hotel, "high up in the Sierra Madre Mountains." Jolson had been widely regarded as the "world's greatest entertainer" and was seldom less than maniacally egotistical about his superiority over competition—or lack of interest in other performers. But veteran Hollywood columnist Sidney Skolsky never forgot and frequently referenced Jolson's genuine rapture over Garland: "I could sit and listen to her all night." As effective as Judy was in the late 1930s and early 1940s, he wisely added, "What she is now [by comparison to what she'll become] is nothing. She's going to be one of the all-time greats."*

Below: *The October 10 premiere of* Babes in Arms *at Grauman's Chinese was launched by Judy's immortalization in the theater forecourt. She is assisted by Rooney, with the ever-watchful Ethel Gumm hovering in the background.*

I wanted to look glamorous that night, as I never had wanted to before or since. Well, I bite my fingernails, and I felt sick because I couldn't have long, glittering ones like Joan Crawford's. So the manicurist fixed me up with artificial ones.

Well, I placed my hands in the wet cement, I went into the theater, and after a while, I thought a creeping paralysis had set in, beginning with my fingers. They felt all numb and heavy. I was in a cold sweat until we left the theater, and then I realized some of the cement had got under my false nails and hardened on the real ones. I went to a party afterward feeling like Dracula's daughter—with talons.

The next day I had to have them chipped off; that was my first and last attempt at being glamorous!

—Judy Garland

the 1940s

With the release of *The Wizard of Oz* and *Babes in Arms*, public delight in (and demand for) Judy Garland reached a new intensity. Future response to her performances and personality would hit even higher emotional peaks, but the enthusiasm for her entertainment throughout the 1940s spurred a decade of cumulative work that few others matched in terms of output and quality.

The forums in which she worked from 1940–1950 were the same as those of the immediately preceding years: motion pictures, records, and radio. The decade began with recognition for her performances as a 1939 screen juvenile when Judy was presented with a special Academy Award Oscar in February 1940. Over the next ten years, she starred or costarred in sixteen additional motion pictures, made guest appearances in four others, and turned up in a couple of short subjects. She achieved rank as one of the top ten box office stars in 1940, 1941, and 1945; eleven of her movies were among the greatest moneymaking product of 1940, 1941, 1944, 1945, 1946, 1947, 1948, and 1949.

Garland films of the '40s can best be categorized in three "mini-eras." The first few years of the decade saw an uproariously successful continuation of her on-screen partnership with Mickey Rooney. Twice more, she joined "the kid from Carvel" in his Andy Hardy series, but the duo was most appreciated for their "let's put on a show!" musicals, all three of which followed the trailblazing pattern of *Babes in Arms*. Understandably, the Mickey & Judy pictures were produced both to showcase their prodigious talents and to milk their topical celebrity, but Metro was also mounting vehicles to highlight Judy alone. She was given the chance to shine in 1940's *Little Nellie Kelly* (in which she played a dual role of mother and daughter) and in 1941's all-star *Ziegfeld Girl*. Judy's was the sole character propelled to fame in the script of the latter picture—competition be damned from the more glamorously bedecked creatures portrayed by Lana Turner and Hedy Lamarr.

Phase two of her 1940s film career was signified by more adult roles and the studio's acknowledgment that Garland was an out-of-the-ordinary box office draw. She was one of the few entertainers who could be billed alone above the title of her films, requiring no costar to ensure ticket sales. Such billing first occurred with *For Me and My Gal* in 1942; so potent was her appeal by this point that her professional and financial worth to M-G-M was editorialized on the front page of the *Hollywood Reporter* trade journal. The box office momentum and critical paeans only escalated with the subsequent release of (among others) *Presenting Lily Mars*, *Meet Me in St. Louis*, *The Clock*, and *The Harvey Girls*.

Meet Me in St. Louis in particular achieved a popular and Technicolor success surpassing (for the moment) even that of *The Wizard of Oz*. Historically, much has been made of the fact that Garland initially refused the assignment; it was

a wise decision on her part, as the early scripts of *St. Louis* were muddled and muddied by extraneous and silly plot complications. But as ultimately refined for production and as glowingly conceived and executed by the assembled members of the M-G-M (Arthur) "Freed Unit," *Meet Me in St. Louis* gave Judy a star showcase in a valentine setting. Her ability to virtually reach out from the screen then presented that gift to thrilled audiences, and the film was acclaimed by no less a highbrow critic than James Agee as "a musical even the deaf should enjoy."

Garland's final "era" at M-G-M produced motion pictures that continued the pattern: commercially successful work that possessed as well a special sheen of artistry. (Or as one contemporary critic decided, "There can be no rivalry for the individuality she brings to a musical film.") Of her last movies of the decade—including *Till the Clouds Roll By*, *Easter Parade*, *Words and Music*, *In the Good Old Summertime*, and *Summer Stock*—only the oddly experimental, avant-garde *The Pirate* failed on initial release to return a profit. She was easily the most highly regarded and respected musical leading lady in Hollywood, alternately described as the quintessential triple-threat talent or as the studio's greatest asset.

The decade also brought Garland increased success and sales as a recording artist. Earlier—between June 1936 and October 1939—she'd cut twenty-one sides for Decca, including the charting and best-selling "Over the Rainbow." Between April 1940 and November 1947, there would be fifty-eight more recordings for the label. The repertoire was varied and imaginative, offering Judy the opportunity to commercially preserve many of her film songs of the era; participate in "original cast" 78 rpm sets of songs from *Girl Crazy*, *Meet Me in St. Louis*, and *The Harvey Girls*; and record popular songs of that time (including "That Old Black Magic," the lyric of which Johnny Mercer wrote when inspired by a love affair with Garland). Thirteen of her 1940s titles charted: "I'm Nobody's Baby," "For Me and My Gal," "When You Wore a Tulip" (the last two as duets with Gene Kelly), "Zing! Went the Strings of My Heart," "A Journey to a Star," "The Trolley Song," "Meet Me in St. Louis," "Have Yourself a Merry Little Christmas," "Yah-Ta-Ta Yah-Ta-Ta (Talk, Talk, Talk)" (a novelty roundelay with Bing Crosby), "This Heart of Mine," "On the Atchison, Topeka, and the Santa Fe," "You'll Never Walk Alone," and "For You, For Me,

---

Opposite: *Top-billed over Fred Astaire in* Easter Parade *(1948), Judy enjoyed the greatest box office success of her career to that date. The film grossed $7 million on an investment of $2.5 million; Judy adored her partner but remembered serving as "his Japanese houseboy" on the set—greeting and charming visitors to get them off the soundstage as soon as possible while the shy, preoccupied Astaire hid out in his trailer.*

a number of cases, these programs were her only opportunity to duet and trade badinage with what would prove to be some of her most convivial costars.

Judy's by-now-legendary sense of humor was also well served by radio. Whether she was breaking up over (or with) her fellow performers or careening through madcap characterizations in sketch comedy, Garland often seemed at her most ebullient during a broadcast. Even her own foibles provided fodder for laughter and self-deprecation: "During the war, [the networks] were doing overseas broadcasts for the troops. [And at that point] I had never worked with Bing Crosby or Frank Sinatra before. So we first got together around the microphone and sorta said, 'How do you do, how do you do?' and so forth. [Now] Meredith Willson was conducting the orchestra, and he had written a special piece of material for the three of us. [Well,] he handed us the music, and we all three went absolutely blank; there was a great lull. And I thought, 'Oh, dear; they probably know how to read music . . . and I don't want to admit that [I don't!]' But there was just no sound coming except great clearing of throats and so on. And finally I said, 'I don't know about you fellahs, but I can't read a note!' And they [blurted], 'Neither can we!' So we all rushed to the piano to learn it by ear!"

In addition to her 1940s films, records, and radio, Judy was a selfless participant in the stateside war effort. She did three tours of duty around the country, singing multiple shows a day in service hospitals and for massed army camps. There was also a 1943 War Bond train trek with a dozen other stars; their whistle-stop appearances and auditorium rallies sold more than a billion dollars in bonds. Finally, when at home in Los Angeles, she made regular appearances at the Hollywood Canteen, which had been established to provide a star-studded recreation hall/nightclub for any of the military passing through town.

If her career was one triumph after another (at least until near the end of the decade), Garland's personal life in the 1940s was sometimes less jubilant. At home, she was forced to cope with her mother's marriage to Will Gilmore, a man to whom Judy objected; he and Ethel Gumm had begun their liaison long before the death of Garland's father. Judy herself suffered through unsuccessful love affairs with musician Artie Shaw, actor Tyrone Power, and producer/writer Joseph Mankiewicz. In July 1941, at age nineteen, she eloped with composer/conductor David Rose, and as Garland's frequent confidante June Allyson simply summarized, "I think she married too young to get away from everybody telling her what to do." (The marriage lasted scarcely two years.) After an on-again, off-again courtship, Judy married for the second time in 1945; Vincente Minnelli was nearly twenty years her senior, but he'd successfully directed her in three films. On March 12, 1946, the union produced a treasured daughter, Liza May, but the artful Minnelli was far from an ideal husband. Allyson later spoke for many when she declared, "It was no surprise when it [couldn't] work out. He was wrong for Judy, totally wrong." The Garland-Minnelli union collapsed for good in 1950; as Allyson sagely reflected, "I think Judy always chose the wrong man. As brilliant as she was about almost everything, she had no sense about men. And I think that came out of her insecurity, her [disbelief that] 'My gosh. He'll marry me!' And she couldn't believe that some man would really want her." Garland's omnipresent lack of confidence about her desirability stemmed from her earliest days on the Metro lot; from the onset, she had been made to feel in competition with the faces and figures of the glamour girls who had nowhere near her talent but who presented the beauty demanded by the screen.

Forevermore" (in which she teamed with Dick Haymes). Also charting were the albums of songs from *St. Louis*, *Till the Clouds Roll By*, and *Summer Stock*; the last two of these were among the actual "Original Soundtrack Recordings" released by M-G-M when it opened its own record company in 1947.

Even while merely recording, Garland frequently and unwittingly manifested her unique charisma. Lyn Murray was Decca's music director for some of Judy's 1945 sessions, and he never forgot the logistics on those dates: "In the recording setup, I was about three feet from her. . . . The chills ran up me when she sang, [and] the orchestra felt it, too."

More immediately ephemeral than film and recording work was the product of Judy's third predominant 1940s career. But radio was in some ways her most fulfilling and ideal forum. She didn't have to worry about the glamour required for making movies, and best of all, there were often live studio audiences during the broadcasts: Baby Gumm was getting a chance to once again sing to the people. Garland did nearly 150 radio shows during the 1940s, not only plugging her films and film songs but performing scores of numbers new to her repertoire; in

Judy's main problem in the 1940s, however, would come with the escalation of her need for prescription medication: the stimulants and sedatives on which she became dependent for energy and sleep. It is now uncertain whether the addictions began with her mother's determination to keep the child "pepped up" or when the studio doctors prescribed the new "miracle drug" Benzedrine to help the four-foot-eleven Garland maintain a camera-thin ninety-five pounds. While most entertainment critics found a less-lean Judy both far more attractive and effective than the wraith Metro demanded, such comment meant little to the front office hierarchy. Meanwhile, to counteract the churning false energy, sleeping pills were prescribed at night. The cycle was soon out of control, the need for larger and larger doses unavoidable.

Compounding the medication was Garland's intense schedule. The overwork demanded of her throughout the decade was consistent (apart from a pregnancy leave while expecting and first raising Liza). She suffered malnutrition, whether from studio-imposed diets or as a side effect of the pills. As the 1940s wore on, she was increasingly unable to meet shooting schedules; there were late

arrivals and missed days—and occasionally even weeks—of work. She endured episodes in psychiatry and sanatoria; in 1948, Judy had her third major physical collapse in five years and had to be replaced in the film *The Barkleys of Broadway*. The same thing happened the next year after she had already begun *Annie Get Your Gun*.

Though far overdue in its attempts, M-G-M did try to provide hospitalization, treatment, and support for Judy in 1947–50. But it was all too little, far too late. In October 1949, she began preproduction of *Summer Stock*; though there were delays along the way, the finished product was only $50,000 over budget and a sensation in its opening weeks of release. By that time, however, Judy was once again on suspension. Her promised eight-month vacation had been truncated after three weeks so that she could replace a pregnant June Allyson in *Royal Wedding*. Best intentions aside, Garland was far from well; she faced minimal compassion from director Stanley Donen, as well as the added tension being spread around the studio by new, unsympathetic honcho Dore Schary. Despite all that, a beaming Garland was cheered by the on-set crew for her chic and radiant appearance during a preliminary wardrobe test for the film. Moments later, however, she was emotionally decimated by a chance, thoughtless crack from preoccupied producer Arthur Freed: "What are you made up for?" He and Judy adored each other; had she been less on edge or he been more sensitive, there would have been no trouble.

The next day, she canceled a basically nonessential rehearsal; the studio dropped her from the film in retaliation, and a briefly hysterical Garland made a minor cut on her throat with a piece of broken glass. There were immediate international headlines and massive sympathy for the star, both from the public and from the vast army of M-G-M coworkers, in front of and behind the camera.

If devastated by the latest developments in her life, Garland nonetheless made a swift recovery. Within days of the "suicide" try, she was visited at home by songwriter Hugh Martin, a cherished friend. "Just a few people were allowed in; I was very honored that she wanted to see me. Katharine Hepburn and Donald O'Connor were there the night I was there. And Gene Kelly. And I remember Judy was already speaking offhandedly about what had happened—as only she could. And humorously, she said, 'Yes, Arthur affects people different ways . . . I cut my throat!'"

Bing Crosby's radio writers enabled Garland to offer an even more cavalier and self-mocking "take" on the situation. Months later, while Judy was broadcasting with Crosby, he was scripted to inquire: "Oh, were you going to be in *Royal Wedding* out at M-G-M?"

Referencing Metro's mascot—the "king of the beasts" whose roar opened every one of the studio's movies—Judy gleefully riposted, "I was, before Leo the Lion bit me!"

The elegant M-G-M star in one of her final portrait sittings at M-G-M.

Getting the Oscar was the most sensational moment of my career [to that date]. The lump in my throat was so big when I sang "Over the Rainbow" that I sounded more like Flip the Frog than the most excited girl in all of Hollywood. And I'll never forget how Mickey came to my rescue. I was so nervous, I thought I would faint. He practically held me up through the second chorus!

—Judy Garland

Despite two later nominations, Judy received what would be her only tangible recognition from the Academy of Motion Picture Arts and Sciences when Mickey Rooney presented her with a miniature statuette on February 29, 1940. The award commemorated her "outstanding performance" as a screen juvenile in 1939; on the same evening, "Over the Rainbow" won Oscars for Harold Arlen and E.Y. Harburg for best song, and The Wizard of Oz original score won a similar accolade for M-G-M's musical mainstay, Herbert Stothart. (Though nominated for best picture, Oz relinquished that honor to Gone With the Wind.) During the ceremonies, Judy sang "Rainbow" for the assembled Hollywood royalty in a performance that the press appreciatively deemed "never more persuasive . . . with a suspicious little quaver in her voice."

At home at 1231 Stone Canyon Road. Garland avowedly built the house to provide for her mother, although at some point, all three Garland girls lived there. (Sue and Lee Kahn were already divorced; she would remarry in 1941 to cornetist Jack Cathcart, who became Judy's musical conductor in the 1950s. Jimmie's first marriage to musical arranger Bobby Sherwood would end in divorce as well, and she would marry another arranger, John Thompson, in 1949.) Judy's private suite included a large daybed, a record-your-own-voice phonograph machine, a large record collection, and photographs of family, friends, and costars.

*M*y mother decorated that house on Stone Canyon, and while Judy was very happy about having it, she wasn't happy about going in and out the front door with her mother saying, "Don't wear this," and "Do that," and "Who's that guy you're going with?" So they built a stairway on the side of the house that went up to her bedroom and put a door there. Judy had her own key—her own dressing room and suite with this private entrance. (All of this because Mr. Mayer heard she was going to move out, and he would not have any of that: she must live with her mother and be a nice girl!)

But she was a dear kid, a dear young girl, a dear lady. You always wanted to do something for her, you wanted to help her, you wanted to make her laugh. And when I was single, she was fascinating—a most interesting, unusual person at every age.

—*Jackie Cooper*

Right: *A one-sheet poster for Judy's return visit with America's preeminent film family. She enthused at the time, "I never was happier than when I found out I was going to play in a second Hardy film." She then referenced the 1938* Love Finds Andy Hardy *as "a picture which is a picture. It was about real people, and the Hardys in real life are real people. I didn't feel I was acting at all."* Andy Hardy Meets Debutante *was actually a stopgap in the teen's film schedule. Arthur Freed had been preparing a remake of the Broadway musical* Good News *as the Garland/Rooney follow-up to* Babes in Arms. *When Louis B. Mayer suggested instead that the producer capitalize on both "swing" music and the growing national patriotic fervor, Freed switched plans. He had a new story created and titled* Strike Up the Band, *using the popular George and Ira Gershwin song standard as its theme. While that script was being written, Judy was assigned the Hardy picture so as to get her back on the screen as quickly as possible.*

Above: *A Spanish herald for* Andy Hardy Meets Debutante. *The film gave Garland one of her great Decca record hits when she revived on-screen and disc the 1921 classic "I'm Nobody's Baby." Her rendition of the Freed/Brown "Alone" was also heard in the picture, although their "All I Do Is Dream of You" and the Arlen/Harburg "Buds Won't Bud" were prerecorded and filmed by Judy but dropped from the movie prior to release.*

Left: *Andy proudly indicates a (borrowed) $400 pearl shirt stud. The fact that he eventually manages to lose it provides one of the script's complications—most of which are left to Betsy Booth (Judy) to sort out before the final credits. Her character is pretty much regarded as a mere child by the too-big-for-his-britches protagonist; by the end of the picture, she impresses him as both vocalist and potential girlfriend.*

Below: *Betsy greets Judge Hardy's family on their New York arrival in this scene from* Andy Hardy Meets Debutante *(1940). From left, Sara Haden as Aunt Millie Forrest, Mickey Rooney as (then and forever) Andy Hardy, Cecilia Parker as his sister Marian, Judy, Lewis Stone as Judge James K. Hardy, and Fay Holden as Mrs. Emily Forrest Hardy.*

Right: *A Danish poster for* Strike Up the Band *(1940). The unabashedly rousing and sentimental nature of the film gave Rooney and Garland a chance to top both the gross and acclaim of* Babes in Arms; *it also reunited them with* Babes *costar June Preisser, once again cast as the vampy, blond "other teen" who temporarily distracts Mickey from duty and Judy. Busby Berkeley reprised his directorial chores as well, providing somewhat more intimate musical numbers than in his Warner Bros. heyday a half-dozen or so years earlier. (M-G-M director George Sidney once summarized in a single sentence the evolution of the movie musical from its beginnings in the late 1920s up to the onset of the "Freed Unit" in 1939: the first musicals, he explained, featured "thousands of girls kicking together . . . until somewhere along the line we found out that you could just have a close-up of Judy [instead]—and let it run for three minutes, because she had talent.")*

Opposite: *Mickey and Judy rehearse Roger Edens's "Do the La Conga" as the teen chorines of Hollywood look on. Apart from the title song and the show-within-a-show medley of classic Gay Nineties ballads, Edens composed all the music for* Strike Up the Band; *producer Arthur Freed then provided the lyric for the film's Oscar-nominated hit, "Our Love Affair" (per Rooney's later description, "one of the most beautiful love songs ever written"). The "La Conga" was a particularly taxing and exciting routine. Roger described the tune and lyric as "designed to cash in on the current dance craze. [Then when] they were ready to shoot, Berkeley decided he wanted to make it a huge number with about five minutes of Judy singing and every possible camera angle . . . and he decided he wanted to do the entire song and dance number in one take. Nobody thought it was possible, but he rehearsed it with a complete crew for five days, laying out every movement step by step, with cameras taking all kinds of angle shots of maracas and trumpets. It soon became like the opening night of a Broadway show. There was the same great tension, because the number could only be shot once. When the morning came to shoot, the whole studio was down there. Everyone was very tense and keyed up—and the result was a real giving performance. The scene went beautifully, without a hitch. Even now, it has an unforgettable something extra about it."*

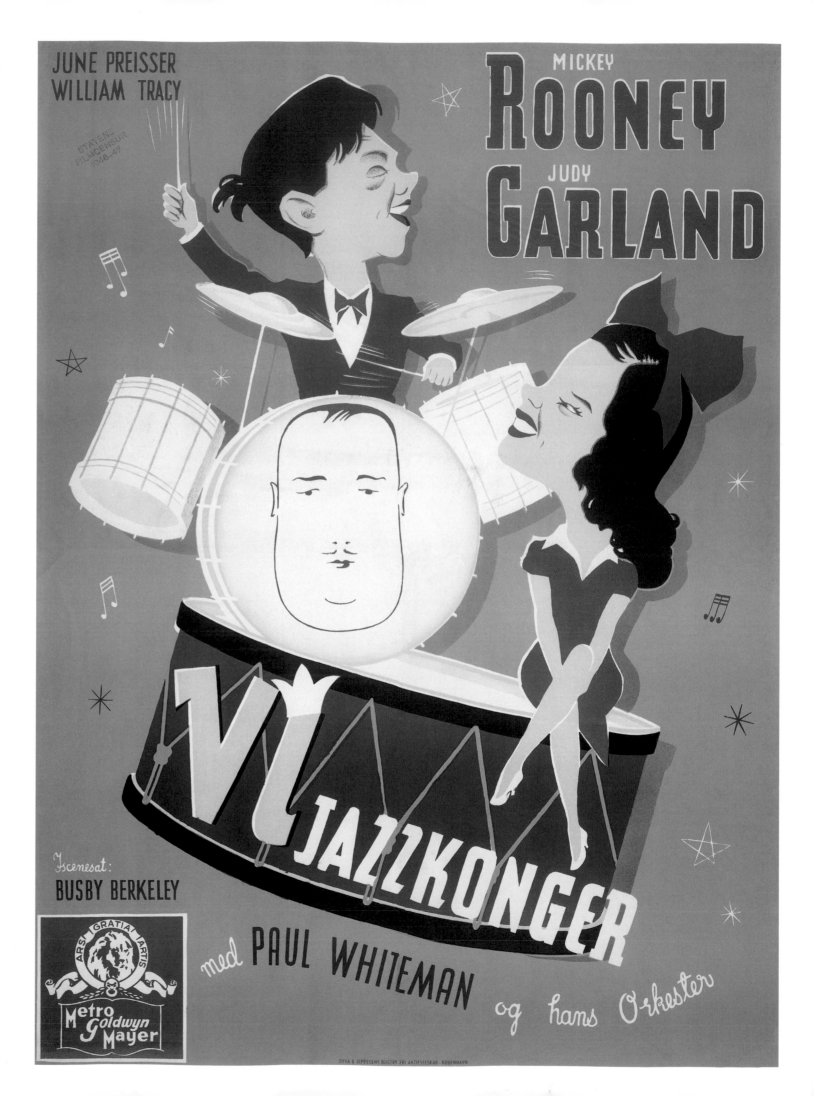

Below: *Director Berkeley hovers as Judy and Mickey rehearse a pivotal scene for* Strike Up the Band. *The clipping that Mary Holden clasps has provided them news of a national high school band competition, to be presented by the legendary maestro Paul Whiteman on his coast-to-coast radio program. In the script, Mickey's Jimmy Connors is a kid drummer and conductor of his own teen aggregation; Mary is his vocalist— and the contest is the kind of opportunity about which the kids have dreamed.*

Left: *Judy leads the ladies of the ensemble in their fund-raising Elks Club musicale,* Nell of New Rochelle. *(The show has been mounted to raise funds for the band's trip to Chicago for the Whiteman contest. In best Metro fashion, however, Mickey and Judy instead relinquish the cash to meet the health emergency of a local youngster.) Flanking Judy to her right is Margaret Early; to her left is June Preisser.*

*J*udy called me "Uncle Buzz" and always wanted me right there when the camera was photographing her. She would not do a scene unless I stood by the camera, and afterward she asked me how she looked and if she had done all right.

She was the sweetest girl—so unspoiled and so cooperative. She and Mickey had great respect for each other's ability. I don't know any two kids who could be better than those two were. Over at Universal, they teamed a couple of very talented kids, Donald O'Connor and Peggy Ryan. And they had Deanna Durbin. But nobody ever topped Judy and Mickey.

—Busby Berkeley

On June 26, 1940, Judy joined the senior class of the local University High School for their graduation ceremonies. She later wrote, "I wasn't one speck different from any of the other 249 girls. I wore a plain blue organdy dress . . . and carried a bouquet of sweetheart roses, just like the others; the flowers were provided by the school. I almost missed my place in line, too, because Mother sent me a lovely corsage of mystery gardenias, and Mickey sent me a cluster of orchids. And I had to dash into the audience and explain to Mom that I loved the corsages but I just couldn't wear them: 'I can't be different from the other girls . . . please don't be hurt, but that's the way it is.'" The press was requested to stay away, although at least one photographer immortalized mother and daughter at the end of the proceedings; he noted that "mobs of kids surrounded Judy when the exercises were over."

Right: *On September 5, 1940—bedecked for final sequences of* Little Nellie Kelly— *Judy and on-screen beau Douglas McPhail stride to their Metro soundstage. He had first played with Garland and Rooney in* Babes in Arms; *his featured role in the even earlier* Love Finds Andy Hardy *was dropped from the script prior to filming.*

Below: *Half-sheet poster for* Little Nellie Kelly (1940). *The original George M. Cohan stage musical was a Broadway success in 1922, but M-G-M producer Arthur Freed kept only its title, the plot point that Nellie was the daughter of a police captain, and one song ("Nellie Kelly, I Love You") in remounting the vehicle for Judy. Another Cohan tune, "You Remind Me of My Mother"— McPhail's solo—was deleted from the film before release.*

Little Nellie Kelly *provided Garland with her only dual role on screen. She begins the picture as an Irish immigrant who eventually dies giving birth to her only child. The baby's early years are dismissed in a couple of quick scenes and a montage; suddenly, the girl is sixteen—and Judy's back! Garland's own heritage was Scottish/Irish, and although she would again offer a Freed/Brown classic ("Singin' in the Rain") as her major number in* Little Nellie Kelly, *Roger Edens capitalized on her ancestry by preparing as well an arrangement of "A Pretty Girl Milking Her Cow." By Garland's admission, that song was an Edens discovery. "an obscure, Irish folk song that fit the picture quite well. So we did it. And they released the picture . . . and the song became an obscure Irish folk song!" She nonetheless included the song in her stage, television, and recording repertoire, but it was another Edens original—"It's a Great Day for the Irish"—that sparkled the most musical magic. His tune, lyric, and Judy's delivery quickly achieved Saint Patrick's Day standard status. (Unfortunately, a tender Garland rendition of "Danny Boy" landed on the cutting room floor.)*

*A*pparently there was a market for "family" pictures in those days. Little Nellie Kelly broke all box office records wherever it played. When the picture was being cast, Judy and I made a screen test with Barry Fitzgerald of the delightful Irish brogue. I thought Barry was fantastic; the producer thought otherwise. "You can't understand him," he argued. "You don't have to understand him," I said. "All you have to do is watch him on the screen, and you know what he's doing." The producer wouldn't buy my argument and gave the role [of Judy's father] to Charlie Winninger. [But] I was proved right about Fitzgerald some years later when he and Bing Crosby made Going My Way. . . .

Judy and Mickey Rooney were [then] the mainstays of the studio. For several years, their films helped keep that giant factory afloat in a sea of increased competition. As a consequence, they were worked far beyond their endurance . . . they were making three or four pictures a year with no rest in between. [Studio head] Louie Mayer really loved those kids as much as if they were his own. He was terribly proud of them and their successes, but sometimes he would forget they were only children.

For little Judy, it was all too much. At a time when other girls her age were having teen-age fun, Judy was constantly working— learning new songs, new dance routines, studying parts. . . . [But] she was a true professional, and I recall a scene she did in Little Nellie Kelly; we were in a hospital, and she was about to die [after] the birth of her only child. I assure one and all that this was one of the greatest dramatic scenes that I have ever witnessed. It took me longer to get over it than it took Judy!

—*G*eorge *M*urphy

Above: *Judy rehearses with future United States senator George Murphy for "Nellie Kelly, I Love You." Garland remains the only woman to have danced on-screen with four preeminent song-and-dance men: Murphy, Gene Kelly, Fred Astaire, and Ray Bolger.*

Opposite: *With the chorus at the Police Ball, during actual filming of the routine.*

Le Fanciulle delle "Follie"

JAMES STEWART
and JUDY GARLAND
HEDY LAMARR
LANA TURNER

JACKIE COOPER
E. E. HORTON

regia di
ROBERT Z. LEONARD

Metro-Goldwyn-Mayer

GRAFICHE I.G.A.P. ROMA

I was, of course, aware of Judy before we did *Ziegfeld Girl* . . . but she didn't work at being impressive when you knew her: she was just darling. There was this sense that she loved everyone . . . and everyone loved her. That was one thing about Judy: she loved to be loved. So she made a lot of mistakes, like everyone does— and I say that very affectionately.

And that was such a heavy workload for her; she was doing three and four pictures a year at that point.

As [contract] dancers, we were expected to do ballet or anything else. But you don't expect the star to dance that way; whoever the star is, you work around her talents. But Judy could dance; and when the choreographer would explain what he wanted, she would catch on very quickly. Her talent was unbelievable.

It was the same with her acting: she could take a script, cold, read it [and perform], and you'd think she'd studied it for two weeks.

—Dorothy Tuttle Nitch,
M-G-M Contract Dancer

Above: *Italian poster for* Ziegfeld Girl *(1941). In addition to the top-billed star power shown here, the picture also boasted the talents of Tony Martin, Jackie Cooper, Charles Winninger, Edward Everett Horton, Ian Hunter, Eve Arden, Al Shean, Philip Dorn, and Fay Holden—all audience favorites of that era. Musical numbers were overseen by Busby Berkeley, including "You Stepped Out of a Dream," a new Gus Kahn / Nacio Herb Brown song that became an instant hit.*

Right: *As dancing partner Señor Orta looks on, Judy adjusts an earring between takes of "Minnie from Trinidad," the Roger Edens specialty routine that provided her major production showcase in the picture. It was, as Roger defined it, the "hot number" Judy always wanted—if, in this case, less than torrid and still pretty tongue-in-cheek (i.e., "They call her Minnie from Trinidad . . . she wasn't good—but she wasn't bad!"). All lavish Berkeley trappings aside, Garland's most memorable musical moment in* Ziegfeld Girl *was a reflective revival of the 1918 "I'm Always Chasing Rainbows."*

Jackie Cooper with Judy; she's in costume for "Laugh? I Thought I'd Split My Sides" for Ziegfeld Girl. He played her boyfriend in the film; it was the only chance the two would have to work together, although they had remained friends since 1935. By 1940, Cooper was more or less watching from the sidelines and trying to help Judy through the throes of her offscreen passion for much older musician Artie Shaw. "Nobody would have wanted her to see him . . . but she would ask me to take her over to his place. And I could see they couldn't wait for me to leave! So I'd go and kill some time and then later pick her up and bring her home. So I was the guy she had the date with—not Artie—as far as Judy's mother and Mr. Mayer and anybody was concerned!"

I think the one difference between my show business family and hers is that mine never pushed me into [a career]. And I think Judy's mother was living out her ideal of what she herself had wanted to be as a singer. She had the three girls, and they were all talented. But Judy by far was the most brilliant . . . and so I think she was pushed a great deal.

And I think the greatest tragedy of Judy's life was when . . . her father [died]. Because she needed that wonderful thing that a father can do for you—that my father [songwriter Richard Whiting] did for me before he passed away. They had had that bond of music and caring; I know that she and I talked about it several times . . . and how unhappy she was about losing that father figure in her life.

— Margaret Whiting

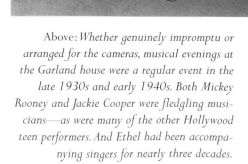

Above: *Whether genuinely impromptu or arranged for the cameras, musical evenings at the Garland house were a regular event in the late 1930s and early 1940s. Both Mickey Rooney and Jackie Cooper were fledgling musicians—as were many of the other Hollywood teen performers. And Ethel had been accompanying singers for nearly three decades.*

Opposite: *Mother and daughters, 1940. From left, on the sofa: Susie, Jimmie, and Judy.*

Above: *A happy second birthday party for Judy's niece, Judaline, held at the Stone Canyon house. Judaline—daughter of sister Jimmie and first husband Bobby Sherwood—is about to disembark from the bottom of the slide. Aunt Judy is helping one of her friends, mid-trip.*

Above: Life Begins for Andy Hardy (1941). *Andy is a hapless high school graduate and Betsy Booth a sleeker, chic-er New Yorker in this, their third and final on-screen encounter. As ever, she lives to help with his problems; for the moment, they encompass joblessness in Manhattan, the death of a friend, the pawning of a car, and the prowling of a "wolfess."*

Right: *Advertising herald. Although Judy recorded four numbers for* Life Begins for Andy Hardy, *they were all dropped from the picture (perhaps so as not to take the edge off the forthcoming Garland / Rooney Babes on Broadway). The picture thus finds her songless but for a brief a cappella rendition of "Happy Birthday."*

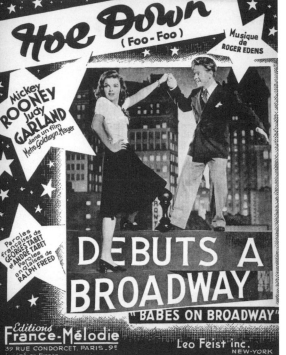

Left: Candid camping during a rehearsal of "Hoe Down," the Busby Berkeley swing/square dance that provided Babes on Broadway (1941) with its production centerpiece. Here, Garland underplays to Mickey Rooney's mugging while featured players Richard Quine and Annie Rooney (no relation) look on over Judy's right shoulder. Another Edens melody (with a lyric by Arthur Freed's brother, Ralph), "Hoe Down" ran more than seven minutes on the screen, amalgamating Garland's vocal, a specialty tap by Ray McDonald, and an auditorium full of jiving chorus kids.

Above: The Edens/Freed title—and the latter's lyric—seem to have suffered (if not died) in translation. Per Georges and André Tabet, "Hoe Down" reached France as "Foo-Foo" ("On dan-se le foo-foo!"). Contemporary French critics reportedly had some antipathy to the Rooney/Garland musicals; small wonder.

*S*even years after I played for one of Judy's
first M-G-M auditions, I was signed to a contract
to write the music for a picture called Babes on
Broadway. *This young kid who was twelve years
old seven years before had now become a giant
star; she and Mickey were the stars of this film.*

*One day, when I was sitting in the commissary
having my lunch, Arthur Freed (who was the
producer of the picture) came by and said, "Burt,
I think you ought to go over to the [sound]
stage . . . and break the kids into the songs." And
when I walked over to that stage and opened the
door, I became aware that someone was running,
running toward me. It was Judy Garland, who
threw herself into my arms and said, "Burt, I
never thanked you for what you did for me
[at my audition]. Thank you."*

*And that was this wonderful, wonderful,
wonderfully talented young girl, Judy Garland.*

*I remember, too, that everyone [at M-G-M]
was very thrilled about the songs for the picture.
The minute we finished "How About You?" we went
to play it for Arthur. It was he who had introduced me to his brother, Ralph, who was a very
good lyric writer . . . and we weren't a team long,
but we did come up with this one big, big hit.*

*Of course, Judy and Mickey were wonderful
together; he was always "on," doing something
outrageous: very imaginative, funny—the life
of the party. But Judy, I think, would have been
a partner to anybody and be wonderful. She had
a tremendous ability to move in any circle and
do the right thing. . . . She possessed this great
instinct in everything she did.*

*And many years later, my wife and I were
having dinner at Chasen's one night when Judy
came in with a group of people. So I brought my
wife over to her table as we were leaving, and
Judy got up, put her arms around my wife, and
she said, "You know, I owe everything I have to
your husband." And I was very touched by this—
the warmth of this affection, so long after the
actual event.*

—*B*urton *L*ane

*Rotogravure pose (1941) with Judy in her
"How About You?" wardrobe from Babes on
Broadway. The song went on to win an Academy
Award nomination for Burton Lane and Ralph Freed.*

Left: *Had the footage survived vault fires, nitrate deterioration, and wholesale discard, several feature-length motion pictures could be strung together using the songs, dances, and routines that were filmed for—but deleted from—movie musicals over the decades. The casualty from* Babes on Broadway *was "The Convict's Return," a comedy sketch written for the 1939 stage revue* The Streets of Paris *and originally performed by Bobby Clark.* Babes *producer Arthur Freed bought the material as a showcase for Judy and (specifically) Mickey: the latter would play a prison warden, a wealthy father, a family butler, and an escaped convict. Judy was the convict's long-suffering, long-anticipatory girlfriend, awaiting news of his flight from justice in "Any News from Armand?" The entire sequence was cut from the picture.*

Right: *One-sheet poster for* Babes on Broadway. *The relentless pace of the picture was matched by the dynamism of Garland and Rooney. To audiences everywhere, the two had long since come to typify "the kids next door"—although, as a journalist has since pointed out, the kids next door didn't have the Garland/Rooney charisma, chemistry, or talent. And if their films were of their time, their talent was timeless.* Babes on Broadway *was highlighted by a melange of new and old musical thrills: Garland infused the banal "Chin Up, Cheerio, Carry On" with a rallying, wartime surge of passion, and she joined Rooney to deliver tribute in song or recitation to such veteran entertainers as Sarah Bernhardt, George M. Cohan, Fay Templeton, Blanche Ring, Sir Harry Lauder, and Richard Mansfield. Mickey wickedly platform-shoed his way through an impersonation of Carmen Miranda. And the entire cast put forth a then-traditional minstrel show, highlighted by Judy's full-throttle "F. D. R. Jones"; she had been singing the song on stage and radio for the preceding three seasons and herein had a chance to perform it for posterity.*

*J*udy had the advantage of working with wonderful people; we all did. Roger Edens would come into the rehearsal hall, always excited with his work. And so everyone else got excited. Kay Thompson would come in—her stole dragging on the floor—and we'd watch [in astonishment] 'til she got to the piano and started playing. . . .

Some of these people were as dramatic as the stars: [choreographer] Bob Alton was famous for offering staging directions while sitting down. He would look around and say, "Now, uh . . . ," and just indicate with his hand. Then he'd put his leg out and he'd point it: "You, over there. You, over there." He did all the directing with his foot!

— *Dorothy Tuttle Nitch*

*R*oger Edens was Judy Garland; he became Judy Garland: his songs, the way he wrote them, the dialogue that he did. And then, of course, he got Kay Thompson in later to work with her. That was all Roger's doing, and Kay taught Judy a lot . . . but it was all basically Roger's doing: all the great arrangements.

— *Ann Miller*

Georgie Stoll conducts the rehearsal while Roger Edens (center foreground, in profile) discusses prerecordings for Babes on Broadway *with—among others—Judy and Busby Berkeley. Garland would later laughingly remember the effort that went into creating, perfecting, and performing the long, medley-prone arrangements in her Metro musicals: "We'd spend weeks. Then Mr. Mayer would come in, listen and watch, and when we were done, he'd say, 'That's great. GREAT! I want four more just like it. By Thursday.'"*

I can't remember who had the party; I know Oscar Levant was there, I think [Ira] Gershwin was there— and all the top people of Hollywood. And I wanted to go to the ladies' room, so I went upstairs to the hostess's bedroom . . . and Judy was sitting on the floor, kind of smiling. I said, "Hey, can I join you?". . . and we had a real one-to-one, woman-to-woman talk.

And she said, "You know the toughest thing for me: I'm at the best studio. I've got the most wonderful directors and cameramen and people to work with. . . . But I'm also at a studio where there's Ava Gardner and there's Lana Turner and there's Gloria DeHaven," and she went through [the list of] all the big stars, Greer Garson and everybody that was [at M-G-M]. And she said, "They're all so beautiful. And I look at myself, and I know I'm not beautiful."

And I said, "Judy . . . You're out of your mind. The way you sing, the way you look with those gorgeous eyes and that wonderful voice and that great personality. I've got to tell you: you're the most beautiful one of them all." And we threw our arms around each other and cried. And then I said, "Come on, let's go back to the party," and that's the way the evening ended.

But I mean, it's true. She was as beautiful as anybody.

— *Margaret Whiting*

Judy—happily married, rising ever higher in her career—in late 1941.

The courtship of Judy and David Rose. A mutual passion for music gave the duo at least a partial foundation for their romance; during their time together, Rose conducted the orchestra for Garland at a half-dozen Decca sessions, on radio, and at benefit shows on many occasions. Judy's mother threw an engagement party for the couple at the Stone Canyon house on June 15, 1941; although they announced they wouldn't wed until the autumn, there was a sudden Las Vegas elopement, and they were married on July 28.

*J*udy had been going with Artie Shaw; she was mad about him. And he asked her to marry him . . . and [then one] morning the headlines read: "Artie Shaw and Lana Turner Wed in Las Vegas." [After] that night, Judy . . . came in my dressing room; we were doing radio that evening. And she really threw herself against the wall; I was trying to shake her, trying to straighten her out. She was sobbing, "How could he do that? . . . ." And I finally said, "I don't know, darling, but there will be others, and they'll be the right ones." And on cue, David Rose—[who] was on staff at NBC—walked in, and he sat down with us . . . and he said, "Let me take you for a drink, Judy."

Meanwhile, of course, she'd been crying and going to pieces. And suddenly they said, "Miss Garland, you're on!" And she said, "Oh! Oh!" And she dried her eyes and went out on the stage and did her bit and sang so brilliantly, I couldn't stand it!

David came along in her life when she needed somebody. Now Artie was a very articulate, brilliant man. Not that David wasn't, but David was kinder, softer . . . and a true musician who used to play marvelous piano. . . . It was a very beautiful love affair but probably couldn't have lasted. For the moment, though, and after Artie Shaw, it was a blessing.

[Later] Judy was terribly in love with Tyrone Power . . . and I think Joe Mankiewicz was probably the love of her life. But of course, he was married, and the studio broke that up.

— *M*argaret *W*hiting

*When she was married to
David Rose, she was young and fresh
and beautiful. And we would sit on
the floor at their house; she'd have
people over like Danny Kaye, and
they'd stand up, and they'd entertain
us. She'd serve spaghetti and wine—
very, very informal. We loved going
to her house; and we loved David.
He was quiet, but he was darling.
And she was a charming hostess.*

—Marcella Rabwin

*More than five months after their marriage,
Judy and David Rose enjoyed what the press
termed "a deferred honeymoon." They are
shown here at the Lord Tarleton in Miami
Beach in January 1942.*

Left: *Judy and David Rose cut short their honeymoon and opted instead to tour for the U.S.O. From Michigan to Kentucky, Missouri, Arkansas, and Texas, she sang and he played or conducted. Between shows, they kibitzed with the boys.*

Opposite: *There's no mistaking the rapt attention of the audience, but the little boy in the second seat off the aisle offers proof positive even then of Garland's cross-generational appeal. (Ethel Gumm Garland is just down the row from him.) Judy's repertoire— in what was usually a four-show-a-day setup—included "Blow, Gabriel, Blow," "This Love of Mine," "Blues in the Night," "Over the Rainbow," "Chattanooga Choo-Choo," and "Abe Lincoln Had But One Country."*

There was nothing like a military audience; you got a chance to go out and meet this marvelous audience of men who were about to go overseas to fight for us. And they were so appreciative; it was just a learning time for all of us.

A star like Judy would go out on a bond[-selling] tour by train . . . she and Mickey Rooney and a bunch of the other stars. They would stop in different little hamlets and big cities, and the people would come to the train stations to see them—and then they'd make appearances selling war bonds at theaters.

And she made appearances at the military bases as well.

— Margaret Whiting

Right: *Judy poses backstage before appearing in a musical revue presented by the Soldiers of the 73rd Evacuation Hospital Unit, West Los Angeles, October 20, 1942.*

*R*oger said they needed one more song for For Me and My Gal. But when Ralph [Blane] and I sang what we'd written for Judy— "Three Cheers for the Yanks"—Roger said, "I don't think they'll take it, because it sounds too current. It doesn't sound like World War I, it sounds like the Second World War." We had a lot of blue notes in it; it was kind of jazzy.

But Roger loved it so much that he said, "Go on out to Judy's house and teach it to her and see what she thinks. So with fear and trembling, we went out; I remember asking Roger, "What's this remarkable singer's range? What's her best tessitura?" And he said, "Oh, I wouldn't take her below an A or above an A; from A to A is about right for her." Well, this song I'd written for her was a two-octave range. And I sort of gulped and said, "That's interesting!" But I wanted it so much to be in the picture that I didn't say, "It's two octaves, Roger; let's forget it."

So he sent Ralph and me out there, and we sang it for her. And she hooted and hollered and loved it. And then she sang it back to us, note for note, two octaves and all. It was the scariest thing I've ever seen! We played it for her once, and she didn't read music. But she'd followed the lead sheet . . . and always landed on the right note somehow. And she said, "I want to do it. And we've got to do it."

And so it was orchestrated and shot. And then it was cut, because it was indeed out of key with the rest of the little World War I songs!

—*Hugh Martin*

Left: *Australian insert poster for* For Me and My Gal *(1942). The film marked a new level of stardom for Garland. She was given solo billing above the title of the picture; it was also her first adult role. And if the vaudeville/World War I mix of plot and song standards was considered corny by some, it was—in the hands of Garland, Kelly, Murphy, producer Freed, director Berkeley, and supervisor Edens— extraordinarily effective entertainment for virtually all.*

Opposite: *Judy sings "How Ya Gonna Keep 'Em Down on the Farm?" in a servicemen's concert sequence.*

I was lucky enough to know Judy. The world has long recognized her incredible, truly enormous talent, her voice, her timing, her sense of humor, and her miraculous understanding of the human condition. This understanding informed all her work. She could be funny, sad, wistful, sophisticated, lusty, delicate, girlish, and womanly. Perhaps only Charlie Chaplin equals her in this—they both danced, but he couldn't sing!

She was [ninteen] when I arrived in Hollywood at seventeen with my brand-new husband, about-to-be-movie-star Gene Kelly. Judy had seen Gene in New York in Pal Joey, and she asked Metro for him to play opposite her in For Me and My Gal. [When] the casting of the film was set . . . we were invited to dinner at Judy and David Rose's house. She was a movie star; I was a girl from New Jersey who had danced in the chorus of one Broadway musical and played the lead in one straight play. Judy saw no difference between us. Her generosity, her sense of fun, her zest for life obliterated any possibility of grandeur or pretension. She was a joy to know. And Gene always publicly acknowledged her vital help to him on his first film when he was the novice.

—*Betsy Blair, Actress*

Right: A Sunday supplement newspaper ad for For Me and My Gal. *Originally, George Murphy was cast as the film's leading man, but Kelly's performing persona was much more in keeping with that character's traits. Garland was instrumental in effecting their switch in roles, and Kelly remained forever grateful for her support. (Even director Busby Berkeley—who was initially opposed to the change in casting—came around to approving Kelly. Despite his signature and landmark Warner Bros. musicals in the 1930s, Berkeley would eventually regard* For Me and My Gal *as his own favorite of the more than fifty films with which he was associated as director and/or choreographer.)*

Opposite: Garland and Kelly at work at M-G-M, 1942. Thirty-two years later, Gene, Fred Astaire, and Judy's daughter Liza Minnelli would gather at Metro for a press conference to promote That's Entertainment! *(1974), a celebratory feature film compilation of musical moments from the studio's archives. When the media asked that day what the two men remembered about their days at the studio, Astaire acknowledged the workload, and Kelly remembered the friendly jockeying between them to get to use "the big rehearsal hall." Someone from the press followed up, "Well, who got it?" The men looked at Liza and smiled: "Judy!"*

Left: *Herald for* Presenting Lily Mars *(1943). Originally purchased as a potential dramatic vehicle for Lana Turner, the Booth Tarkington story was considerably softened and turned into a musical for Judy. If massively clichéd, the plot contains a realistic twist: When temperamental European star (Marta Eggerth) storms out of the lead in a Broadway operetta, inexperienced chorine Garland is thrust into the role. But she's such an all-American girl from Indiana, she can't summon up the regal and foreign attitude to make the character believable—and Eggerth returns to replace her for the opening. (By the film's finale, of course, Lily Mars has the lead in her own, suitable musical comedy.) In addition to some splendid vocal star turns, Judy was especially effective duetting a tender "Every Little Movement Has a Meaning of Its Own" with an elderly theater charwoman played by Connie Gilchrist.*

Below: *Costume, makeup, and hair test reference photo for* Lily Mars; *Garland's modern wardrobe was designed by Howard Shoup, and his clothes were particularly becoming to the young woman she was now allowed to be on the screen.*

Opposite: *Garland with Van Heflin in* Presenting Lily Mars. *It's quite possible Judy never looked more beautiful onscreen than in this film; Liza Minnelli privately gives it as her own favorite of her mother's movies. Costar Heflin made a fine vis-a-vis, and he remained a lifelong Garland fan. One of his own favorite memories followed* Lily Mars *by a dozen years and occurred at the home of June Allyson and Dick Powell. Allyson gleefully admits that she had "made Dick buy me a great, big, baby grand piano, and I gave party after party—just so I could hear Judy sing." On one such occasion in February 1955, most of the guests had departed early; it was a Hollywood weeknight, and they had early studio calls. But Garland—accompanied by Johnny Green with Powell chiming in on either sax, trumpet, or vocals—sang from midnight until almost dawn. Despite his approaching workday, Heflin sat entranced, dismissing his wife's quiet admonitions that he should get at least a little sleep before heading to his film location: "Sleep I can always get; something like this comes along only once in a lifetime." Just before 6 A.M., Judy said, "Well, I think that's about it; I'm a little tired now." And as the Heflins drove down Mandeville Canyon with an out-of-town journalist who'd been a fellow guest, Van could only marvel over and over, "Once in a lifetime do you ever get to hear anything like that."*

My feeling then and today is that this lady could do anything on the screen; she had talent that would not quit. She didn't need to prepare and study and have somebody work with her; whatever it was that was needed, she had the talent to bring it right to the surface then. And she seemed to enjoy it, whatever it was. That was the great part. And it made it enjoyable for all the rest of us. And so often we were all laughing as we went into a scene or came out of a scene over something she had said. Now the remarkable thing about that is that she was really quite shy to be around on the set. She did not hang out with us. . . . But when the lights went on and the camera started, we were all buddies; we'd all been friends for life. She made it that way.

She wasn't a trained dancer, and this was obvious—as one dancer looking at another dancer. But it didn't matter; she carried it off with ease. I'm sure the audiences thought she was doing it all just perfectly. She had a style, and she certainly had a flair.

I had the privilege of working with a number of stars at M-G-M: Greer Garson, Marlene Dietrich—even a dance number with Greta Garbo. They're beautiful, but Judy was so far apart from them; these were big stars, but Judy went beyond that . . . and given a role could surpass them all.

—*Dorothy Gilmore Raye*, M-G-M Contract Dancer

Above: Van Heflin, director Norman Taurog (seated center), and Judy on the set of Presenting Lily Mars. *She is in costume for Lily's unique approach to Lady Macbeth and the sleepwalking scene.*

Right: The original Lily Mars finale, "Paging Mr. Greenback," was built around a number that M-G-M patriotically touted as "one of the best bond-selling songs of the year." Despite a chorus of 200 men and women (and a scenic backdrop left over from Babes in Arms*), the E.Y. Harburg/Sammy Fain/Lew Brown routine was dropped and replaced by the more lavish Edens treatment of "Where There's Music" and a medley of standards.*

*J*udy wasn't a dancer, but she could pick up a step instantly. And as a singer, she was incredible— she had only to hear a melody once, and it was locked in her mind. We used to call her 'Ol' Tin Ear.'

It was Judy who pulled me through our first picture together; her screen technique taught me virtually everything I learned. I knew nothing about filming when we started, and I was scared. But by the time we finished, I had picked up quite a lot of know-how, thanks to [Busby] Berkeley and thanks to her. She was very kind and helpful, more than she realized, because I watched her to find out what I had to do. She pitched her voice and her gestures very low, because she knew—which I didn't—that the soundtrack and camera pick up everything. I was amazed at her skill; she knew every mark and every move.

She was a very relaxed, marvelous person . . . the most talented performer we've ever had. And my favorite partner.

—*G*ene *K*elly

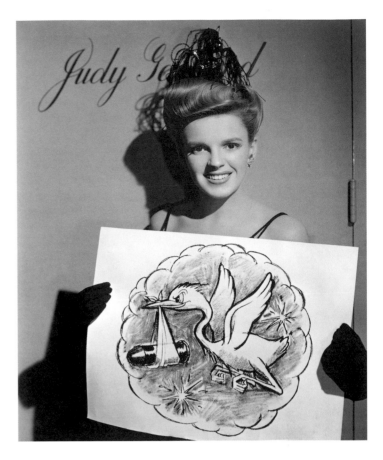

Above: *In March 1943, Judy prerecorded and filmed the new Lily Mars finale in this gown. The photograph was taken outside her on-set dressing room; she holds a cartoon in commemoration of one of the two World War II bomber planes named in her honor: "Imagine me bombing Hitler twice a day."*

Left: *Gene Kelly and Judy clown with the young Zero Mostel outside an M-G-M soundstage. The men are in costume for Du Barry Was a Lady, and Judy wears her "Greenback" gown from Presenting Lily Mars.*

Opposite: *Garland and Kelly in a graceful—if posed—whirl for the camera. One of the national magazines had planned a major photo feature on Garland's "average day" at the studio; a photographer shot these pictures and dozens of others on the "Greenback" set—before, during, and after the shooting of that number. When the song was dropped from Lily Mars, the negatives were thought worthless; now they provide an extraordinary glimpse of life at Metro in late autumn 1942.*

Below: *When wartime restrictions limited the number of elaborate movie posters that could be printed, hasty substitutes were issued by independent companies. Thousands Cheer (1943) was an M-G-M all-star Technicolor musical; the plotline was carried by Gene Kelly, Kathryn Grayson, Mary Astor, John Boles, and (in his screen debut) José Iturbi. But the film's selling point was an army camp show finale featuring much of the Metro roster. Mickey Rooney served as emcee and introduced songs, dances, and sketches by (among others) Red Skelton, Lena Horne, Eleanor Powell, Lucille Ball, Frank Morgan, Margaret O'Brien, Virginia O'Brien, June Allyson, Gloria DeHaven, Kay Kyser and His Orchestra, and Bob Crosby and His Orchestra. Judy had the climactic solo song, paired with pianist Iturbi in the Roger Edens/Hugh Martin/Ralph Blane number, "The Joint Is Really Jumpin' Down at Carnegie Hall." Even though the amount of time she, Rooney, and Skelton were actually onscreen in the picture is minimal, the independent poster company knew that it was their images that would bring in the cash customers. (The sketches were adaptations of those done for M-G-M by the renowned Al Hirschfeld.)*

$\mathcal{J}$ust before the war, we went to a party held by some patriotic group—the American Legion or something. And she sang, and she was wonderful as only she could be, moving the audience. At the end, she did "God Bless America." And as she sang it, tears started running down her face. And they picked her up on their shoulders, and they marched her around; it was one of the most exciting evenings of show business I can remember. And later on, I said, "How did you do that, Judy? How do you make the tears?" She said, "Well, Bobby, I just look up into the big spotlight, and it makes my eyes tear up!" So it's a combination of simple technique and this magic she had. . . .

A little later, I joined the navy. I was in there four years. And when I came back on leave, you'd be surprised how few people know who the heck you are. You call up girls you used to know before, and they're busy, and they've got their own romances, and there just ain't anybody there for the old sailor coming home. Judy, no matter what she had to do, would always cancel that for me: there she was. And she was my date over my leave . . . a gifted, wonderful talent and a dear, loyal friend.

—*Robert Stack*

Left: *In autumn 1942, Judy participated in this publicity photograph that urged the public to provide a Thanksgiving home away from home for servicemen during the holidays.*

Opposite: *One such serviceman on his leave, with his date—Judy and Robert Stack during the war.*

I had one quick song in Girl Crazy. And how Judy and I got to know and love each other so much, I'll never know. Because after that picture, they immediately tried to pit us against each other for film roles. When I got to Metro, they would say to me, "Well, if you don't behave yourself, you know we've got Judy. We'll put her in the picture; she can do anything." And they'd say to Judy, "You know, if you don't behave yourself, we've got this new kid on the block who can just step right into your shoes." Which was all silly, really. Arthur Freed knew if there was no Judy, there would be no picture. If they could have put Judy in every single picture they made, they would have! Because—I promise you—she had more talent in one little finger than all of us put together. When I think of a star, Judy immediately comes to my mind. Although she's never left it. She could tell a story that would last an hour and you'd never get bored . . . you just loved to watch her face when she talked. And she would do these imitations of people that were just right on. And sometimes she wasn't very kind— which was even funnier!

— *June Allyson*

Right: *Italian poster art for the last major Garland/Rooney musical,* Girl Crazy *(1943). Direction for the film was begun by Busby Berkeley, who had to be relieved of his duties when he insisted on overburdening the "I Got Rhythm" production number with cannons, whips, pistol shots, and extraneous activity. He was replaced by Norman Taurog; Charles "Chuck" Walters took over most of the musical staging.*

Opposite: *Who could ask for anything more? Rooney and Garland meet the music and words of George and Ira Gershwin—and the accompaniment of Tommy Dorsey and His Orchestra—in "I Got Rhythm." Rooney played Danny Churchill, Jr., eastern playboy sent West to school as a punishment by his father. Dad's non-coeducational concept dies aborning when the first person his son meets is Garland's Ginger Gray, granddaughter of the dean at the (otherwise) all-male Cody College.*

*J*udy didn't like Buzz . . . and neither did I! But I think the reason she didn't like him is that he made her nervous. He was always saying, "Open your eyes!" God, how big can you open your eyes?! He was a very strange, cruel man. . . . He'd work the hell out of his dancers and Judy and Mickey. I personally think he was terrible, and I think anybody that's honest would say that he was. No talent; all he had to do was pick up a kaleidoscope, and he had his routine. (I know I sound like I'm being bitchy, but I'm not!)

I worked all the Judy / Mickey pictures with Buzz; the last one I worked on with her was Girl Crazy, when she and Mickey were [being lifted] up and down, up and down. And she went out of her mind, she was so frightened. She was afraid of the gunshots. . . . But she'd been a very nervous child—extremely nervous and high-strung and sensitive. And Mickey was wonderful—they were very close, and he was very kind. Every time the shots would go off, he'd grab her and tell her not to worry.

—Dona Massin

Above: *Contemporary newspaper caricature of Garland with conductor Andre Kostelanetz. He led the Philadelphia Robin Hood Dell Orchestra in accompaniment when Judy gave her first formal concert on July 1, 1943. Her portion of the program consisted of a Gershwin medley ("Someone to Watch Over Me," "Do, Do, Do," "Embraceable You," "The Man I Love") and a selection of her film hits: "Strike Up the Band," "You Made Me Love You," "Our Love Affair," "I'm Nobody's Baby," "For Me and My Gal," and "Over the Rainbow." Audience response led to two renditions of "The Joint is Really Jumpin' Down at Carnegie Hall" and a final encore of "But Not For Me" from the score of the forthcoming Girl Crazy.*

Right: *The day prior to the show, Judy rehearsed with accompanist Earl Brent in her suite at the Warwick Hotel. Brent traveled from Hollywood to serve as her musical adjunct, but all Garland's orchestrations and vocal arrangements were overseen by Roger Edens prior to her departure.*

JUDY GARLAND DISPLAYS AMAZING SENSE OF RHYTHM AT DELL

Everybody expected that Judy Garland would be a great success . . . but nobody could have accurately imagined what really took place at that usually dignified shrine of music. Cyclonic is the only word to describe with any degree of accuracy the twenty-one-year-old, redheaded film star's success. To begin with, all records in attendance at Robin Hood Dell were broken. Fifteen thousand persons paid for admission and were somehow within the Dell, while thousands were turned away from the gates [and] filled the neighboring fields and hills. . . .

Very charming and youthful she looked as she modestly took her place by Mr. Kostelanetz' side to the lusty cheers of her many admirers. We had been told that [she] was "awfully nervous and scared to death," but there was no evidence of this as the young singer sang her opening group of Gershwin songs with a poise and assurance that must have won the admiration and respect of all those onlookers. . . . She projected her songs with all the verve and sincere good will for which she is beloved by thousands of fans all over the country. In her own particular way, she is an interesting stylist . . . what she did with that marvelous Gershwin tune, "Strike Up the Band," was an experience in rhythmic vitality.

The young lady was unmistakably "in the groove," as she sang, crooned, and swayed to the rhythmic clapping of her thousands of admirers. . . . The usually sedate orchestra gave a first-rate impression of a jive session.

— *Max de Schauensee,*

Philadelphia Evening Bulletin, July 2, 1943

Left: *In September 1943, the Hollywood Bond Cavalcade enabled Judy to join forces with Mickey Rooney, Dick Powell, Harpo Marx, Greer Garson, Lucille Ball, Betty Hutton, José Iturbi, James Cagney, Kathryn Grayson, Paul Henreid, Kay Kyser, his orchestra and specialty singers Ish Kabibble, Harry Babbitt, and Sully Mason. They are shown here as they prepare to leave Los Angeles on a sixteen-city fund-raising tour.*

Right: *Garland, Kyser, and Ball pose with a representative of the Third War Loan Campaign at a stop on their cross-country trek.*

Opposite: *Judy waiting in her jeep for the festivities to begin in San Antonio. In every city, the stars left their train to participate in a motorcade parade, conduct a press conference, and present a full-length evening show in the largest available local venue. Audiences "bought" tickets to the show by purchasing war bonds; this tour alone sold more than one billion dollars' worth.*

*W*e all agree that Judy was one of the most talented women that ever worked in show business—in many different angles. But what really hasn't ever been mentioned very much is the fact that she was a tremendously gifted comedienne . . . and liked fun and good times and laughs. I worked with her quite a bit, on radio and at benefits, and I found her one of the most amusing women I have ever known. Her sense of humor was delicious. She was a good, low comedienne—baggy pants stuff. Did all kinds of dialects: Italian, Southern, whatever you wanted. She was a great storyteller.

I had some wonderful times with Judy and always enjoyed working with her. And I think she enjoyed working with me. I hope people . . . think of Judy as I think of her: as a joyous, talented, dear girl. She was unquestionably the most talented person with whom I ever worked.

—Bing Crosby

Above: *With fellow M-G-M star Walter Pidgeon as they prepare for the* Lux Radio Theatre *broadcast of* A Star Is Born *on December 28, 1942. The sixty-minute program was an adaptation of the acclaimed 1937 screen drama starring Janet Gaynor and Fredric March. Judy later suggested to Metro that they revamp the property as a movie musical vehicle in which she could play; they rejected the idea as too adult and unseemly for Garland. (She would prove them wrong, but it would take twelve years and a contract with Warner Bros. to accomplish that.)*

Right: *With Groucho Marx, recording* Mail Call, *January 1943. Along with* Command Performance, G. I. Journal, Everything for the Boys, *and* Personal Album, Mail Call *was one of the regular Armed Forces Radio Service programs transcribed on disc and shipped to military installations all over the free world to entertain the men and woman on the World War II front. Garland did more than a score of such volunteer recordings.*

Opposite: *With her* Meet Me in St. Louis *songwriter Hugh Martin at the piano, Judy and Bing Crosby intently await a rehearsal for radio's* G. I. Journal, *circa April 1944. A year later, Garland and Crosby would cut a Decca Records duet of Martin's "Connecticut," written with partner Ralph Blane.*

*Meet Me in St. Louis wasn't
just another job. There was something
different about the way it all came
together and the way we felt about it
in learning—along the way—our
involvement in the story . . . not just
a dance number. And that made a
big difference. You felt a very strong
influence by the other people and
by the coordination of bringing us
together and having us tell a story. I
don't know that I would have realized
it was going to be a big hit . . . but
there was a tremendous difference.*

*Also, Judy enjoyed the picture
and working on it. Although there
was one time when we were all in
our positions for shooting, and there
was a number that Judy did with
Margaret O'Brien. Now at that time,
Margaret had no teeth up front, so
she had to have a plate put in there
and held. O Well, she'd be singing and
kicking along, and the plate would
come flying out. So we'd have to go
back and start all over again!*

—Dorothy Gilmore Raye

Right: *A combination caricature and collage, drawn and designed by Al Hirschfeld and reprinted as artwork unique to the intra-industry M-G-M journal,* The Lion's Roar. *His sketch heralded Judy Garland's finest screen role and most important motion picture since* The Wizard of Oz: *1944's* Meet Me in St. Louis. *Her portrayal of a seventeen-year-old girl circa 1903–04 served as the musical and dramatic center of Vincente Minnelli's masterful recreation (or happy reinvention) of fin de siècle life in the Midwest.*

Below right: *In costume for the penultimate sequences of the film. Judy's dress was designed by Irene Sharaff and her makeup created for the first time during this film by the masterful Dottie Ponedel, who became a lifelong friend.*

Opposite top: *Reviving a classic vaudeville turn, "Under the Bamboo Tree" with seven-year-old Margaret O'Brien. The child adored Judy, who treated her like a little sister off-camera as well. (Dorothy Gilmore Raye, who reminisces about* Meet Me in St. Louis *at left, is the brunette standing just to O'Brien's right.)*

Opposite below: *A contemporary advertising herald for the film.*

There was a spot in the picture where Arthur Freed said he wanted Judy to sing on a trolley. I really thought he wanted a song that was like "Cuddle Up a Little Closer" or "Play That Barbershop Chord"—something from that period that Judy could show off doing. I didn't know he wanted a song about the trolley, because Arthur was a little inarticulate. So once a week, we'd come in with a song for her to do on the trolley. And he'd say, "No. Go back and write another one."

And finally [my partner] Ralph Blane caught on that he wanted a song about the trolley, so he went to the library and came home with a little clipping of a trolley from that period. And the caption underneath it said, "Clang, clang, clang went the jolly little trolley." Well, we were so happy; we'd been so frustrated at not being able to please Arthur. So when we went in and did ["The Trolley Song"], for once in his life, Arthur whooped and hollered and threw his hat in the air.

—Hugh Martin

Opposite: *A desolate Judy— as Esther Smith—regrets that "the boy next door" missed the trolley to the fairgrounds.*

Left: *With Lucille Bremer as her older sister, Rose Smith. A charming dancer, Bremer was the protégé of St. Louis producer Arthur Freed.*

It was a long shoot, but it really was a lot of fun. And Judy and all of us got so seasick on that darn trolley! We'd start at 5:30 in the morning, and we'd start shooting at 8 or 9 . . . and sometimes we'd work fifteen or sixteen hours a day. And we'd get off that trolley at the end of the day, just weaving and weaving! But you'd had to be beautiful and wonderful at the work [whether] eight o'clock in the morning or eight o'clock in the evening.

Margaret O'Brien was adorable—a darling actress. But I think she scared us because that role was a little weird for a child: all those fanciful ideas and terrible things about her dolls. Judy was very aware: one time she said to us, "That poor little girl; she's not having any childhood!"

—Dorothy Tuttle Nitch

Now Ralph wrote in one room and I wrote in another. We never collaborated. We just shared credit as a team for whatever the other did. I wrote in a room with a piano, because Ralph didn't play. And I had written a few bars of a song, but I couldn't figure out how to end it; I couldn't even figure out a bridge, so I thought, "Let's go on to something else." So I switched gears and started writing other things, but after a couple of days, Ralph couldn't stand it anymore, because he heard everything through the walls, and he liked the partial tune. He asked, "Whatever happened to the one that sounded like a little madrigal?" And I knew instantly which one he meant. And I said, "I threw it away." And he looked at me: "Oh, no; that's so lovely! We've got to find it!" We found it in one of my notebooks; I hadn't really put it in the wastebasket, I just put it aside. But then I wrote a lyric that Judy refused to sing: "Have yourself a merry little Christmas. It may be your last. Next year, we will all be living in the past." It fit the plot, but as she said, "They'll think I'm a monster, singing that to that little girl [Margaret O'Brien]." "Have yourself a merry little Christmas. Pop that champagne cork. Next year, we will all be living in New York." Perfect for the book, terrible for Judy's image.

But I just held my ground; I was stubborn and arrogant in those days, and I wouldn't change it. I said, "I'll write you another one, Judy." She said, "All right, but I did like that one." And finally Tom Drake could stand it no longer, and he took me aside one day and said, "Hugh, you're being a stupid son of a bitch! Now listen to me." He sat me down over a cup of coffee and convinced me that it could be an important song. But nobody ever thought of it as a hit song. That came years later and much to the surprise of everyone.

—Hugh Martin

Above: *Newspaper supplement ad art for M-G-M's triumph as it prepared to open around the country. Early reviews had already announced to hundreds of thousands that* Meet Me in St. Louis *was "a picture that represents sheer unadulterated enjoyment"—so wrote Kate Cameron in her four-star rave in the* New York Daily News. *Bosley Crowther in the* New York Times *labeled the film "a warm and beguiling picturization . . . done in a manner calculated to warm and enthuse the heart." The direction, design, scripting, and songs won unanimous praise, and all recognized Judy as the spearhead of a splendid ensemble cast. Crowther spoke for many when he referenced her "rich voice that grows riper and more expressive in each new film."*

Left: *"I feel like the ossified woman in the side show" was Esther Smith's scripted comment about the effects of a corset; even resting between takes, Garland's demeanor aligns with that of her character. Nonetheless, she came to regard* St. Louis *as one of her career highlights.*

Left: *Though their off-camera romance
died aborning in 1943, Judy's fondness
for "boy next door" Tom Drake endured for
decades. Some twenty years after* Meet Me
in St. Louis, *he attended the taping of one
of her CBS-TV series shows; her jubilant
reaction when she unexpectedly found him
in the audience was apparent to everyone,
and she warmly introduced him to those
in the studio.*

Below: *The British sheet music for
one of the movie's three new song hits.*

THE BOY NEXT DOOR

Words and Music by

HUGH MARTIN
and RALPH BLANE

Featured in

"Meet me in St. Louis"

A Metro-Goldwyn-Mayer
Picture

Starring

JUDY
GARLAND
with
MARGARET
O'BRIEN

MARY ASTOR
LUCILLE BREMER
TOM DRAKE
MARJORIE MAIN

Directed by
VINCENTE
MINNELLI

Produced by
ARTHUR FREED

THE SUN MUSIC PUBLISHING Co. Ltd.,
23, Denmark St. London. W.C. 2.

JUDY GARLAND Y VINCENTE MINNELLI

Above: *The back cover of the Spanish* Primer Plano *magazine for November 3, 1946. Garland is shown onset between takes of "An Interview" for* Ziegfeld Follies *(1946). Despite the captioned identification, Minnelli is nowhere to be seen; Judy is flanked by cameraman George Folsey (left) and a studio technician.*

Right: *Color portrait of Garland in costume and guise for her satirical sketch in* Ziegfeld Follies. *Her routine— written by Roger Edens and Kay Thompson for (and rejected by) Greer Garson—spoofed any "Great Lady of the Cinema" as she gave an affected and grandiose interview to the press. The press, in this case, was played by the male Metro singing and dancing corps, and Judy ultimately led them into a hypersleek number to extol the merits of the woman she plans to portray in her next picture: Madame Gretchen Crematante, "the inventor of the safety pin." It's a measure of Garland's off-screen humor and burgeoning sophistication that she was able to so convey such mischief; the number was staged by Chuck Walters and filmed by Vincente Minnelli.*

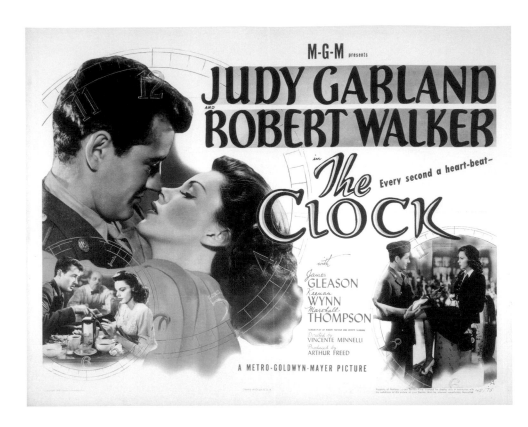

Left: Half-sheet poster for The Clock *(1945). Originally begun under the direction of Fred Zinnemann,* The Clock *was to be Garland's first straight dramatic role. As such, Judy felt that it "had to be done just right . . . but somehow it didn't [come] together. After a while, the studio shelved it. I wasn't happy about it, and I kept going over it in my mind. One day, I went to the officials and told them I knew what the picture needed: Vincente Minnelli." With Minnelli on board, the project flourished and was received and respected as a low-key gem of truth about the vagaries of life and love in wartime Manhattan.*

Below: Costar Robert Walker and Garland in a scene filmed for but deleted from The Clock. *This still was taken during the early days of Zinnemann's work as the film's director. Minnelli would have Judy's hair and makeup softened before he began the picture again.*

She adored Vincente and needed him because he took care of her . . . as a star. He had such imagination and brilliance—and when he came to Hollywood and became her director, he loved her. And he put all that he felt about her into making their films. I think they had a great love and affection . . . and God knows, they had a wonderful child.

—*Margaret Whiting*

One could analyze Judy's phrasing and timing and her distinctive emotional throb and still not capture her essence. She believed every word, and her sincerity made believers of us all. Her whole being was suffused with emotion.

I eventually could tell Judy what I wanted her to do [in a scene] with just a look, but at first I had to find the key words to get her to react. What seemed obvious to me was perplexing to her. [But] once she grasped the motivation, she was as brilliant in dramatic scenes as she'd been in musical numbers.

— *Vincente Minnelli*

Judy and Robert Walker. During the filming of The Clock, *Walker was performing under the stress of a crumbling marriage to actress Jennifer Jones; it often fell to Judy and her makeup woman Dottie Ponedel to track him down on sodden late nights and sober him up in time for his morning call. Yet there was great, quiet on-camera sincerity in their interplay, deftly guided by Minnelli. The director's concept envisioned New York City as the third "character" in the triangle of their story: a corporal visiting Manhattan for the first time meets, loses, finds, and marries a girl—all within his forty-eight-hour leave.*

The wonders of M-G-M and what could be wrought at that greatest of all "playgrounds" for adults of exemplary talent. Although exteriors of New York were duplicated by process photography, the studio built and recreated the necessary interiors on the Culver City lot. These included the lobby of the Astor Hotel, sections of the original Pennsylvania Station, and a variety of museum galleries— as in the chamber shown here. Ironically (and despite the obvious care and expense involved in its setting), this sequence was deleted from the film in order to tighten its running time.

Left: *In her garb for* The Harvey Girls *(1946) ("the apron must be spotless from the collar to the hem"), Judy relaxes on the set staircase of the bawdy Alhambra bar and "house." Her enthralled company: actors Van Johnson and Esther Williams (top), her secretary, and ace cameraman George Folsey.*

Right: *Italian poster for* The Harvey Girls—*another instance when the name Judy Garland, alone above the title of the film, was deemed exciting and magnetic enough to create box office magic, anywhere. The film's theme of the good versus bad girls of fictitious Sandrock, New Mexico, is everywhere apparent in the background artwork; naturally, the good (Harvey) girls win out . . . which was essential plotting were M-G-M to win the necessary legal permissions from the still thriving Fred Harvey Company to release the film. (The appellation "Harvey girl" was coined in the late nineteenth century to describe any young woman hired to staff a growing restaurant chain along the western railroad route of the Atchison, Topeka, and the Santa Fe.) A 1942 novel about the wild and woolly early days of some of the Harvey employees was purchased by Metro as a possible vehicle for Lana Turner. With the success of Broadway's* Oklahoma! *(1943), the Harvey property was appropriated by Arthur Freed and Roger Edens for its similar overtones of Americana and quickly adapted as a Garland musical.*

JUDY GARLAND

LE RAGAZZE DI HARVEY

JOHN HODIAK · RAY BOLGER · ANGELA LANSBURY

PRESTON FOSTER · VIRGINIA O'BRIEN

Metro-Goldwyn-Mayer KENNY BAKER · MARJORIE MAIN · CHILL WILLS

PRODOTTO DA ARTHUR FREED

DIRETTO DA GEORGE SIDNEY

George Sidney got Judy's section of "Atchison, Topeka" all set and rehearsed with the stand-in, just the way he wanted it. And Judy watched this one time, when he was ready to shoot. Then she walked in and did it without a retake, everything exactly when and where it was supposed to happen. Of course, one arm went on the girl in the front, and the other one on the girl in the back. And I thought we'd have to take another camera shot, because we'd all be a blur: her hands were shaking so. But it's true, she didn't need rehearsal; she could just go do it.

And of course you hear about her supposed temperament. Then and afterward. Well, we were with her every day, month after month. I never saw Judy angry on any occasion. If she was, she must have gone outside the door and fussed . . . but never did I see it; I don't even know if she had a temper!

—Dorothy Gilmore Raye

The grand finale of the film's eight-minute production number, "On the Atchison, Topeka, and the Santa Fe." It was Freed's idea to build an introductory song around "the arrival of the train," and the routine served to introduce much of the principal cast in special material prepared by Edens, vocal arranger Kay Thompson, and lyricist Ralph Blane. (The basic song itself would win the Academy Award for Johnny Mercer and Harry Warren in 1947.) Protagonist Garland is top and center. Just below, to her left, is Wizard of Oz "Scarecrow" Ray Bolger; on the bottom right, in her first major screen role, is comparative newcomer Cyd Charisse. The "Harvey girls" themselves were primarily played by the exemplary dancers from the studio's stock company. Below Garland on her right (and standing on the Harvey Co. box) is Dorothy Gilmore Raye; to Raye's right, on the same level, is Dorothy Tuttle Nitch.

The Harvey Girls was six months of work; we were a family by the end of it. George Sidney was a wonderful director, although years later when she saw the picture, his wife at the time teased him about me and Dorothy Gilmore Raye. George liked using us in a lot of shots; usually when he called "Dorothy!" we'd both turn up. So we were on camera a lot; when you see The Harvey Girls, we're almost there all the time. And his wife kidded him [about our screen time], "What about those two Dorothys? Did you have an affair with one of those Dorothys?" And George said, "How could I? They were always together!"

And the fight scene! We—the Harvey girls—were the waitresses and goody-two-shoes. And the Alhambra girls were just the opposite . . . and some of them were really kind of rough gals. So I didn't particularly want to tangle with them, especially on camera, because they were really looking forward to "getting" the Harvey girls! Anyway, as soon as George called, "Action!" Cyd Charisse dove under one of the gaming tables, and I went under the other one. And because I established that at the start of the scene, I got to stay there through the entire fight; they all wondered why I didn't have a scratch on me. But I wasn't going to fight those girls!

So we worked hard . . . but most everything we did was a lot of fun. Then sometimes—after we'd worked with Judy on ["March of the Doagies"] for a number for days—they'd say, "Well, you know, we don't need that!" But at least we had the fun of doing it.

—Dorothy Tuttle Nitch

Above: *A contemporary, promotional souvenir postcard, distributed by the proud-as-punch Harvey Company.*

Right: *Garland as Susan Bradley, being "slated" aboard the train to Sandrock. She's traveling in response to a matrimonial ad but will instead join the Harvey girls. (Susan ultimately reforms and wins local gambler Ned Trent, played by John Hodiak; the role was originally planned for Clark Gable.)*

Opposite: *A climactic confrontation between the Harvey contingent and the Alhambra "dance hall girls"; the latter euphemism covered a multitude of talents. Dead center, Judy squares off with saloon hostess Angela Lansbury (who, only twenty-one, won the role over Lucille Ball and Ann Sothern). Cyd Charisse is just behind Lansbury, and beloved character actors Marjorie Main and Chill Wills can be seen far right.*

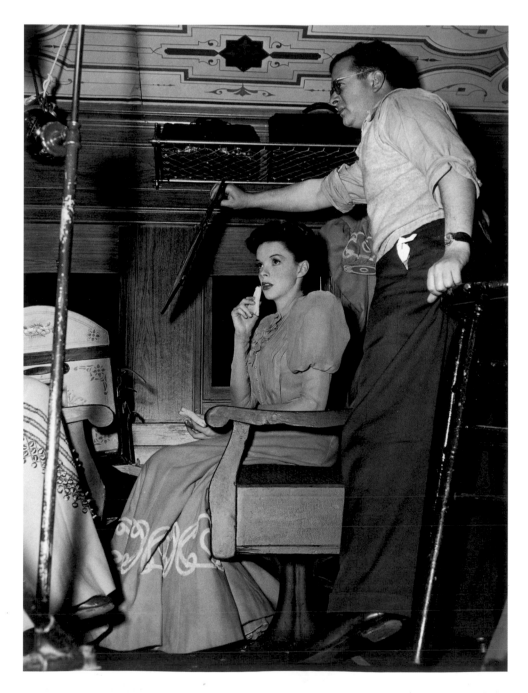

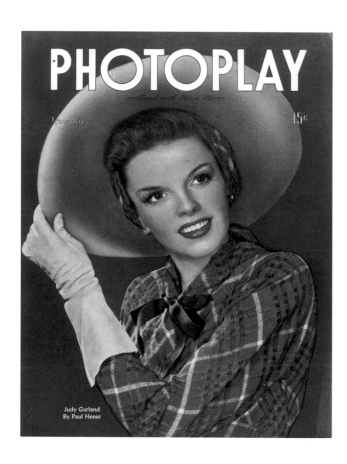

Above and right: *By the mid-1940s, Judy Garland had begun to evolve into a leading lady—with a special beauty to match that she'd so often envied in other female stars of the time. She was coaxed to this self-image by the makeup techniques used by Dottie Ponedel and the judicious molding and support of Vincente Minnelli. Though they'd begun to date during the making of* Meet Me in St. Louis, *the association ended soon thereafter, and they didn't emotionally align again until he was assigned to rework* The Clock. *By the end of 1944, they were engaged. The pose at right was taken around that time by famed fashion photographer George Hoyningen-Huene.*

Opposite: *Judy Garland and Vincente Minnelli were married on June 15, 1945, at her mother's home. Lyricist Ira Gershwin served as best man; Judy's publicity adjunct, the duplicitous Betty Asher, was maid of honor. Surrogate father and studio chieftain Louis B. Mayer (only symbolically) gave away the bride. The newlyweds entrained the same day for a ten-week New York honeymoon; by the time she returned to Metro in September, Judy was pregnant.*

Vincente's artistry was just unbelievable. He would imagine all these great things; then they would create them, and we would just do it! In the circus scene of Till the Clouds Roll By *(1946), we were ballet dancers, they had these big elephants, and Judy was going to sing; she had a ballet tutu on. Now we were behind the curtains—there were very large curtains on the stage—and the elephants were right in front of us. Well, the poor elephants had never heard a big, loud, musical playback: the disc started, the curtains opened, and the elephants went crazy: up on their hooves [turning] around to us. We were in a cart; it was going to be a parade. Well, you never saw ballet dancers scurry any faster!*

—Dorothy Tuttle Nitch

Right: The stunning artwork for this insert poster was drawn by Al Hirschfeld. Though billed alphabetically, Garland is given top/center prominence.

Opposite: The opening of the mammoth production number accorded the Kern/Oscar Hammerstein II/Otto Harbach song "Who?" This portion of the routine—the verse of the song—was deleted from the release print of the film; Garland is either rehearsing in a dressing gown or wore an evening coat over the dancing costume she sports in the remainder of the number.

Right: *Metropolitan Opera tenor Lauritz Melchior joins Judy and Danny Kaye for an Armed Forces Radio Command Performance, circa August 1944. Garland's natural ebullience carried as effectively over the airwaves as her voice; by 1945, she was hoping to limit future film work to a single picture a year and devote most of her time a radio series of her own. That plan never came to fruition, and it's perhaps unfortunate. Such a schedule would have been infinitely easier for her to maintain. Her scores of surviving radio transcripts are invaluable, however, as they not only preserve for posterity the dozens of songs she never performed elsewhere but offer as well almost countless glimpses of what seems to be the genuine Garland personality: quick to laugh, happy to sing, delighted to be working with those she admires to an audience that never fails to rise to her communication.*

Left: *Tom Drake, Margaret O'Brien, and Judy reunite to reprise their original film roles in the* Lux Radio Theatre *presentation of* Meet Me in St. Louis, *December 2, 1946. (The role of family patriarch Alonzo Smith—played in the motion picture by Leon Ames—was taken by radio personality Gale Gordon, later a mainstay of television's* Our Miss Brooks *and comic foil to Lucille Ball in several of her teleseries.)*

Opposite: *At a radio rehearsal break with Frank Sinatra, 1945; the two singers would share a life-long (if occasionally volatile) fealty. Though Sinatra would at one point criticize Judy's vocal technique, he remained both a fervent fan and a friend at hand. Garland would invariably offer Frank as a prime example of her own favorite singers and gratefully acknowledge his generally ready ssistance. (For the record, Judy's own tastes in vocalists were varied and included at one time or another an avowed admiration for Tony Bennett, Kate Smith, Mabel Mercer, Peggy Lee, Billie Holiday, Ella Fitzgerald, Barbra Streisand, Jack Jones, Ann Sothern, and her daughters Liza Minnelli and Lorna Luft.)*

Without getting all saccharine and gooey, may I say simply that I am very glad to be my mother's and father's child. I was an enormously happy little girl. My parents instilled in me a sense of heroism—a you-can-do-it mental focus. They were both wonderful like that. My father gave me a mad sense of fantasy; my mother taught me nothing was impossible. So I was given this great sense of color: I was always taught to see the beauty in every situation—even when things were awful.

Mama had a terrific brain and a great sense of humor. Even when she was going through hell, she could step outside herself and see something funny about it. I had a tremendous amount of love from my parents. Mama was always there. I can't think of a question I haven't answered about my family. We couldn't do anything without the whole world knowing—or thinking that they knew. When I got older, we used to sit around and read what we were supposed to be doing—and laugh and giggle.

—*Liza Minnelli*

Opposite, above, and right: With daughter Liza May Minnelli, 1946–48. In the photograph at right, the little girl sports one of the costume creations that her father had made for her; Mama looks on as Liza opens her Christmas presents. June Allyson remembers how "absolutely thrilled" Judy was to become a mother. "And everyone was thrilled for her; I think everybody thought, 'This is so wonderful because now Judy will have time to enjoy her life. She won't be just a worker. She'll have the family to care about and someone to care about her—just because she's Mom.'"

With lifelong friend Kay Thompson, November 21, 1946. Judy was in rehearsal for her dramatic performance on the CBS Suspense Theatre *radio program*, produced by Thompson's husband, Bill Spier. The Spiers served as godparents to Liza May, and they and the Minnellis were frequent companions during Kay's 1943–47 tenure as vocal arranger, coach, and writer at M-G-M.

146

Left: *In contrast to her natural capacity to kick back the traces and whoop, Judy had learned by the late 1940s to evolve into the sophisticate as well. Daughter Lorna later remembered, "It fascinated me to watch her turn into a movie star," and Liza concurred: "It was Mama being elegant—and she could do it!"*

Below: *Sylvia Sidney and the Vincente Minnellis at Ciro's, 1947. Actress Sidney was then married to Carleton Alsop, who would become a strong buffer for Judy in her soon-to-increase confrontations with the M-G-M hierarchy. Given the eager insistence of Metro, its parent company, Loew's Inc., and Minnelli himself, Judy had signed a new five-year contract with the studio effective in late 1946. Within weeks, she regretted the move and its portents of pressure, prescription medication, and servitude. Garland had successfully eliminated pills from her life immediately after marrying Minnelli in 1945; the slowly growing realization by 1947 that the marriage was perhaps ill advised and the knowledge she'd bound herself back to M-G-M as well meant increasing frailty, illness, and an even greater pharmaceutical dependence on what she wryly described as "the bolts and jolts."*

I think one of Vincente's attractions to Judy was a total, creative Trilby / Svengali sort of thing— for him to develop this singer into an actress. I feel, too, that she had tremendous need of support as a young actress . . . the little girl who suddenly became a star. She still was a little girl in some ways and needed the support of a powerful director.

They always came to the parties at our studio and at one of them, Oscar Levant was playing the piano, and Judy and Kay Thompson were singing together. She said, "Oh, Kay, let's just sing real loud!" (That became one of our family statements when we really wanted to have a good time; we would say, "Oh, let's sing real loud!")

And Judy never had to be begged to perform. She and Kay and Roger Edens would sometimes invent, too, which was the most extraordinary treat of them all . . . where they'd change some of the words and some of the rhythms. It was an incredible time because the talent was so active.

—*Tony Duquette*, M-G-M scenic designer

Right: Three-sheet poster for The Pirate (1948), which, on paper, seemed glorious entertainment. Between the expertise of Freed and Minnelli, the songs of Cole Porter, the customary lavish M-G-M production, and the star power of the studio's preeminent musical stars, the production promised a new height of achievement. Unfortunately, and as Kelly himself later admitted, "It didn't occur to us until the picture hit the public that what we had done was indulge in a huge inside joke. The sophisticates probably grasped it—all three of them—but the film died in the hinterlands." It was the only picture Judy made at M-G-M that lost money.

Above: For all its tongue-in-cheek misfires, The Pirate contained many effective sequences. One of the wildest was a slapstick battle between Garland and Kelly in which an entire room of artifacts was demolished as she attempted to thwack him with tossed crockery and smash him with random decor.

Of course, Judy looked simply gorgeous in the part, but she wasn't well. And we were very upset about it, because we all knew it was the studio's fault. I think people who knew Judy realized at this point that it was the [pressures of the] studio that made her ill. She was not temperamental at all. If she was well, she could do anything; if she was ill, she was ill.

And there was a huge "Voodoo" song and dance. Now, Gene Kelly was a genius—and a very sexual person. And this was a very, very sexy number and very well done; it was supposed to be pretty wild and wonderful. And Judy was great; she and Gene enjoyed working together, and she liked the challenge of doing something different. But Louis B. Mayer wanted every [picture] a family picture—the number could not be that sexy, so it had to be changed a bit.

And they did it again. And then they cut it out anyway!

—*Dorothy Tuttle Nitch*

Right: *Gene Kelly mesmerizes Judy at the onset of the controversial "Voodoo."*

Above: *In the role of Manuela Alva, Garland rehearses the posturing that marked the beginning of her routine. She would literally and figuratively let down her hair as the six-minute song and dance became more manic and abandoned; unfortunately, all film footage of "Voodoo" was lost in an M-G-M vaultfire several years after its deletion from* The Pirate.

A nita Loos was supposed to write The Pirate; she did some work, and one Sunday morning, we all trooped over to Cole's house to hear Anita read her screenplay. I had never met Anita Loos; all I knew was that she had written Gentlemen Prefer Blondes, and I guess she was pretty hot stuff.

Well, we all sat down in Cole's lovely living room—Arthur and Vincente and Gene and Roger and I— and in came Anita. She sat in an enormous chair and sort of tucked her feet under her . . . and she started to read. And in Anita's version, Gene was José or Gomez or someone—and he wasn't even a pirate; he was a fisherman!

So Anita was reading along, and she came to the part where Gomez and Manuela meet. And she said, "When Gomez sees Manuela, he drops his nuts—uh, NETS!"

Well, I thought I would die; I was in hysterics. But I looked around, and everyone else was terribly serious. They hadn't heard a thing.

Well, you know Vincente. . . .

— J udy G arland

Between takes. Garland was frequently ill and absent from the set during filming of The Pirate; her instincts told her that Minnelli, Kelly, and vocal arranger Kay Thompson were creating a film for which a mass audience quite possibly didn't exist. (As so often on other occasions, Judy's estimation was spot-on; after highly mixed "sneak preview" reaction to the finished film, there would later be several weeks of retakes, deleted or replaced musical numbers, and simplified arrangements.) Still, the film contained one immediate song hit, Cole Porter's "Be A Clown."

Above: *Husband and wife on the set. If not herein the all-American girl next door that audiences demanded, Garland (and Kelly as well) rose to the occasion whenever the songs and scenes of* The Pirate *provided the opportunity. The finished product contains many of Judy's wittiest film moments, and Minnelli deserves much of the credit for encouraging the expansion of her screen image and persona.*

Right: *Al Hirschfeld's promotional caricature of the stars of* The Pirate.

Judy was a real pro. She always knew what she was doing when she walked out there; if she was late on the set, she saved time by not having to do it over and over to get it right. Now, every time a star somehow delays production, the budget goes up that much higher. But this woman was worth it, and the studio was wise enough to know that. She ranks tops—but really tops—and I think she'll go down in history as one of the greatest performers we've ever had. And she was so down-to-earth; she wouldn't even know what the phrase "Queen of the Lot" meant.

She just loved to laugh. I don't think she ever had enough laughter in her life; maybe that's why she was such a great cutup and clown.

—Ann Miller

Right: *Publicity artwork by M-G-M mainstay Jacques Kapralik for* Easter Parade *(1948). His innovative, collage-like renderings were assembled, photographed, and used to promote many Metro pictures; this one was perhaps the sunniest and most romantic musical comedy of the Garland career. Easter Parade now ranks second only to* The Wizard of Oz *and* Meet Me in St. Louis *in terms of timeless appeal and long-term success. Gene Kelly and Cyd Charisse were originally assigned the roles ultimately played by Fred Astaire and Ann Miller, but a broken ankle suffered during a touch football game (Kelly) and ligaments torn during another film project (Charisse) quashed their involvement. Thus Kapralik depicts Garland and Astaire at the base of his art, with Miller and Peter Lawford across the top.*

Opposite: *"A Couple of Swells"... and in the exultant memory of director Chuck Walters, "Garland and Astaire as a couple of deadbeats! All I had to do was let it happen!" Their madcap duet was the highlight of* Easter Parade—*and arguably one of the most memorable of the seventeen Irving Berlin songs that happily laced the picture.*

Left: A gallant Peter Lawford helps Judy across M-G-M's "New York Street," which had been tarped-in and overlaid with pipes to create the rainstorm suitable for their Berlin duet, "A Fella With An Umbrella." As ever, Metro was determined to enhance the reality of the set, and the design and construction forces implanted an actual freight elevator into a portion of the sidewalk as an integral aspect of staging for the number.

They had spent a lot of money to make this practical—this elevator that comes out of the sidewalk—so that it would come out; it wasn't just there. I'd rehearsed for about three weeks; Judy [only needed] a day!

So we came to shoot the number. Bells are ringing, and we're marching along. I'm singing, "I'm just a fella, a fella with an umbrella…." Rain's pouring down. Oh, it was horrible! Meanwhile, the crew is shouting orders to each other [over the prerecorded playback of the song]: "Okay, let the elevator go, Charlie!" So up it comes, clang-grinding. And we just make it [across the raised platform]; it was supposed to be a shot where we stop and turn and do a "take" when we realize we didn't drop into the hole.

Now, when we went to see it on the film, they had had the wrong lens on the camera—a close-up—and you never even saw a sidewalk or the elevator. And we'd been worried all day long about falling about the shaft!

—Peter Lawford

Judy's the greatest entertainer who ever lived— or probably ever will live . . . an amazing girl. She could do things—anything—without rehearsing and come off perfectly. She could learn faster, do everything better than most people. It was one of the greatest thrills to work with her.

—*Fred Astaire*

Left: *Insert poster for* Easter Parade, *again featuring artwork by Hirschfeld and promoting the Irving Berlin song catalog showcased in the picture.*

Above: *Judy and Fred in "When the Midnight Choo-Choo Leaves for Alabam'." Fifteen years later, singer-dancer Ken Berry met Garland at a party; when he shyly confessed his admiration for that particular dance duet, she got him up out of his chair and taught it to him, recalling virtually every step.*

The first time I read the script of Easter Parade, I knew the ending was all wrong. . . . I was just heartbroken: this beautiful Irving Berlin music and all of this glorious M-G-M Technicolor was just going to go down the drain with this cockamamie ending!

So I went up to the [executives]—Mr. Berlin was there, too—and I really laid it on them, kindly but firmly, about this bummer of an ending. Well, they listened; then I was told: "That's our department!" [So] my dander got ruffled a bit. "Wait a minute," I said. "This is not the time to be concerned with departments. I'm in this film, too, you know . . . and we're all going to be in trouble unless that ending is changed!" Then I explained to them what was to me a very simple script solution, but they just repeated themselves and shouted: "Out!"

Well, Mr. Berlin had just stood there quietly, taking all this in. Then he finally opened his mouth: "That little girl happens to be right, you know. Her suggestions are exactly on the nose." They started to protest again, and this beautiful gentleman simply said, "We can do it her way, or you can do it without Irving Berlin."

In a matter of hours, we had the new ending, and everybody was smiling again . . . and I fell in love forever with darling Irving.

—*Judy Garland*

On the set with director Chuck Walters, who remained a lifelong friend. In the 1950s, Chuck helped direct several of Judy's stage acts, including the first elaborate presentation at the Palace on Broadway in 1951. (On opening night, the planned partner for Garland's re-creation of "A Couple of Swells" was not yet comfortable with the routine—so Walters went on and did the number with her.)

From left: Irving Berlin, Louis B. Mayer, Judy, and Arthur Freed in a publicity pose for Easter Parade. Berlin agreed to do the film at M-G-M solely because of the chance to work with Garland; he later went on record with the statement "No one has ever sung my songs better than Judy Garland."

"Words and Music"
JUDY GARLAND · MICKEY ROONEY
JUNE ALLYSON · TOM DRAKE

Left: Screen Stories *for January 1949. The issue contained a brief novelization of M-G-M's* Words and Music *(1948), the wildly fictionalized biographical film about songwriters Richard Rodgers and Lorenz Hart. Tom Drake played the former, Mickey Rooney the latter, and their prominent billing on the magazine cover is understandable. But Garland only had ten minutes in the film (and Allyson even less); her placement here is proof positive that the editors knew whose popularity would best market their product. (It's an even greater commendation when one realizes that* Words and Music *was an all-star effort; others in the cast included Gene Kelly, Lena Horne, Perry Como, Betty Garrett, Cyd Charisse, and Ann Sothern.)*

Right: *With Lennie Hayton conducting, Mickey and Judy prerecord "I Wish I Were in Love Again" for* Words and Music. *She played herself in the film, attending a Hollywood party and duetting with Larry Hart; the song marked the final screen appearance of Garland and Rooney as a team. Judy fell ill before her second number in* Words and Music *could be decided upon, and the picture was completed and sneak-previewed without it. When audiences reacted so strongly to her appearance with Rooney, Metro reopened the production and, three months after "I Wish I Were in Love Again," she sang and filmed "Johnny One Note" for insertion in the final edit.*

Opposite: *Garland during the holidays, 1948.*

The first week we were at M-G-M, Roger Edens and Kay Thompson had a joint birthday party. Everyone was there . . . but we didn't know any of them! And that's when we first met Judy. She was already this sort of legendary figure, but we just had to talk to her for two minutes before we found out she had this brilliant, outrageous sense of humor. Such spirit and great warmth and fun and lovability and love coming from her.

And at first, we just knew her at parties; we hadn't written anything for her at that point. But we'd meet at the Gershwin's or at Gene and Betsy Kelly's or at one of our places—whether in California or in New York. And everyone performed at these parties . . . not to be "on" or to impress anybody but just to have fun. It was just part of the evening.

When she did sing some of our things later on, she had a very exciting, theatrical way of doing a song—the music being changed slightly and going through progressive keys. It was just Judy; you can't ask for any more.

—*Betty Comden & Adolph Green*

Right: Garland and costar Van Johnson "meet cute" in a don't-watch-where-you're-walking collision for M-G-M's In the Good Old Summertime *(1949). During the film's opening sequence, Judy's entire ensemble and hat were systematically dismantled at Johnson's hands; the routine was a masterpiece of interplay devised by veteran comic actor Buster Keaton, also in the* Summertime *cast.*

Above: Irene's sketch for Garland's costume, pre-collision.

In the Good Old Summertime *marked the screen debut of two-and-a-half-year-old Liza Minnelli, who appeared for a few fleeting seconds at the end of the picture, typecast as the daughter of Garland's character. Judy would later joke that Liza was paid $47.50 for her one day of work: "That's a lot of money for a three-year old. . . . I never forgave myself for letting her hang around the house for the first two years of her life doing nothing." Originally set to be produced as* The Girl From Chicago *with June Allyson and Frank Sinatra,* Summertime *was a remake with songs of the 1940 Metro classic* The Shop Around the Corner. *(In that incarnation, it had starred Margaret Sullavan and James Stewart.) With the locale switched from a European perfumery to a Chicago music store, Judy was given the chance to sing six songs, one of which was deleted prior to release. The supporting cast was once again crammed with adept favorites; in addition to Keaton—whose violin-smashing bellyflop is a split-second acrobatic/balletic highlight of the film— the stars are complemented by treasurable S. Z. "Cuddles" Sakall, buoyant Spring Byington, and stalwart Clinton Sundberg.*

Right: *A publicity pose with costar Van Johnson. He and Garland had become instant friends when he first arrived at M-G-M in 1942, and they dated informally on many occasions thereafter. Johnson was an early choice to play "the boy next door" in* Meet Me in St. Louis, *but the military requirements of World War II took him out of Culver City at that juncture. He would later appear with Judy on television in 1966 and 1968; he also proudly presented her to (and shared her with) the cast of* The Music Man *when he played the title role in that stage show in London, and Garland came to see him work. Johnson's wardrobe assistant remembered Judy praising Van for his performance—particularly the fast-paced "Ya Got Trouble" song; she then proceeded to sing the entire routine back to him in his dressing room!*

Below: *Between takes with secretary Virginia Paine.*

Opposite: *Judy in orbit, slamming across "I Don't Care." Her freewheeling exuberance during this revival of the 1905 hit was so effective that the initial movie audiences for* In the Good Old Summertime *were impelled to applaud the screen as if Garland were appearing in person.*

Left: *Judy adored choreographer Robert Alton, and his presence helped sustain her through the couple of months she invested in* Annie Get Your Gun.

Below: *Judy in costume and wig for her first sequence in* Annie Get Your Gun *(1949). The project seemed cursed from the onset. Per Judy, "I had my heart set on doing the picture," but she knew she wasn't well and begged for a vacation prior to production. This was deferred. She had separated from Minnelli, who—after the debacle of* The Pirate*—didn't seem to be able to provide what was best for his wife on-screen or off. Compounding everything, Arthur Freed inexplicably assigned Busby Berkeley to direct, and his was precisely the approach to completely annihilate what was left of Garland's reserve energy. Within a month, Freed realized this and replaced him with Chuck Walters, but within days of that decision, Judy was fired as well and the production was shut down. (When filming resumed, George Sidney was the director and Betty Hutton starred in the picture.)*

The first time I sang "They Say It's Wonderful" with Judy, she just made me cry. I had been in the business only three years, and to do something with Judy Garland. . . . ! I just never thought I'd ever do anything like that. But I didn't actually shoot with Judy except one day on the backlot—because a horse fell with me on stage and broke my ankle. So they shot around me for six weeks, and Judy was exhausted; she just fell apart. They should have given her a rest . . . Annie's a tough musical, a lot of work—hard work. And she would have been wonderful if she'd had the energy for it.

—Howard Keel

I was in my dressing room in costume for the "I'm an Indian, Too" number, and I was wearing war paint, moccasins, and a lot of Indian beads and feathers. [The front office] sent me a note; some stooge delivered it. The note said: "Your services are no longer required." I was so mad, the only thing I could say was: "You can't do this to me. With this makeup on, I don't even know what tribe I belong to. What reservation do I go to?" The man didn't say a word. "Let me get this war paint off and this feather out of my head and get my nice dress on—then fire me. But don't fire me as a Navajo or whatever I'm supposed to be." The man didn't even laugh. I saw the humor of the situation, but even humor can't cure what I was going through.

—Judy Garland

GENE KELLY
Judy GARLAND

TECHNICOLOR

LA VALLÉE
HEUREUSE

"SUMMER STOCK"

"HET GELUKKIG DAL"

avec
EDDIE BRACKEN
GLORIA DE HAVEN
MARJORIE MAIN
PHIL SILVERS
Mise en scène
CHARLES WALTERS

I was on the set when she shot "Get Happy" with that little black fedora, and her little black tuxedo top with her long black stockings and her five-inch black heels. She was so adorable.

And Liza was on the set as well; she was only about four years old, and she was running around [making noise] until Judy yelled out, "Annie! Grab Liza and make her sit in your lap!" So I sat with Liza in my lap and watched Judy shoot "Forget your troubles, c'mon get happy. . . ." Actually, it was one of the best numbers she ever did.

And she was a very good mother— just devoted to her children.

—*Ann Miller*

Left: *A Belgian poster for* Summer Stock *(1950). Though a difficult shoot, the film brought Judy back to M-G-M after a couple of months at Peter Bent Brigham Hospital in Boston. Plotwise, it was a throwback to her early pictures with Mickey Rooney, who was briefly considered for the role opposite Garland. Instead,* Summer Stock *reunited her with the highly supportive Gene Kelly and Chuck Walters, old friends Phil Silvers and Marjorie Main, and the appreciative Eddie Bracken. The final product remains an immensely enjoyable—if not major— motion picture, and Garland and Kelly share probably her greatest screen dance duet in* "The Portland Fancy." *They each have a classic star turn as well: his newspaper dance to* "You, Wonderful You" *and her tour-de-force with* "Get Happy."

LM17441

Opposite: *"Get Happy"—in action. The vocal arrangement of the song was prepared by Saul Chaplin, and Judy performed it sporadically on stage and on television for the next nineteen years. It was the opening song in the last three concerts of her life in 1969.*

Below: *Judy perches on Chuck Walters's lap. They were delighted to add "Get Happy" to* Summer Stock *at the end of the production; he had staged a sexy version of Irving Berlin's "Mister Monotony" for her in* Easter Parade *two years earlier—in which she first wore what would become the "Get Happy" wardrobe—but the number had been deleted from that picture. (In the background: dancer Nita Bieber and choreographer Nick Castle.)*

*W*hen we were making Summer Stock, there was one incident where Judy wasn't there for about three weeks. I thought it was wonderful, because I was getting paid; I was paid by the week. And then I heard Dore Schary and the other executives talking: if they can't get her to come in, they're going to cancel the picture. And I asked "What's wrong with her?" And they go on and on about how difficult she is. And I finally asked, "Do you mind if I call her?" And Schary says, "No, but it won't do any good." He laughed at me, really. But I called Judy: "I know you're feeling terrible, and you haven't been able to come in to finish this picture. But I've got another job on Broadway, and if I don't do this, my career is going to be hurt. Could you somehow or another try to gain enough strength to get in here and knock off this scene? And maybe we'll finish the picture?"

And she said, "Okay. I'll be in at 10:00." And she was in at 10:00, and we finished the picture. Now that's Judy. She would do anything for a friend, I don't care who they were. If she loved you, no what matter you asked, you got it. So I can't help but love and respect that girl. She would sometimes fight with the upper echelon: those authorities who were yelling at her, telling her to do this! yelling at her to do that! And she refused to do it. Now, if someone had asked her nicely, it would have been done in one second. That was the difference with Judy Garland: a wonderful, wonderful, wonderful girl. I named my first daughter after her—and you've gotta love someone to want her to be part of your family.

Judy was my patsy. If I did a double take, or I raised my brow in some ridiculous way without trying to be funny, she would fall on the floor. In the scene where I was proposing to her—but my father was sitting between us and interrupting and actually doing the proposing—she could not stand looking at me. She would start laughing and couldn't stop. Chuck Walters, our director, was going out of his mind trying, but there was no way you could talk to her seriously. The more seriously you talked to her, the funnier it became!

—*Eddie Bracken*

On the set of Summer Stock. *Making Judy laugh was something Eddie Bracken could always do . . . and she loved him for it.*

*H*er laughter was raucous. It was funny. It was vital. She'd just throw her head back and laugh. And you felt great because if you told her a joke, and she laughed like that, you [thought], "I've made it. Judy really likes it!"

For a long time, she was a happy woman, and I heard that laugh a lot. The funniest time ever, we were going to lunch at the Beverly Hills Brown Derby. She picked me up in the car, and we went behind my house through an alley to get back to Wilshire Boulevard, and she said, "Look, I need a Kleenex." So I reached in the little compartment, and I brought out a little box and asked, "What is this?" She said, "I don't know; throw it away." So I tossed it out the window.

And all of a sudden, screech went the brakes! She said, "Oh, my God! My teeth!" Everyone had dental work done for pictures; they had special teeth—caps—they'd put on. So she backed up, and I got out and rummaged around and came back and said, "Here's your teeth, Granny." And she laughed. She laughed all through luncheon.

— *Margaret Whiting*

Above: *One of Judy's emotional mainstays for many years, Dottie Ponedel remained Garland's champion until her own death— publicly refuting the many far-fetched and exaggerated aspects of the legend. Between 1943 and 1950, they completed ten films together, and the association and friendship endured far beyond M-G-M. These birthday photographs with her friends are among the last ever taken of Judy Garland at Metro-Goldwyn-Mayer. She would pose for wardrobe, hair, and makeup test pictures the following week, but on June 17, the studio suspended her for the third time in three years when she canceled a rehearsal.*

Left: *Flanked by Minnelli (with whom she'd reconciled the preceding autumn) and Freed, Judy celebrated her twenty-eighth birthday a day early on Friday, June 9, 1950. The late-afternoon party was held in one of the M-G-M rehearsal halls after several hours of work on Royal Wedding. Many of the chorus kids who'd danced with Garland in the past were in attendance, as were Gene Kelly and Saul Chaplin.*

the 1950s

Judy Garland was released from her M-G-M contract on September 29, 1950. At that time, even major Hollywood motion pictures had begun to be assembled in a sort of efficiency-expert panic. With the encroaching popularity of television and the government-ordered divestiture of studio-owned theater chains, economy was paramount on every lot; whatever their job, workers were ordered to crank out the goods in the least amount of time imaginable. Even (or especially) high-salaried performers were far from exempt, and Judy humorously remembered the unspoken politics of it all years later: "I was the first, 'trial' [firing]. Dore Schary came in to Metro and wanted to prove that stars weren't necessary. So he fired me—after sixteen years. I kind of kidded him afterward and asked, 'What are you going to do? Put your wife's name on the marquee?' And he said his idea was that the writing of [any] picture was more important. So I was a test case. Then, eventually, *everyone* was in exodus!"

Leaving M-G-M was a mixed blessing: the pressures were suddenly gone, but so was Judy's home base. Both her personal and professional friends rallied, however; within days of the firing, she appeared on the first of numerous radio shows that season, happily reunited with Bing Crosby and Bob Hope. But it was the variety stage on which she and her management set their sights; by early 1951, Garland was booked into the London Palladium for four weeks beginning April 9.

It was the logical progression. After an almost sixteen-year "detour" in motion pictures, Baby Gumm was returning full-time to her natural habitat. (Appropriately, all but four or five of the twenty-eight feature films in which she'd thus far appeared had cast her as either a singer or an aspiring singer.) Additionally, starring at the Palladium carried with it the prestige of starting at the top. London's premier variety house booked only the best—and had the capacity to make or break anyone, from a small-time novelty act to a major Hollywood name.

Despite opening night nerves (she literally fell and sat down square on the stage when attempting a bow), Judy was received with heartfelt hysteria by London audiences. There was critical approval as well: "Her charm," exulted the notices, "is a complete absence of affectation. . . . She did what she was born to do—sing—[in] an extraordinary mix of humor, vitality, and . . . passionate, blinding sincerity." On that opening night, the star herself came to a happy realization: "Judy, you're back where you belong—in the theater." Given such approval, and bolstered by the encouragement and presence of new manager and boyfriend, Sid Luft, Garland spent the summer appearing in Glasgow, Edinburgh, Manchester, Blackpool, Liverpool, Dublin, and Birmingham. She varied her repertoire to suit each venue, reviving songs from *Little Nellie Kelly* in Ireland and tossing off "Loch Lomond" and an impromptu highland fling in Scotland. Audiences continued to rise and cheer—this during an era when

standing ovations were rarely accorded to even the best of classical music performances. And whether one read the popular press or the private circuit reports filed by theater managers along her tour route, the appraisals were much the same: there was an almost stunned disbelief among the professionals as they tried to explain Garland's singular abilities and effect on the crowds.

Even those successes were to pale, however, when Judy returned to New York and it was arranged for her to appear at the most famous of all United States variety theaters. The Palace had opened in 1913; almost immediately, it became the Broadway goal of every vaudevillian—or, per Roger Edens's special material—"the mecca of the trade." By the early 1930s, when live variety shows had finally given way in popularity to films and radio, the Palace began to present instead a halfhearted melange of movies and small-time acts. It was Luft's idea that Judy take over the theater as the star of a full, traditional vaudeville bill, and Roger Edens and Chuck Walters quickly assembled for her a heady and theatrical presentation of undiluted Garland. In addition to portions of the Palladium act, they added special material about Judy, the Palace, and some of the early performers associated with the theater; two fully staged re-creations of Garland's movie numbers; and a male backup chorus à la the "Madame Crematante" reporters from *Ziegfeld Follies*.

The scheduled four-week engagement opened on October 16, 1951, and ultimately played nineteen weeks and 184 performances. Only when Judy wanted a vacation and the chance to take the show on tour did the Palace agree to let her go. In an era that predated most forms of audience and journalistic hyperbole, all who saw the act scrambled to rapturously, adequately describe what they'd beheld. "Judy at the Palace" was the first of many occasions over the next eighteen years that would be described—whether by the press or by Garland herself—as the high point of her life. The critic for the *New York Post* could only acknowledge, "Those who planned and worked on her [show] were out to make this the greatest act to have ever played the Palace. I am sure they succeeded."

That success was repeated during sellout engagements in Los Angeles and San Francisco in the spring of 1952, but a further tour was eliminated by Judy's pregnancy and June marriage to Luft. By the time daughter Lorna was born on November 21, everything was in place instead for Garland's film return: *A Star Is Born* was prepared from conception as a premier showcase for Judy's new level of versatility and fame. The title had been first brought to the

---

Opposite: *"Your face is just dandy . . ."* So Esther Blodgett—soon to be Vicki Lester—is told in A Star Is Born (1954) when the excesses of Hollywood makeup are about to be wiped away. It's an object lesson about Judy Garland's beauty as well; certainly during 1953–54, when she was filming the remake of Star, Garland had never before appeared more piquant, pert, or persuasive.

Above: A pensive and private Judy. With her M-G-M dismissal at hand, she found the escape to New York both therapeutic and invigorating. Additionally, Manhattan seemed adaptable to every mood—and her own highly charged nature would thrive on that compatibility. The future, she wrote in 1950, "seems good, golden, and glorious."

Opposite: "Does anyone still wear a hat?" Judy poses for John Engstead, 1957. When the M-G-M musical compilation film, That's Entertainment!, *first hit theaters in 1974, one of its highlights was a truncated version of Judy's final song and dance on the lot, "Get Happy." At one Midwestern matinee, a woman who had been audibly sighing and laughing and enjoying herself throughout grew suddenly hushed. As Judy completed the routine on-screen, the woman was heard to marvel, "That lady can do more with a hat . . . !"*

screen as a 1937 drama overseen by David O. Selznick and William A. Wellman. The Lufts formed their own company to coproduce a musical remake of the property with Warner Bros. and quickly assembled a remarkable creative team: director George Cukor, scenarist Moss Hart, composer Harold Arlen, and lyricist Ira Gershwin. All were personal friends of Garland, as well as rabid admirers of her professional acumen.

Given *Star*'s monumental ambitions, there were commensurate problems in its making. Judy labeled herself, Cukor, and Luft perfectionists in their attempts to have everything exactly as they wanted, whatever the potential time and cost overruns. Warners junked the first couple of weeks of footage when CinemaScope—a new filming process that provided a longer, wider film image—was deemed essential to the project, and the production started again from scratch. There were staff problems and replacements, most specifically in costume design and cameramen. Although Arlen and Gershwin contributed seven songs to the picture's rough cut, the eighth number they'd written to close the first half of the film was found unusable; Roger Edens and Leonard Gershe were brought in to provide "Born in a Trunk," a fifteen-minute production medley that stylistically reflected on Garland's act at the Palace. Finally, the star herself—working as she was under the stresses of diet, mammoth responsibility, and attendant medication—would some days find it impossible to perform, her emotional stability and energy resources having completely bottomed out.

The shooting schedule for *A Star Is Born* ran from October 12, 1953, to July 29, 1954, but the final $4.8 million budget seemed entirely justified when both West and East Coast premieres, the opening reviews, and the first week's box office were described by *Variety* as "little short of phenomenal." Critic Philip Bradford summed up the general media reaction to the film's star: "Everything she does attains perfection [with] greater magnetism, voice projection, poise and emotional depth than ever before." Unfortunately, Warner Bros. had decided at the last minute to release the 181-minute film on a continual-run basis, without the planned intermission. Within days of the opening, exhibitors advised the studio that a shorter *Star* would mean an extra performance each day—and the opportunity to capitalize on the initial glowing reviews and public appreciation. Almost mindlessly, Warner Bros. recut the picture, eliminating roughly thirty minutes from every release print and then ordering the destruction of the now-excess footage. *A Star Is Born* had seemed a potential box office champion, a probable Academy Award winner, and a Ten Best–list honoree for the year. Instead, personal and press word of mouth bemoaned the deletions, box office fell off (most cities were never provided the chance to see the complete film), and the picture lost money and year-end accolades. There was some consolation the following spring; although the Best Actress Oscar went to Grace Kelly for *The Country Girl*, Judy got both a nomination and a new son—Joseph Wiley Luft, born on March 29, 1955.

Despite the disappointment of *A Star Is Born*, each year for the rest of the decade brought Garland an astounding level of professional acclaim. What would have been all-time pinnacles in any other career were merely de rigueur achievements for Judy Garland; just a summary of her annual workload from 1955 to 1959 provides ample evidence of the effort and response for which she was responsible:

1955: A seven-city tour of the West Coast, from San Diego to Vancouver. A best-selling record album, *Miss Show Business*—the first release of her decade-long association with Capitol Records. A television performance debut as the star of *Ford Star Jubilee*, a ninety-minute "live" production that won the highest ratings to that date for a "spectacular" on the CBS-TV network.

1956: A second Capitol album, *Judy*, on which she worked for the first time with orchestrator par excellence Nelson Riddle. A second highly rated CBS-TV special—this time a half-hour "live" concert. A five-week engagement at the Las Vegas New Frontier that made Garland the highest-paid entertainer in the desert to that date. A front-page-headlined New York return to the Palace for a seventeen-week engagement that ran into 1957.

1957: A Capitol "concept" album of ballads, *Alone*, reuniting Garland with Gordon Jenkins, with whom she'd worked at Decca. A three-week return to Las Vegas at the Flamingo, followed by engagements in Detroit, Dallas, Los Angeles, Washington, D.C., and Philadelphia. A triumphal return to London for four and a half weeks at the Dominion Theatre. A royal variety show Command Performance for Queen Elizabeth II at the Palladium.

1958: A Capitol album of romantic songs, *Judy in Love*, orchestrated by Nelson Riddle. A special "return" to Minnesota for an appearance during the state's centennial celebration. An extraordinary two-week run at the Los Angeles Cocoanut Grove, closing night of which became Garland's first "live" recording for Capitol. A record-breaking stand at Chicago's Orchestra Hall. A Las Vegas engagement at the Sands.

1959: Another concept album for Capitol—*The Letter*—with an original score by Gordon Jenkins. A Miami Beach debut at the Fontainebleau Hotel. A lavish and ambitious stage revue designed to play the Metropolitan Opera House in New York; the show also toured to Baltimore, Chicago, San Francisco, and Los Angeles. A week at the Las Vegas Sahara.

Amidst these outstanding successes, however, Judy faced a disproportionate amount of difficulty. The strain of producing the kind of performance professionalism she demanded of herself led to physical depletion, periodic laryngitis, and canceled concerts. There were bookings in Las Vegas and Brooklyn that were aborted mid-engagement because of rows with audiences or management. Though a ratings delight, her television appearances had found Garland in less-than-great vocal shape, which led to some disparaging public opinion; this was augmented when a 1957 television special was abandoned in the planning stages amidst a morass of accusations from CBS and subsequent legal action against the network.

There were personal demons as well. Even though the women had been estranged for several years, Judy was emotionally devastated by the death of her mother in January 1953. In 1956 and 1958, Garland brought divorce suits against Luft (although their reconciliations were quick to follow). Despite the top-dollar salary she commanded, Judy increasingly faced horrifically mounting debt; songwriter-scenarist Gershe later summarized: "Something was wrong. She did not live expensively, she did not entertain lavishly, she didn't have Rolls-Royces, she wasn't extravagant in any way at all. Where was the money? She was the biggest star of her time; where was the money? It couldn't have all gone to taxes; the tax people say she didn't pay them!" Finally, there were Judy's age-old problems with weight and medication; on a couple of occasions, there were attempts at suicide when the cumulative effects of her pills meant that she literally did not know what she was doing.

By November 1959, all the years of excess coalesced. The pressure, overwork, substance abuse, and psychological malfunction manifested themselves in a virulent case of hepatitis. Garland was hospitalized in New York, and her recovery was seriously in doubt. Even beyond that—and whatever the physical outcome of her illness—the doctors were definitive in their consensus that her career was over; she couldn't possibly work again.

How typical with Judy Garland that the best was yet to come.

Left: *Groucho Marx, Judy, Jerry Lewis, and Gordon MacRae during rehearsals for* The Big Show, *radio's ninety-minute weekly attempt to hold an audience that was rapidly fragmenting in favor of television. Other guests on this edition of the program—broadcast live on February 11, 1951—included Dean Martin, Joan Davis, and The Andrews Sisters. In addition to the power of such all-star casting,* The Big Show *proved to be a sizable (if brief, two-season) sensation because of its mistress of ceremonies. Tallulah Bankhead hosted each show, and her considerable talent and unstoppable personality fascinated listeners. Even Tallulah was fallible, however. On this episode, she stepped to the microphone and grandly proclaimed: "Darlings . . . here she is. The one. The only. The most vibrant young singer in show business today—singing 'Get Happy' from her latest M-G-M picture,* Summer Stock *. . . Miss Judy Holliday!"*

Right: *Judy with columnist Louella Parsons and her announcer, circa March 1951. Over the years, Garland did several broadcasts with Parsons, perhaps most notably in 1948 (at which time she sang* "Over the Rainbow" *and included the seldom-heard verse of the song) and in 1954 (when Parsons played the soundtrack recording of* "The Man That Got Away" *three months prior to the premiere of* A Star Is Born*). Radio was Judy's primary contact with the public in late 1950 and early 1951; between the cancellation of her Metro contract and her departure for England the following March, she was heard well over a dozen times. There were eight guest stints on Bing Crosby's program (plus a slot on his twentieth-anniversary show); an appearance with Bob Hope; a couple of variety shows; and four* "radio plays." *The latter included the straight dramatic adaptation of the 1936 Katharine Hepburn screen vehicle,* Alice Adams *(a role Judy would be offered again in a never-to-be-realized 1956 film musical), a rhymed adaptation of* Cinderella*, and her only post-1939 appearance as* "Dorothy Gale from Kansas" *in a Christmas 1950 broadcast of* The Wizard of Oz.

Right: *Rehearsing with Fred Astaire for the Screen Guild Players radio adaptation of* Easter Parade, *March 22, 1951. The sixty-minute presentation also included Peter Lawford re-creating his film role; Monica Lewis filled in for Ann Miller. Truncated as it was, the program included at least nine Irving Berlin songs; Judy's selections included solo turns on "I Want to Go Back to Michigan," "I Love a Piano," and "Better Luck Next Time," as well as duets (with Astaire) to "Snooky Ookums," "Ragtime Violin," "When the Midnight Choo-Choo Leaves for Alabam'," and the title song.*

Left: *Leaving ABC studios after the* Easter Parade *broadcast. There are countless pictures of Garland accepting or cradling bouquets of roses over the spectrum of her career; she became so associated with that flower that an award-winning rose was named for her in England in 1975. The Judy Garland Rose—which bloomed yellow-tipped with crimson-orange and matured to a full red blossom—was then successfully imported and grown in the United States as well.*

Arriving in Southampton, England, aboard the Ile de France—April 5, 1951. Nearby ships spelled out her name in nautical code with their horns, disembarking passengers waited for Judy's departure to cheer her on, and more fans waited in London to greet her as she left the boat train. Four nights later, she opened at the Palladium.

There was no dementia in the tremendous roar of welcome that greeted Miss Garland as she walked onto the stage. The warmth of that welcome was genuine, kind, and understanding—greater and deeper than ever would have been given to her when she was the madcap princess of the movies. And genuineness was met by genuineness. This sturdy young woman bowed and smiled as the cheering went on, but there were no tears, no trembling of the lips or wobbling of the chin. She was a trouper who had come to give a perform-ance. That was what mattered to her.

She possesses a real voice, a voice which even has beauty in its softer moments, and her face is expressive because it plays no tricks.

In fact, she is an artist.

—*Beverly Baxter,*
The Evening Standard, April 11, 1951

*E*veryone in town was going to see Judy at the Palladium. And I said, "Boy . . . I gotta go down there!" I didn't have very much money, and I remember standing in line for hours to buy a ticket for the third balcony. [From that angle] Judy looked absolutely tiny . . . but she wasn't. She filled that place. After the show was over, we were just screaming. Everybody was screaming. And I went home and said to myself, "I've just seen the legend. I was lucky enough to see her when she was tremendous. Voice was wonderful. She looked great." She was an enormous success in London at that time.

— *N*orman *J*ewison, Director

Left: *Opening night at the London Palladium, April 9, 1951.*

Right: *Mother and daughter reunited in Birmingham, July 1951. To share and experience the joy of Judy's triumph, Liza joined her near the conclusion of the post-Palladium tour. Garland had given some three months of performances in the British Isles by this point; both her audiences and her peers were jubilantly dumbstruck by her power. Although they were only slightly acquainted in 1951, James Mason enthusiastically acclaimed Judy "without doubt, the greatest success of the year. She has a tremendous, exciting, dynamic talent. I've always thought she would be great as a dramatic actress as well as a singer." Two years later, his suspicions would be confirmed on the set of* A Star Is Born.

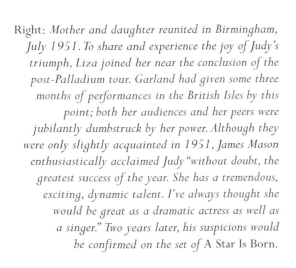

*S*inatra's opening at the New York Paramount—pandemonium. *Carol Channing coming down the*
stairs singing "Hello, Dolly" for the first time opening night—Caruso singing Pagliacci—Mazeroski's ninth
inning home run in the seventh game of the World Series to beat the Yankees—Can't-anybody-here-play-
this-game, the Mets winning their World Series, Citation taking the Triple Crown—he ran that one without
his feet touching the ground, Clark Gable arriving in Atlanta for the premiere of Gone With the Wind,
standing in the door of the plane while the whole Confederacy gave rebel yells. All that is to qualify myself
as having heard ovations.

    Judy Garland's opening night at the Palace.
    There has never been anything like it.

—*A*dela *R*ogers *S*t. *J*ohns

Below: *Director/choreographer Chuck Walters takes Judy's stance in a Los Angeles rehearsal hall during preparations for the "Get Happy" sequence of her Palace act. He is appreciatively appraised by Garland, coworkers, and members of her "Boy Friends" dance corps. From left: Hamil Petroff, Hal Bell, Jack McClendon, Jack Boyle, and (on the floor) Bert May.*

Opposite: *"Get Happy" as it looked from a stage-side box seat at The Palace Theatre. The number was lifted virtually intact from its staging in* Summer Stock, *backdrop and all. On opening night, Judy lost her fedora mid-routine and yelled out (with her best Baby Gumm-informality): "Whoops! Wait a minute!" She retrieved the hat and then continued the number.*

Opposite: *The finale of the Palace act. No one who saw Judy Garland sit on the apron stage and sing her theme song could ever forget it; for decades after, critics, commentators, and fans tried to explain the emotion. In Holiday, Clifton Fadiman could only offer: "When she breathed the last phrases of 'Over the Rainbow' and cried out its universal, unanswerable query, 'Why can't I?' it was as though the bewildered hearts of all the people in the world had moved quietly together and become one, shaking in Judy's throat, and there breaking."*

Above: *Judy and Hugh Martin at the Palace. He was composer, lyricist, vocal arranger, accompanist, and Garland's great support—whether helping her back on with her high heels or (as here) helping her off with her barge-sized tramp boots.*

Right: *The first twenty-five minutes of Judy's act were staged in concert format as she sang early vaudeville favorites and her own movie hits.*

*I*t made me a little nervous to call her after so many years . . . but she gave me a very warm reception. So I had the courage to say, "Do you think I could get house seats for opening night?" She replied, "I have a better idea. Why don't you sit on the stage with me and play for me?" I could not believe my ears. She said, "I didn't ask you [earlier] because you were writing shows, and I thought you'd think it was beneath you to play in vaudeville." But I said, "Well, I'd just love it"; I thought, gee, I can take three weeks out of my life. I didn't know it was going to go into nineteen weeks! But it was extraordinary to watch this marvelous, overwhelming, heaven-kissed genius twice a day for nineteen weeks. Then she found out that my dressing room was way up in the flies, and she said, "Oh, Hugh, that'll never do. . . . Besides, I feel so comfortable when I'm near you; I'm not scared." And I asked Sid if it was all right. I said, "We can pull a sheet down as a partition, like Claudette Colbert and Clark Gable." But in a sense, it was an answer to his prayers, because she was very frightened, and I was a little security blanket.

At dress rehearsal, when I wasn't needed onstage, I went upstairs in the balcony. And they hadn't put the microphones in yet, and Judy was singing "Over the Rainbow" with the orchestra, and I was hearing it. And I came back down, and I said, "Judy, this is going to sound crazy to you, but why don't you do 'Over the Rainbow' without the microphone . . . just your own sweet voice?" And she looked at me as if I'd gone absolutely mad and said, "I think that may be the nicest, sweetest thing I've ever heard of." It was a very tender, wonderful moment which wouldn't have been quite the same with the microphone. I'm very thrilled that I contributed that little, tiny thing.

On opening night, I just stayed in the shadows. A lot of wonderful people came to the dressing room; I could hear them through the sheet! I didn't want to meet them, but it was fun hearing the Duke and Duchess of Windsor and Marlene Dietrich. They were all so excited and loving it so. And she was in total disbelief; she couldn't believe that it had gone so marvelously well.

She had this running gag when she'd come onstage and see me, she'd say, "Is that you, Hugh? You look twelve tonight!" And then on another night, she'd say, "You look twenty-two." She'd change it every show. And then she'd kick her shoes off because her feet hurt. And the audience loved that. . . . Then, when it came time to put them on again, she couldn't really without me. And I left the piano bench and went over and put her shoes on for her. And that became a nightly occurrence.

—*Hugh Martin*

I saw her Palace act when she brought it out here to the Philharmonic. I mean, everybody from M-G-M was there that night. When she sat in the footlights and sang like a little urchin—"Over the Rainbow"—she just ripped that audience to pieces. Just tore the house up. There wasn't a dry eye in the house each time that I saw her. When she walked out on the stage, she had what psychics call a force field around her that was so powerful that it would reach the back of that house. She didn't need a microphone—she had such a force field of energy that hit the audience. It was like mystical electricity; all great performers have that . . . and when you have it, it gets to the audience. Call it charisma, call it star quality; you don't see it very often, but Judy was electrical. She was dynamite.

—*Ann Miller*

The Sixth Annual Tony Awards: March 30, 1952, at New York's Waldorf Astoria Hotel. Helen Hayes (center) presented the medallions that evening. The honorees flanking her here include, from left: Oscar Hammerstein II (lyricist and librettist of the "outstanding musical," The King and I), Gertrude Lawrence ("distinguished musical actress" in The King and I), Richard Rodgers (composer of the "outstanding musical," The King and I), Phil Silvers ("distinguished musical actor" in Top Banana), Judy ("for an important contribution to the revival of vaudeville through her recent stint at the Palace Theatre"), and Yul Brynner ("distinguished supporting or featured musical actor" in The King and I). Silvers later remembered attending Judy's show on the night before his own opened; Top Banana would be a happy hit, but Garland's success made him wryly question his own potential: "Her performance was extraordinary; her show was dazzling, emotion-charged. How could I possibly measure up to her kind of mass hysteria? I felt I didn't even belong in the same city with Judy!"

Left: *During her Los Angeles engagement, Judy posed for photographer John Engstead; he did a dozen or more sessions with her over the years, and his appreciation for her was no less than hers for him:"She was always agreeable and almost always happy . . . she would stay as long as was necessary. And she loved her children—enjoyed doing sittings with them. Often she would call home and have them brought down."*

Above: *Near the stage entrance to the San Francisco Curran Theatre, where the Palace act played for four weeks, beginning May 26, 1952.*

Opposite: *Replacing Frank Sinatra's tie at the Biltmore Bowl, June 29, 1952; he was about to sing "You Made Me Love You" to Judy at the Friars Club testimonial dinner in her honor. Garland was only the second woman to be so honored by that all-male show business fraternity (Sophie Tucker had been the first), and among several speakers and performers, Olivia de Havilland was most succinct in her summation: "I salute [Judy] for her ability to take a stranger's heart and make it her own."*

Above: *With Sid Luft at Romanoff's after the Philharmonic opening, April 21, 1952. The "Welcome home, Judy!" aspect of the evening was underscored by the mix of show folk and Los Angeles society in the premiere crowd; the press filled columns with their lists of those in attendance. Among the notables: Mr. and Mrs. Henry Ford II (who flew in for the occasion on their private plane), Metro alumni (Louis B. Mayer, Mervyn LeRoy, Eddie Mannix, Arthur Freed, Joe Pasternak, Esther Williams, Van Johnson, Jimmy Stewart, Jeanette MacDonald, Johnny Green, June Allyson, and Dick Powell), and—as Time would later describe the crowd at a Garland appearance—"stars, starlets, starlettes, and lesser celestial debris" (George Burns and Gracie Allen, Danny Kaye, Jack Benny, Lucille Ball and Desi Arnaz, Humphrey Bogart and Lauren Bacall, Eleanor Parker, Jack Warner, Jean Simmons, Jane Wyman, Marge and Gower Champion, Claire Trevor, Ezio Pinza, and Louella Parsons). And a host of others.*

Right: *At her wedding dinner, June 8, 1952. Although Luft arranged for a secret ceremony at the Hollister (California) ranch of a discreet friend, Louella Parsons managed to discover what had happened and broke the news four days later.*

Opposite and left: *Judy and daughter Lorna, 1953. The girl had been born the preceding November 21 and remained name- less for several days while her parents debated the merits of such appellations as Amanda and Nora. Eleven years later, Judy would plan a musical salute to all three of her children as part of a television concert. Liza had been named for a Gershwin/Kahn song, and Garland had long been singing "Happiness Is a Thing Called Joe" in honor of her son (who was born in 1955). But she discovered, as of early 1964, that "Nobody ever wrote a song about 'Lorna'! And we looked everywhere: we found songs [about] Linda and Lily and Lola and Lorraine and Lulu and, of course, Cincinnati Lou. Even 'Lydia, the Tattooed Lady.' But we couldn't find a Lorna!" The problem was solved when "A Song for Judy" (Mort Lindsey's lush theme for Garland's TV series) was deemed wonder- fully worthy of a lyric. Judy dispatched the show's executive producer Bill Colleran to Detroit, where Johnny Mercer was in the pre-Broadway throes of the Bert Lahr musical, Foxy. In a drowsy all-night session— the show-weary Mercer kept nodding off between couplets—"Lorna" was born.*

Left: *Judy arrives to headline the Blue Grass Festival during Derby Week in Lexington, Kentucky, April 1953. She brought the entire audience to its feet at the close of her act by singing a hushed rendition of "My Old Kentucky Home" to the accompaniment of a single violin. Per the admiring Variety, "It was one of those moments."*

Below: *At Romanoff's with Jack L. Warner, Warner Bros. studio head, 1953. Warner had announced "official" plans the preceding autumn to remake A Star Is Born as a musical film for Judy, although actual shooting wouldn't begin until October 1953. (The project was initially rumored to costar Tyrone Power, employ William Wellman to re-create his 1937 direction of the original Star, and feature a score by Richard Rodgers and Oscar Hammerstein II. Those names would be supplanted by James Mason, George Cukor, Harold Arlen, and Ira Gershwin by the time A Star Is Born began preproduction.) Though the picture proved to be an expensive proposition, Warner remained a Garland fan. In 1956, Judy turned down the title role in his production of The Helen Morgan Story; the disappointed Warner saw to it that the singing voice of the film's eventual star, Ann Blyth, was dubbed by that of Gogi Grant; Warner felt Grant had a more Garlandesque sound.*

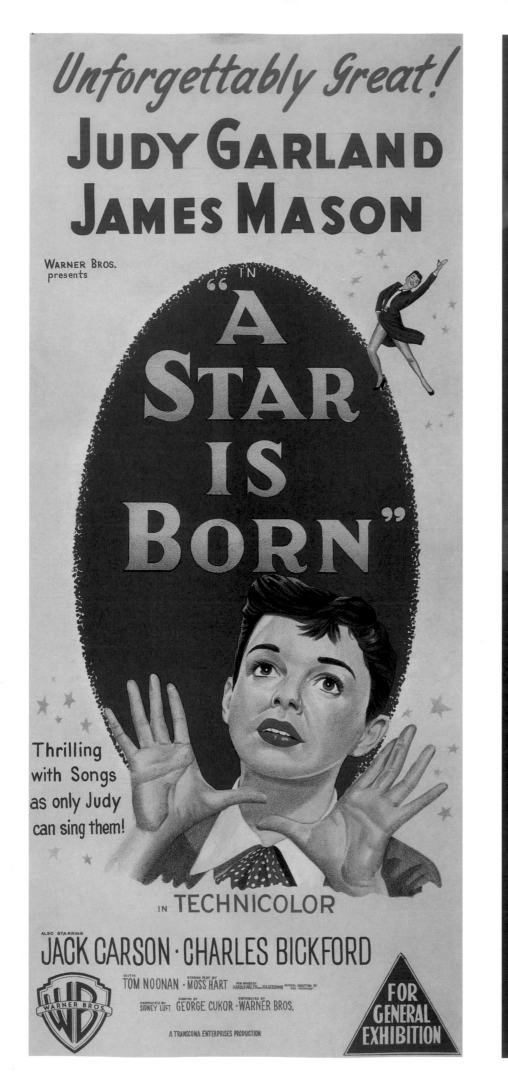

Right: *Australian insert poster for Judy's greatest screen achievement (1954).*

In A Star Is Born, Judy appears as big band singer Esther Blodgett, seen first in a benefit performance of "Gotta Have Me Go with You." She and her dancing partners (from left) Don McCabe and Jack Harman are interrupted midroutine by drunken screen idol Norman Maine (James Mason); Esther's quick thinking makes the actor seem to be part of the number.

With director George Cukor (right) and ace cameraman Sam Leavitt during preparations for the suicide sequence of A Star Is Born.

Regardless of what Judy felt internally, she never showed it on the screen. But when it was finally a wrap for the day, she would many times ask me to take her home because she was so wrung out from the concentration. You can just wring so much out of the dish rag. Director George Cukor was one who would do takes over and over and over. Especially the scene in her dressing room when she was breaking down crying. I don't know how many times I put those freckles back on her—because she'd cry and rub them all off. What was seen on the screen in that six-minute scene was actually shot over two or three days. So the big process for an actress and the director is to get the performance up to that level every time. Meanwhile, the crew would have to take an hour or whatever it took to relight the whole set to get a different angle. Then Judy would rehearse and rehearse and bring herself up to the same pitch again.

Now there were days when we didn't do any [filming], because they were rehearsing with Judy. And they were rewriting stuff; there were delays for that. And if Jack Warner or any of the powers that be would question the lack of footage and say, "Hey, we got to move," they'd say, "Well, Judy's not feeling . . ." I mean, she was the escape hatch; I saw them use that quite a few times. They would put the blame on Judy, because they knew it wouldn't go any further than that. No one would go and ask her; everybody assumed, "Oh well, [we've] got a temperamental star, so we'll make the best of it."

—Del Armstrong, Makeup Artist

Publicity portrait for A Star Is Born, *1954.*

*I*n the spring of 1954, Roger called and came by and said, "I had lunch with Sid Luft today; they need a song for A Star Is Born." I thought it had been finished . . . but they were missing a song. Roger asked if I had any ideas—and I had had a little refrain going through my head for almost a year: "I was born in a trunk in the Princess Theatre in Watusacalla, Idaho. . . ." I sang that to Roger; he asked me to sing it again and to write down the words. Now I'd heard it as a fast song, and I never could get past that little refrain; I never could figure out what the next line should be. He took it away, and he made it much slower. And he turned Watusacalla into Pocatello, which was so much better; there is no Watusacalla—it just came along with the music. And before Roger wrote anything more, Sid ran the picture for us, the finished picture. So we could see where the number was to go.

Well, they were indeed in a lot of trouble. . . . You had Judy and James Mason driving to a preview of Vicki Lester's first movie, and she's so nervous and so frightened, they have to stop the car so she can be sick. And then they went to the theater . . . and you had a shot of her and him, and you saw the flicker of the screen on their faces. And then you went outside the theater, and everybody was coming out after the preview saying, "This is the greatest thing we've ever seen!" "Vicki Lester!" "A star is born!" But what did they see?! There was nothing there. And to compound it, there's a party afterward where . . . the head of the studio reads the preview cards: "Vicki Lester is the greatest singer and dancer in the world that ever . . ." Well, what did she do?! Indeed they needed a number, and they needed a big number. You couldn't just have her singing "Embraceable You" or even "The Man That Got Away"; it had to be a production number. There was none [elsewhere in the picture] except for "Lose That Long Face"; everything was sung on a soundstage or in front of a band or in a hotel room.

So Roger wrote [the first sixteen bars]; he made it a ballad. And then he gave it back to me to finish. The first time we performed it was a night at Judy's house with Judy and Sid and [associate producer] Verne Alves and Jack Warner—just the four of them. Roger sang, I turned pages and, knock wood, they loved it. And it became like a separate little movie done and then put into this already finished main picture. Now if I had been asked to musicalize A Star Is Born, that would have been the first number I would have written, the number that shows what made her a star. And Ira and Harold did write some songs . . . but they just weren't right for that spot. And "Born in a Trunk" was.

—*Leonard Gershe*

Above: *The hit song from A Star Is Born would be "The Man That Got Away," which was photographed multiple times in three different dress styles before perfectionists Garland, Cukor, and Luft were satisfied. This is the earliest version.*

Opposite: *Garland and company let 'er rip in a thrilling Roger Edens vocal arrangement of "Swanee," the final song in the "Born in a Trunk" medley. Judy had recorded a simpler "Swanee" for Decca fifteen years earlier; she added Roger's treatment to her concert repertoire from 1955 to 1968.*

Young Patricia Rosamond and Bobby Sailes flank Garland in the guise of a New Orleans newsboy, extolling local Louisianans to "Lose That Long Face." The upbeat, extended vocal and tap routine was specifically written and staged to frame a dramatic dressing room speech in which Esther breaks down between takes of the song, confessing her growing ambivalence about husband Norman Maine to studio head Oliver Niles (Charles Bickford). The entire "Long Face" number was cut from A Star Is Born *after its premiere; the footage remained lost for almost thirty years.*

Below and right: *Garland and Mason
on the beach in Laguna, filming a sequence
in which Esther Blodgett and Norman Maine
celebrate the location of their Malibu dream home
with a picnic. The charming, lightly humorous scene
would be deleted from* A Star Is Born *prior to release.*

*The final result is a remarkable
work of art. It captures an essence of
Hollywood, an essence of achievement,
of struggle, in that crazy business
that no other film has ever captured.
It also captures the backstage excitement
of the movie business like no other
film, before or since.*

—*Rex Reed*

*The Los Angeles world premiere of
A Star Is Born, September 29, 1954.
From the Pantages Theatre for the
screening to the Cocoanut Grove for the
party, launch festivities for the Garland/
Luft production were lauded as the most
elaborate, exciting, star-studded event
in Hollywood history to that time.*

I think that I ought to tell the folks that it was I who named Judy Garland "Judy Garland." Not that it would have made any difference; you couldn't have hid that great talent if you'd called her Tel Aviv Windowsill. But her name when I first met her was Frances Gumm, and it wasn't the kind of name that so sensitive a great actress like that should have. So we called her Judy Garland—and I think she's a combination of Helen Hayes and Al Jolson and maybe Jenny Lind and Sarah Bernhardt.

— *George Jessel*, Master of Ceremonies
for the *A Star Is Born* Premiere Telecast

Above: From left: George Jessel, Judy, Sid Luft, and Jack L. Warner at the Pantages Theatre prior to the premiere.

Right: Judy and A Star Is Born *choreographer Richard Barstow with his sister at the New York premiere of the picture, October 11, 1954. The film was considered so important and such a potential moneymaker that it debuted and played simultaneously at both the Paramount and Victoria theaters in Times Square. Barstow went on to stage portions of Judy's live performances in 1957, her 1959 Opera House show, and her 1967 return to The Palace. In 1969, he remembered, "It was a joy to work with her, because she had such talent, and because she was such a thorough professional. [She had] tremendous capabilities for exciting the public. She trusted me. I think Judy tried all her life to find people she could trust. And she didn't find many."*

Left: *Judy, Marlon Brando, and Edmond O'Brien at the Golden Globe Awards, February 1955; Garland was honored as best actress in a musical or comedy. Among her other accolades for* A Star Is Born *were the* Film Daily, Box Office, *and* Picturegoer *awards. The first two were voted by hundreds of national motion picture critics and exhibitors; the latter was the result of a readers' poll conducted by that celebrated British publication.*

Below: Look *publisher Gardner Cowles and his wife, Fleur, congratulate Judy and Bing Crosby on being selected as best actress and best actor by that magazine. The* Look *Awards were presented "live" on the CBS Red Skelton television program on March 8, 1955; Judy was then in her ninth month of pregnancy. Skelton enthused, "I hope it's a girl, and it sings just like you," to which Judy inquired, "What if it's a boy?" Red beamed, "Then I hope it sings like Bing Crosby!" (Judy: "What about Eddie Fisher?" Red: "I hope he sings like Bing Crosby, too!") Bing was honored for his performance in* The Country Girl, *a role that won him an Academy Award nomination as well. When both he and Judy lost the Oscar later in March, he sent her a telegram that read, simply, "I don't know about you, but I'm renewing my subscription to* Look." *(Garland, Crosby, and fellow 1954 Academy Award nominees Humphrey Bogart and Sammy Cahn all lived on Mapleton Drive in 1955. When Cahn was the only Oscar winner of the four of them that year—as lyricist of the best song, "Three Coins in the Fountain"—the other three wired him: "Thanks for not letting the street down.")*

I really hated the [Motion Picture] Academy that year. Judy should have won that Oscar; she really should have. She took a chance doing this film, because the original was such a fantastic success. But she made it come alive. Everybody knew she was going to win the award. I know we all voted for her. And when Grace Kelly was announced, it was like "I beg your pardon?!" Not that I don't think well of Grace Kelly, but she got it for Country Girl. *And she didn't do that much in* Country Girl. *(Grace Kelly seemed always to fall into something. Somehow or another, she got a gold record; she sang one line with Bing Crosby, and it sold millions!)*

— *June Allyson*

E*verybody has a sense of humor to some degree or another, but not everybody has a sense of silliness. Judy could be silly; she had a wonderful sense of the ridiculous, and that's what got her through so many trials and tribulations—like the night that she lost the Oscar. She could laugh about what happened to her.*

She had just given birth to Joey the morning before. And she was lying there in bed, and all these technicians just walked in and took over. They put up all these lights, there was a cameraman [on a platform] outside the window, focusing; they were practicing putting up and down the blind, they were telling Judy to practice smiling.

[So] they're all there, all these technicians waiting breathlessly to see if she'd won. And then they heard over the television, "The award goes to Grace Kelly."

Boom! Out went this light! Out went that light! Up went the blind! Down came the window! Nobody said good night, nobody said good-bye, nobody said, "We're sorry." She was just dead in the water to them. She just sat there, and they all disappeared. In two seconds, she was all alone.

And she roared with laughter at it.

—L*eonard* G*ershe*

Judy and Joseph Wiley Luft, early 1956; Wiley was the middle name of Judy's brother-in-law, Jack Cathcart. The boy was born on March 29, 1955; he wasn't expected to live but rallied after about thirty-six hours. Garland always referred to him as her own special Oscar.

We just all decided we were going to see Judy because we loved her. We weren't doing it for publicity; even people who weren't at M-G-M wanted to be there for Judy. And we knew that there would be a parking problem, so we just hired this huge bus; we all got aboard and sang, ate sandwiches. Swapping stories, just having a wonderful time.

Debbie Reynolds was there. Frank Sinatra, Peter Lawford, Dean Martin, Sammy Davis—that's the Rat Pack, you know. And Betty Bacall and Bogie. Van Johnson, Edgar Bergen, Mike Romanoff, Eddie Fisher, David Wayne, Johnny Green. Betty Hutton. Leslie Caron.

Some bus!

—*June Allyson*

Frank Sinatra and Humphrey Bogart with Judy in Long Beach, California, July 9, 1955—the second stop of her month-long seven-city tour. Sinatra charted a bus to cart a couple dozen of Garland's friends to the municipal auditorium for the show; their presence made for an impromptu all-star finale. After her last encore, Judy announced that Sinatra was in the audience, and he leapt up to join her. In turn, they invited Bogart to the platform, and the evening then sailed happily out of control. The remainder of what Frank affectionately termed their "idiot friends" were heralded one by one, and all of them lined up onstage for ten minutes of badinage. The spontaneous mélange hit its peak with a Dean Martin/Sammy Davis Jr., duet; the latter imitated Martin's absent partner, Jerry Lewis.

One of my goals with Capitol Records was to record for posterity so much of the great, classic talent that had been around for a long time and whose earlier records were such bad [audio] quality by comparison to what could be done in the 1950s. And I was a great admirer of Judy's—I wanted her in our catalog. She brought Jack Cathcart in—her choice—for the first album, Miss Show Business. But we were very high on Nelson Riddle at the time; we had put him with Sinatra, and we next put him with Judy. Nelson was the favorite of all the singers, because he had a capacity for enhancing their vocals and knowing how to accompany, as opposed to [providing] an orchestra unto itself.

Repertoire was decided jointly by Judy and myself. Obviously, she would want to approve whatever she did. Sometimes, she'd come in with an idea, or we would bring a song to her or a concept for an album. We didn't approach her as a hit-single record maker; we never thought of her that way. [Instead,] she would do an album which had a running theme, which would make sense for her in view of who she was professionally . . . and what she had done in the past.

Judy needed tremendous encouragement to get her into a studio. It was very hard for her to face up to come in and make records, or to come into the office to sit down and discuss what we might do. And the amazing thing is that once she got there, it was like she was perfectly at home—and sang like a trouper.

The musicians, of course, didn't face up to [any] problems leading to the session. All they knew was that she would come in and record, and everybody was terribly impressed and had great pleasure in working with her. Once she was in the studio, she was a different person.

—*Alan Livingston*, President, Capitol Records

August 1955: Judy records her first album for Capitol Records, Miss Show Business.

Judy rehearses the opening moments of her television performing debut for the CBS "spectacular," Ford Star Jubilee, September 24, 1955. She began the program by singing "You Made Me Love You"; the rest of the show was primarily drawn from her Palace act. Critical notices were mixed, as Garland was plagued with laryngitis for the live telecast, and the quality of the production that surrounded her was uneven at best. Nonetheless, when the phone calls, telegrams, and ratings were tallied, Judy had achieved what CBS judged "the greatest personal triumph in the history of the network." By the end of the year, they had signed her to an exclusive television contract, calling for a show a year for the next three years. The deal guaranteed her nearly $100,000 annually.

She was in a beautiful evening gown, and she also had on a body stocking and panty hose. [After "Rock-a-Bye"] she ran off stage in the blackout so the audience would never see her. In the wings, she just extended her hands, and a makeup man, a hairdresser, a wardrobe lady, and two wardrobe girls, just zipped! Off came the dress, because it was all Velcro—just one jerk and it came off. And they already had the clown suit all put together. They messed up her beautiful makeup, gave her a little burlesque tooth, and I had to put a semblance of a beard on her—all the while keeping in mind that she had to be done in a couple of minutes; this was a live telecast. And she was standing in the wings with two seconds to go . . . and she went out and did the tramp number.

—*Del Armstrong*

Above: *Between rehearsals for* Ford Star Jubilee. *The Ford-sponsored series would continue on the network on a semi-monthly basis until November 3, 1956; for its final telecast,* Ford Star Jubilee *presented the television debut of M-G-M's* The Wizard of Oz. *The film was hosted "live" from New York by Bert Lahr (the Cowardly Lion) and ten-year-old Liza Minnelli.*

Right: *At the cast party with David Wayne, following the* Ford Star Jubilee *telecast. A Broadway and Hollywood star, Wayne was then perhaps best known for his roles in* Finian's Rainbow, Mr. Roberts, *and* The Teahouse of the August Moon. *He served as emcee for the Garland* Jubilee, *and partnered her on "For Me and My Gal" and "A Couple of Swells."*

I was at Capitol Records in 1956; I think Voyle Gilmore was Judy's producer, and the company asked if we would do an album together. She had a very good friend at M-G-M, a fellow named Roger Edens who sketched out many of her routines, and he was involved in a pretty well-known tune that we did, "Come Rain or Come Shine." Roger wrote the vocal part for her, and I had to fit the orchestra around that.

Judy had a strong voice; there were hardly any songs that didn't rise to some sort of emotional peak. (There are a few exceptions to that, and I found them very charming.) But it seems that when singers have the equipment, they are irresistibly drawn toward using it: if you've got a big voice, the world will know!

I remember a couple things she did—I actually did two albums with her—that were so pretty . . . just pretty ballads: "More Than You Know," "Just Imagine," "April Showers," "Memories of You." Anything that someone like Judy does that is a direct contrast to their usual approach is even more effective; it's the unexpected that makes it so great. And she had a round, warm sound. A very appealing face, centered on a couple of very captivating eyes. When she would sing, even a happy song, you were immediately involved with her emotionally.

— *Nelson Riddle*, Orchestrator/Conductor

Above: In rehearsal with pianist Leonard Pennario, who was scheduled to play and accompany Judy on her second CBS telecast in April 1956. When time constraints dictated that his solo number be partially cut, the musician withdrew from the telecast and was replaced by jazzy Joe Bushkin.

Right: Dancer-choreographer Peter Gennaro (left) joins Garland for "Come Rain or Come Shine" during her "live" telecast on April 8, 1956. A much less formal production than her first CBS show, this half-hour program gave Judy the chance to sing seven of the eleven Nelson Riddle arrangements she had just recorded for her second Capitol album, Judy. The show was another ratings champion, although Garland was once again in only fair voice. (By contrast, her vocals on the Capitol disc won accolades; the New York Times reviewed Judy as "one of the finest recordings of this type of popular singing that we have yet had . . . a fascinating ollection of songs projected with glistening polish.")

208

With photographer Richard Avedon at the Capitol Tower studios in Hollywood, March 1956. This would appear to be one of the sessions for the Judy album, as the sheet music for "Just Imagine" can be seen in the background. Avedon was at that time working on Garland's April telecast; the end credits cite "Production Created by Richard Avedon."

*S*he knew many, many songs in her relatively short life—but it wasn't that short musically; she started very, very young. I seem to remember that she always came very prepared [to the sessions]; now, whether she undertook this preparation in her home or in a separate studio at Capitol, I don't know. But she was never one to come to the recording session and learn the song. I never saw her warm up, never heard her warm up.

And she had great phrasing. We did one side called "Last Night When We Were Young," which is a tour de force. It is so tough; I did it with Frank [Sinatra], which took thirty takes. And I did [it] with Judy, which took fewer takes. But she phrased in a totally musical way, the true musical way, which is not to listen to where the phrase in the music is, but to read the lyric and find where you can breathe that will least interrupt the train of thought. I suspect that she either arrived with that ability, or at least was aware of it. She was very canny, not just emotional. A very bright lady. When they sometimes speak of areas in her life where she was less than mature, that can only be attributed to her meteoric rise, and to whatever malevolent creatures lurked in her immediate surrounding . . . [who] were more intent on what she could make than what they could make of her.

—Nelson Riddle

Judy did seventy performances during her five-week Las Vegas "debut" in 1956; after the opening, Daily Variety delighted in reporting that "she went several notches above her previous best." Laryngitis kayoed Garland's throat on just one evening, and Jerry Lewis did the show for her. At his request, however, she stayed onstage virtually throughout, playing silent partner to his madcappery.

A blues "ballet" served as the framework for "Any Place
I Hang My Hat" when Judy and eleven Boy Friends
returned to the New York Palace in autumn 1956;
Walter Kerr's comments echo every other review.

*S*he knew what she was there for. Not to
take us back down Memory Lane—as thirtyish
performers now have an alarming habit of
doing—with a catch in the throat at each
historic milestone. Not to review her own
troubled times with appropriate reference to
how the show must go on anyway. . . .
She was there to sing.

And that's what she did. Whatever has
made Judy Garland's blaring gramophone of
a voice a cherished and unforgettable echo of
our life and times was in soaring good spirits
and spectacular good health. You listened to
the calliope blast of the opening bars of "New
York, New York," and you knew that steam was
up in the boiler. But how about some nice
jazz refinements? In a moment, Miss Garland
had come to the word "sidewalk" and had sent
a single, soft, and very lonesome note scooting
upward into the reaches that used to be
inhabited only by Ethel Waters. If the calliope
was in working order, so was the butter knife.

As the party went on . . . the sense of
conscious style, of precise vocal placement, of
sleek and exuberant command continued to
grow. In a moody dalliance with "Any Place
I Hang My Hat," Miss Garland made use of a
vibrato that had best be called a quaver. But
it was, if you'll pardon the phrase, a secure
quaver, a quaver that had got into the song
by the front door and was going to stay there
just as long as it was doing the song some
good. When it was time for the tune to steady
up, and swell into forthright statement, there
was no trace of fresh effort. Miss Garland
simply took off with the ease of an aerialist
who likes it at the top of the tent.

"You Made Me Love You" was straight silk,
"Happiness Is a Thing Called Joe" took on a
reflective quality that made it sound like the
major work of a minor poet, and a percussive
treatment of "The Trolley Song" found Miss
Garland dramatizing the ditty with a rising
conviction that suggested she'd never heard of
the thing before and was startled to discover that
anyone had written such an interesting tune.

— *W*alter *K*err,

New York Herald Tribune

October 16, 1956: On the fifth anniversary of her Palace premiere, theater management announced onstage that they were mounting a gold plaque backstage to christen the "Judy Garland Dressing Room"—and they presented the star with a gold key to its door. After the show and ceremony (and still in clown makeup from her closing numbers), Judy gazes out at "the house where I was reborn."

*J*udy was the most generous woman I ever knew in giving to other performers; usually, stars are living in their own little vacuum. But she had such respect for people with talent. We had an act on during the first half of the Palace show, a team of Spanish clowns called Pompoff, Thedy and Family—with the big shoes and the orange hair. They were wonderful. And the show was running long, and I was a big hit, so [the producers] gave me more time . . . and—unbeknownst to Judy—Pompoff, Thedy and Family were canceled.

Now every night before the show, I'd get to the theater early and kibitz with her a little, pick up her spirits. And I knew how to get to her. So this night, I walked in and said, "What a shame. Isn't that a terrible thing about Pompoff, Thedy . . . ?" And she jumped up; she thought something had happened to them. I said, "They've been canceled." She said, "They've been what?!" I said, "Well, the first act is running long . . ."

She stormed out of that dressing room, screaming at the top of her lungs for Luft and Sol Schwartz, the head of RKO: "Nobody cancels anybody in my show! Nobody gets canceled from my show!" And I was standing over in the corner, smiling; that's the way she was.

—*A*lan *K*ing

Left: *With Pompoff, Thedy and Family backstage at the Palace. They were one of five acts making up the first half of the Garland show; comic Alan King was one of the others. This engagement marked the beginning of his three-year association with Judy.*

Above: *A Palace tea break mid-performance. The relaxation and liquid were throat restoratives for Garland, whose full-throttle singing eight times a week often left her drained.*

*Judy and the Boy Friends in the "Be a Clown"
finale. For a finish, she climbed atop an all-male
pyramid, and it collapsed to the stage floor, taking her with it. (In their earlier "Lucky Day" song
and dance, the boys scooped up Judy and yanked
her off-stage sideways.)*

The Sunday night shows at the Palace harked back to the early days of vaudeville, because all the legit houses were closed; they went dark on Sunday. So every Sunday night, all of the other stars came to see Judy: Helen Hayes, Bing Crosby . . . Julie Andrews was in My Fair Lady, and she came every Sunday. Every Sunday. In fact, one night from the stage, Judy looked down at Julie in the audience and teased her, "Do I have to introduce you again?"

One night, she was not well, but she did her performance. And I was in her dressing room right after the show, and she didn't want to see anybody—she was very upset over her performance. And I said, "Judy, Georgie Jessel is outside." She said, "Okay, bring him in." And I'll never forget: Jessel looked at her, and she started immediately, like all of us do, "Oh, it was a bad show; I wasn't in good voice," or whatever. And Jessel, in his own inimitable style, said, "Judy, when you're good, you're the greatest entertainer I ever saw." He said, "You're like sex. Even when you're bad, it's not too bad."

—Alan King

Right: *At Capitol, between takes for the* Alone *album, February 1957. Her conductor/orchestrator for this recording (and many subsequent stage appearances) was Gordon Jenkins. All twelve tracks for* Alone *were completed in three evenings; as Alan Livingstone later pointed out, "In those days, you'd go in with a twenty-five or thirty-piece orchestra and do the whole session 'live,' in effect. You could do retakes, obviously—as many as you wanted—but it was all done at once. Today, they do a rhythm track, and then add whatever they want to that, piece by piece—most of it electronically. And they spend hours and days and weeks. [In Judy's day] we'd go in and do a whole album in three or four sessions; that was it."*

Below: *Posing for album art for the* Alone *record jacket, 1957.*

*J*udy's my doll; I love her madly. She never gave me any trouble, nor did she ever miss a show when I worked with her because I know how to handle her.

Few of the many articles about Judy have pointed out what a tremendous musician she is. I have never known her to make a hesitant or faulty entrance, and the whole band could tune up to her pitch—a quality that is sadly lacking in some of our other singers, who need a Seeing Eye dog and a pitch pipe to even approximate a real performance.

Judy, like all great stars, is inclined towards moodiness, which is to me as natural as rain. I believe that anyone who gives as much to the world as Judy does has a perfect right to be out of sorts if she feels like it. An artist without temperament is more likely to end up as a plumber than a star. It would be impossible for Judy to sustain the level of her performances throughout her daily life: it's much too high a pitch, too close to perfection for her not to be allowed an occasional imperfection afterward. I have always believed that the occasional discords in Judy's professional life were caused by only one thing—the people around her didn't love her enough or try to understand her. I think that all Judy ever wanted during some of those troubled days was to have a friendly arm around her.

There will always be more of everything about this miraculous person: more songs, more laughter, more happiness, more tears. Above all: more talent than any of us shall live to see again. Judy walks with music, and I hope it's a long, long path with never an end.

— *Gordon Jenkins*, Orchestrator/Conductor

I think I was in Hawthorne School in Beverly Hills when I first heard the other kids saying terrible things about my mother. Some of the stuff they said I didn't even understand; I don't think they did, either. They heard their parents talking about her, and they would repeat the same things to me. Once, a movie star's kid said, "Your mother's a big, fat pig." I cried all the way home from school. [But] when I told Mama, she told me what to say back to this kid. She said, "The next time that boy says your mother's fat, look him dead in the eye and say, 'My mother can get thin anytime she wants to, but your father couldn't get talent if he took twenty years' worth of private lessons from Sir Laurence Olivier.'"

I did as she said. It worked beautifully.

—*Liza Minnelli*

Left: *Onstage on tour, 1957. By 1956–57, all three children had begun to periodically participate in their mother's live performances. It was generally just for one number: "Swanee" (to which Liza would, as here, duet and dance), "Happiness Is a Thing Called Joe" (during which the baby would be held), or "Rock-a-Bye Your Baby with a Dixie Melody." ("Lorna," explained Mama, "likes the loud ones.")*

Below: *Garland's stage acts were revamped virtually every year so that new songs could alternate with the demanded, expected standards. During her 1957 engagements, "The Man That Got Away" replaced "Any Place I Hang My Hat" as a muted-movement set piece with the male dancers.*

*W*e were together for three years; whenever Judy called, I came! We toured the United States in 1957, and then she wanted me to go to London with her. I said, "Judy, I can't go to London. I'm a Jewish comic. I'm lucky if I get laughs west of the Hudson River; if it's not a B'nai B'rith convention, I'm dead!" She insisted; I said, "Judy, I really can't."

Meanwhile, I'd promised my wife a trip to Europe. We were in a hotel in Rome when Sid Luft called. He said, "Alan, Judy's opening at the Dominion Theatre. And we just can't send [an advance man] over. You know the show inside out. Could you stop off in London on part of your trip and go over the cues and everything?" And I said of course; I owed so much to Judy and Sid.

We get to London; the J. Arthur Rank organization picked me up with the big Daimler. They said, "Do you want to see the theater?" I said, "No, take me to the hotel. I know what theaters look like." They drove me by the Dominion Theatre, and there, six stories high: JUDY GARLAND AND ALAN KING.

She tricked me into opening with her . . . and it was probably the greatest single success of my life. And when I came off after the first performance, there was Judy—this little girl—jumping up and down in the wings: "I knew you'd do it! I knew. . . . Go back, go back, go back!"

—*Alan King*

Left: *Judy at her London press conference, October 1957. Katharine Hepburn later drily recounted a similar occasion in England when "Judy found a photographer sitting on the floor below her with camera poised, and she asked very politely, 'What do you want?' And he said, 'I'm waiting to get a picture of your double chin.' I adore the press!"*

Below: *With orchestrator/maestro Gordon Jenkins in London, October 1957. He also arranged two of Judy's "concept" albums for Capitol and conducted the fifty musicians who made up her backing during the 1959 Opera House tour. Though renowned for four decades of work with many preeminent vocalists of the twentieth century, Jenkins later admitted, "I'd give them all up for Garland."*

*G*ordon Jenkins was the slob of the world—one of the great emotional guys. Now every night in London, we'd stand in the wings. And we wouldn't watch Judy, we'd watch Gordon Jenkins in the pit. And the minute Judy would start to sing, tears were rolling down his cheeks.

And I dressed with Gordon. And one night I said, "Gordon, do me a favor. Judy's told me this on a hundred occasions: you're getting to be a pain in the ass. Stop crying! 'Cause she's gonna start to laugh!" He said, "I don't mean to! I don't mean to!" I said: "Tonight. Work on it."

And he came out there, and I told this to Judy. She started laughing, she looked down: tears rolling down his face again. And she broke up in the middle of one of her prettiest ballads!

—*Alan King*

*N*ot sleet nor snow nor a flooded Belt Parkway that sent Manhattan tourists scurrying to Brooklyn gas stations for directions could dampen the enthusiasm of the multitude that showed up last night at Ben Maksik's Town and Country for Judy Garland's long-awaited opening. After it was over, the Cadillacs were nodding to the Volkswagens as their masters glowed in a kindred aftermath of exhilaration. . . .

One lives with emotion in a Garland performance. The notes pulsate through her throat as if from a meadow lark as she gets her bearings. . . . The program hits its peak with "By Myself," as she tried to teach her heart how to sing; with "Rock-a-Bye," and with the inevitable "Over the Rainbow." A portrait of a performer, a biography of emotions was told bewitchingly in song by Judy Garland last night.

—*R*obert *D*ana, *New York World-Telegram & Sun*, March 21, 1958

Left: *With Bobby Van, her onstage partner at the Brooklyn Town and Country; the pair duetted "When You Wore A Tulip," "I Guess I'll Have to Change My Plan," and "A Couple of Swells." Although everything started out beautifully, Judy's illness, her struggles with debt, and her separation from Sid Luft led to the cancellation of the engagement after just ten nights.*

*T*here I was on a platform in the middle of a football field, with a row of kings and princes and other dignitaries behind me and the Minnesota Symphony Orchestra in front of me. The foreign royalty behind me couldn't understand English, and they must have thought I was a damn fool up there, stamping my feet and screaming. And I forgot the words. Roger Edens had written some special lyrics to the opening number for London, and I started singing the London lyrics, instead of the Minnesota lyrics! I had to stop and start over again. And I wanted to be so good!

—*J*udy *G*arland

Right: *Baby Gumm goes home. Climaxing the Minnesota State Centennial Celebration on May 11, 1958, Judy headlined the outdoor afternoon festivities at Memorial Stadium. As her memories above indicate, the performance was not without incident. But when she admitted her lyrical flub, the 20,000 spectators cheered, and keynote speaker Secretary of State John Foster Dulles encouragingly tipped his hat to her.*

Below: *At the Cocoanut Grove party, following her opening night performance, July 23, 1958. She worked without chorus boys or costume changes, and the pure sixty-minute concert presentation had a laser-direct impact on the audience. Critic Wylie Williams noted that "many stood to clap and cheer to bring her back for more, there was stamping on the floor, and shouts of 'bravo,' an unusual demonstration for the Grove."*

Opposite: *"Judy and Frankie and Dino . . . They were bigger than craps or Keno . . . Sound, O psalters—crash, O cymbals—blare, O trumpets as ye may—there ain't any combination of ear-teasing and eye-pleasing sounds and sights anywhere to compare with the onstage carryings-on of Miss Garland and the Messrs. Sinatra and Martin after Judy's last show Saturday night!" (Mike Connolly in the* Hollywood Reporter*). Judy's concert-style show galloped from the Grove during the summer to Chicago in September and Las Vegas in October. She was joined there by Sinatra and Martin in one of those spontaneous encore sessions that audiences never forgot.*

At the Met, she must have weighed about 200 pounds. And someone in his great wisdom had put her into a red velvet dress that flowed; and boy, it flowed all over that stage. [Now] there was no air conditioning in the old Metropolitan Opera House . . . and I remember having a girdle on that night and thinking what a fool I was to come to the Opera House in anything like this! The perspiration was just pouring off us; it was one of those grand nights in New York. The place was crowded, and the seats were velvety and hot—it was just horrible. And there was this obese woman on the stage with some back-up that was not very good. And the show went on and on, and you thought: I have come to see the end of everything.

And then . . . by George. After the interval, she came out. And she had on that old tuxedo outfit, with the top hat, and the legs that were simply fabulous in the black stockings. [Later] she went into "We're a Couple of Swells" and wound up all smudgey, sitting on the edge of that stage. Well, hitherto, we'd all been a little damp—but now it was the eyes. I then knew what "there wasn't a dry eye in the house" meant. It was fantastic.

—*Judith Crist*, Critic

By the end of 1959, she had hepatitis; she was finished. She couldn't work, talk, sing—she couldn't do anything. And the doctors came to her one day in the hospital and said, "Miss Garland, your career is over. You'll never sing again." And when she heard this, she lay back on the pillow and said, "Whoopee!"

But she loved to work—even as she sometimes hated the pressures of it all. But she was more alive, more real on stage than in any other part of her life. And she knew she was great. And she knew what all her flaws were: she was very tough—tough-minded about herself.

She'd been exploited all her life by all kinds of people—probably her mother originally, who put the kids in show business. Then [some of] her husbands managed to do it. And M-G-M . . . worked her unconscionably. That was the beginning of her constant life of highs and lows, ups and downs, weight gain and weight loss. All that contributed to the hepatitis, and to the kind of total physical burnout she experienced at the age of thirty-seven. And the doctors said, "It's over. You can never recover from this."

So she recovered!

—*Shana Alexander*, Journalist

the 1960s

"I knew the doctors were wrong; I just felt too good." Given an almost miraculous recovery, Judy Garland was probably in better health in 1960 than ever before in her adult life—and poised to achieve the greatest professional successes she'd ever know as well. Virtually medication-free, Garland faced only minimal professional commitments for the first half of the year: a song for the soundtrack of an all-star Columbia film, *Pepe* and a new album—*Judy/That's Entertainment!*—for Capitol. In July, she flew to London where she re-recorded her greatest hits and taped new material in stereo for a two-disc set.

Those London sessions would pave the way to an entirely new stage career. Sid Luft booked his wife into the London Palladium for her first one-woman concert on August 28: no supporting acts, no backup chorus—just Garland, a full orchestra, and a nearly three-hour program of thirty songs. Such a pure, unencumbered approach was the most potent presentation she'd ever offered. Judy's obviously robust health, her new maturity, and her voice (described a few months later by Shana Alexander in *Life* "as rich as caramel, as unrestrained as lava") created a new level of cross-generational hysteria wherever she worked. Garland toured the program to Paris, Amsterdam, and a half-dozen British locales over the succeeding four months, but if the concerts were taxing, the schedule was comparatively easy.

The "new" Garland returned to the United States on New Year's Eve 1960; Luft then relinquished her managerial reins to Freddie Fields and David Begelman, two entrepreneurs in the process of forming their own talent agency. Propelled by the Fields/Begelman ambition and her own desire to achieve financial stability, Judy embarked on what would become an almost nonstop three-year work schedule. Within the first few months, however, she'd already achieved in the States the same high level of artistic and popular acclaim that she'd known in Europe. And though the 1960s offered far less media hype than that which became commonplace for stars in succeeding decades, Garland's talent and charisma didn't need it. If the 1950s had won her billing as Miss Show Business and a reputation (however sometimes burdensome) as "a living legend," she was by 1961 quite simply the "world's greatest entertainer."

Judy sang her one-woman concert some forty times that year, from the Newport Jazz Festival to the Hollywood Bowl. But the single greatest success came with an April 23 appearance at Carnegie Hall. Before a jammed-past-capacity crowd of 3,165 (including the assembled New York press and scores of Broadway, Hollywood, and international stars), the rested, ebullient Baby-Gumm-grown-up gave what was arguably the performance of her life. Capitol recorded the concert in its entirety, and when released in June, *Judy at Carnegie Hall* became the fastest-selling two-disc set to that time.

In addition to her concerts, Garland returned to the screen in 1961 with a dramatic, pivotal cameo role in the all-star Stanley Kramer production *Judgment at Nuremberg*. Her appearance as the blameless victim of a prewar Nazi plot won her another Academy Award nomination, this time as best supporting actress. (The Oscar would go to Rita Moreno for *West Side Story*.) At the opposite end of the performance spectrum, Judy also recorded a blithely amusing voice-over that November as she morphed into Mewsette, the pussycat heroine of *Gay Purr-ee*. A full-length musical comedy cartoon, the project found its special potency in an eight-song score by Harold Arlen and "Yip" Harburg.

The resurgent Garland next returned to starring roles in two films made in 1962. She shared top billing with Burt Lancaster in another Kramer enterprise, *A Child Is Waiting*, for which John Cassavetes directed the moving (if not box-office-potent) script about a school for mentally retarded children; Garland played their music teacher. She then had Dirk Bogarde as her costar in the subsequent *I Could Go On Singing*, but that drama with songs was virtually a one-woman showcase in which Judy played an American concert singer working at the London Palladium while attempting to rekindle an old romance and reclaim her long-abandoned illegitimate child. Though far from a great moneymaker and dismissed for its soap-opera plot, *I Could Go On Singing* brought about yet another, higher level of critical respect for Garland's work; per *Time*: "If the Judy who once stole Andy Hardy's heart has gone somewhere over a rainbow of hard knocks and sleeping pills, Garland the actress seems here to stay."

Perhaps her greatest popular success of 1962 came in a February CBS-TV special in which Frank Sinatra and Dean Martin paid court in support. But the show and the night's honors belonged to Judy. It gave worldwide audiences the chance to watch Garland put across excerpts from the Carnegie Hall album; the ratings, reviews, and public exultation provided an exclamation point "punctuation" to her current comeback. Garland's peers were just as exultant; one of them cabled (with tongue-in-cheek reference to Sinatra and Martin):

Opposite: *"She was forty years old, the toast of television, an Academy Award nominee . . . and back from the living dead." So began a United Press International news story on Judy Garland in February 1962, and although the syndicated release added a year to her age, every other word was accurate. Garland had been near death—and at best a candidate for invalidism—just twenty-seven months before; she told UPI: "Not very long ago, I would have never dreamed that I would be seeing all this. If I thought about being nominated for anything, it would have been for the 'first in the unemployment line' award. . . . The fact that I'm a very happy woman has a great deal to do with my comeback." This portrait from that era is a peaceful reflection of her statement.*

JUDY DEAR THERE ARE NO WORDS TO TELL YOU HOW WONDERFUL YOU WERE SUNDAY NIGHT. I LOVED YOU SO AND THE SHOW THAT EVEN DUFFY AND SWEENEY LOOKED GOOD.

FONDEST LOVE, SPENCE[R TRACY].

By late 1962, Fields and Begelman had parlayed Garland's return into a huge and thriving business, drawing other stars into their agency on the strength of their accomplishments for her. But it was the success of the TV special and Judy's casual but equally exciting December appearance on *The Jack Paar Program* that provided her managers the ammunition for their coup de grace proposal: a weekly Judy Garland TV series, beginning in September 1963. All three networks entered into negotiations, and on December 28, Judy capped the year by signing a four-season, $24 million offer from CBS.

Before beginning preproduction for the series in late spring, Garland taped another successful special for the network; attended the *I Could Go On Singing* premiere in London; and—while in England—appeared as a guest on the top-rated TV variety hour from the Palladium. But the ongoing activities of the preceding thirty months had exhausted her, and she'd again become dependent on prescription medication to maintain her schedule. There had been delays in her 1962 films when she was unable to summon the strength or nerve to reach the set, and she'd been forced to abandon a Lake Tahoe engagement in February 1963 when briefly hospitalized with slight paralysis. Through everything else, the marriage to Luft was off and on and off and on again. But Garland was nevertheless upbeat, envisioning in her TV series a real home base and steady income for the first time since her days at M-G-M.

The Judy Garland Show served as a glorious summation of Judy's concert years. She learned and performed dozens of songs new to her repertoire; there was also memorable duet work with contemporaries (Tony Bennett, Lena Horne, Vic Damone, Ethel Merman, and Peggy Lee), newcomers (Barbra Streisand, Jack Jones, Bobby Darin, and Liza Minnelli), and old friends (Mickey Rooney, Ray Bolger, and June Allyson), among others. But the network saddled her with a thankless time slot from which they then refused to move the show. They stuck Garland with a phony format, fired first producer George Schlatter, forced second producer Norman Jewison to plot the show as a banal variety hour, and then finally allowed the third producer, Bill Colleran, to implement an all-music format. By then, however, the show was scheduled for cancellation after its twenty-sixth episode, a victim of the omnipresent ratings game that even then ran rampant.

To give due credit to the many talents involved, there were memorable shows under all three regimes. Although the demise of the series meant to Garland a devastating loss of both steady nontouring employment and an established home with her children, *The Judy Garland Show* was even then recognized as a quality achievement. Terrence O'Flaherty of the *San Francisco Chronicle* spoke for many in his blunt appraisal: "I cannot recall any [musical series] in television's history where the production was so polished or where the star burned with any brighter intensity."

Drained by the workload but with her children to support, Judy returned to the road. In May and November 1964, she successfully concertized at, respectively, Sydney, Australia, and the London Palladium. The latter shows were joint efforts with eighteen-year-old daughter, Liza, then on the threshold of her own remarkable career. Over the next twenty-two months, there were well-received, extended Garland engagements at the Thunderbird and Sahara in Las Vegas and at the Fontainebleau and Diplomat in Florida. She sang in Toronto, Charlotte, Chicago, New York, suburban San Francisco, and Houston. Most of these shows were uproariously successful, with Garland's audiences more than ever a mixture of all ages, all enthusiasms. But there were also canceled performances and rough nights along the way: a late arrival and an inability to cope with a partially belligerent crowd in Melbourne, Australia; a fever of 103 degrees that knocked her out at intermission in Cincinnati; a broken arm after a great opening in Los Angeles (which meant that four of six scheduled shows were scratched); and such laryngitis after two nights in Mexico City that she was forced to forgo the remainder of a two-week booking. Naturally, all such bad news was bandied with somber glee by much of the press.

Between December 1964 and May 1966, Judy also made a dozen special guest appearances on television. But given the fate of her series, she seemed to regard the TV medium with much more fear than ever before; thus, the quality of her performances fluctuated even more than it did at some of the concerts. As journalist Randall Henderson later summarized in *Emmy*: "[Television] viewers might still find Judy looking reasonably well, in fairly good voice, or in high spirits, but it was harder and harder to find all three at the same time."

The vacillating nature of her work could certainly be traced to Garland's intake of or abstinence from medication. During this era, she again tried several times to rid herself of the dependence, but the pressing need for money always meant she had to return immediately to work; there was never the chance to strive to retain or maintain her health. There was also the stigma of having such an addiction in the first place. As June Allyson explained in 1996: "In those days, if you were addicted to drugs, you wouldn't dare say it out loud, even though [other] people talked about it. You couldn't publicly go to a Betty Ford Clinic; they didn't have a Betty Ford Clinic! They had little psychiatric places in the hospitals . . . if they could sneak you there without anybody knowing." Additionally—and despite all her professional effort and success—Garland was ever more in debt as well. Unpaid taxes (and accruing interest) from the 1950s and 1960s were by this point in a standoff against the government attachment of any current salaries; thus, there were often no funds with which to pay her bills. (In 1966, she filed a multimillion-dollar suit against Fields and Begelman, charging them with embezzlement; she dropped the case two years later to obtain an $8,000 residual check they were holding for her.)

In February 1967, Judy was offered an exploitative film role in the 20th Century Fox feature *Valley of the Dolls*, and by April, she'd been fired for failure to perform. The dismissal meant another negative headline, another blot on her professional reputation, but it was even then acknowledged that this was one movie she was smart to forsake. And true to her tradition, once really down, Judy rallied: from June until December 1967, she came back with a major concert tour, booked for her by Sid Luft. (Though rancorously divorced from Luft in 1965, she had nowhere else to turn for career management in 1966. Her intermediate association with actor Mark Herron had collapsed that May after six months of marriage and despite a twenty-two-month courtship.) In Luft's eighty-three-performance schedule, she missed only four shows—one on receiving news of the death of "Cowardly Lion" Bert Lahr, the others when hospitalized with bronchitis.

Her work in 1967 often found Garland in dry voice but never lacking in an electric showmanship that galvanized audiences and the vast majority of critics. Highlights of the tour included an open-air concert to 108,000 people on the Boston Common (Judy's single largest live audience) and an immediately preceding four-week return engagement at the Palace. As in her two previous stands, Garland's appearance turned Times Square into a cordoned-off mob scene on opening night. She worked twenty-seven consecutive evenings at the Palace, breaking her own box office record on succeeding weeks and sharing the stage for part of the act with daughter Lorna, age fourteen, and son Joe, age twelve.

The energy, determination, and goodwill she summoned up in 1967 was regarded as miraculous by those close to her, but most of her income was yet again attached by the government. A Judy broke and bereft of solution drifted through 1968. There were only a handful of concerts—some excellent and some embarrassingly the result of overmedication. By autumn, Luft and the children had retreated to California, and after a handful of New York television talk show appearances in December, Judy and new fiancé Mickey Deans flew to London, where she was booked to appear for five weeks at the Talk of the Town supper club.

Though almost translucently frail, she gave full value through most of the engagement. Her constant support in England, Lorna Smith, worked backstage nightly and noted Judy's determination to nail every show—"sometimes in full voice, sometimes with a voice which she described to her audience as having been 'left at the hotel,' sometimes struggling against flu, but always with a spontaneous quip or wisecrack." Garland was often late to the club as she fought to summon the strength and mind-set to perform; on one especially late evening, a handful of rowdy patrons verbally assaulted her during the initial songs, eventually throwing rubbish onstage. When one of them wrested the microphone away from her and another shattered a glass across the platform, Judy walked off; she returned to ovations four nights later and completed the engagement in jubilation.

In March, she married Mickey Deans and performed three extremely well-received concerts in Sweden and Denmark; there were plans to further tour Europe and South Africa, to record an album, and to film a documentary in London. But by June, Judy Garland had—in the later, explanatory phrase of "Scarecrow" Ray Bolger—just worn out. Frail to the point of malnutrition, she was unable to rally from her normal, necessary dose of sleeping pills and passed away at her London cottage on June 22, 1969. A subsequent autopsy offered proof positive that her death was accidental; she remained a headlined, worldwide news feature for a full week as millions mourned and 22,000 attended her New York City wake on the twenty-sixth and twenty-seventh.

Variety was almost prophetic when it began its obituary: "Whether they remember her because she was Dorothy of Oz, Andy Hardy's girlfriend, or a girl tramp to Fred Astaire's boy tramp; whether they're thinking back to the birth of a star, born in a trunk, or a tired little woman at the Nuremberg trials . . . or a tiny, talented mite knocking the hell out of 'em on the stage of the Palace—they do remember Judy Garland." The following February, *The Wizard of Oz* received its by then-annual national telecast in the United States; in a special, pretaped introduction to the film, actor Gregory Peck offered an even simpler and—as it turned out—timelessly true appreciation: "Judy Garland left behind her a legacy of performances perhaps unequaled by any star of our time."

"I'm a woman who wants to reach out and take forty million people in her arms." Onstage at the O'Keefe Centre in Toronto, February 1965.

Opposite: *Cover art for the album that commemorated Judy's return to a Capitol recording studio. The twelve songs for Judy/That's Entertainment!* were new to her repertoire and were taped over three nights in June 1960; four of the orchestrations had been prepared for her by M-G-M's Conrad Salinger, who'd been effectively (and often magically) underscoring Garland vocals for two decades.

Left: *Judy at the Palladium. The perform-ances began in London in August 1960, and between then and December 1961, she went on to create happy hysteria in France, Holland, the British Isles, Germany, Canada, and across the length and breadth of the United States. The one-woman show that Garland assembled and presented during this era came to define her unique approach to entertainment—as well as set levels of audience anticipation and fulfillment that it iss quite possible no other popular singer has yet to achieve, never mind surpass. The programs read, simply: "Act One: Judy. Act Two: More Judy." Each roughly fifty-minute segment consisted of about a dozen arrange-ments; as a break from the fully orchestrated numbers (or, as she self-mockingly described her repertoire at the time, "very sad, tragic songs; marches; and holiday songs"), Garland would also swing out with a nine-piece jazz combo in the first half and croon with just a piano during a sequence in the second. All this led not to the conclusion of the show but to the onset of encores: the three, four, five or more additional songs for which the audience would roaringly summon her back. At the end of Judy's live appearances from 1960 on, hundreds of enthusiasts would invariably swarm to the footlights, lining the edge of the stage to be joyously nearer to her, to reach out and touch her, to shake her hand ("as if," commented one of countless wondering and worshipful reviews, "she were a great faith healer"). In many venues, man-agement would finally try to quell the crowd by turning up the houselights and dropping the curtain —generally to no avail. Even when Judy had sung all thirty or so numbers for which she was carrying the musical arrangements, the overwhelming insistence of the audience would commandeer her into a reprise of a song from earlier in the evening.*

Prior to the election in November 1960, Mama had campaigned for John Kennedy in Europe; she really believed in him. I had just come home from the hospital [after] an emergency appendectomy. And I was lying on the couch in the living room, Liza was sitting on the foot of the couch, and I think Joe might have been in bed. And the phone rang, and Mama picked it up. And suddenly she started to scream, laughing, and she shouted, "He did it! He did it!" And Liza started to laugh, because Mama looked so funny jumping up and down.

Now the one thing I could not do was laugh, because if you have an appendectomy, that truly hurts. And I remember lying on that couch, watching my mother jump up and down, Liza laughing, and me praying that they would stop, because it really hurt me to laugh!

—*Lorna Luft*

Above: *Judy played two Paris engagements in October 1960, first at the Palais de Chaillot and then (by popular demand) an immediate return appearance at the Olympia. In commemoration of her success and their friendship, veteran boulevardier Maurice Chevalier honored her with a reception and luncheon at his home.*

Right: *On the campaign trail, October 26, 1960. At the request of two friends—Peter Lawford and wife Patricia Kennedy Lawford—Judy flew to Germany to vocally encourage United States servicemen to cast their absentee presidential election ballots for John Fitzgerald Kennedy.*

I thought she was a wonderful mother. And she was a working mother, a woman on the road, leading a life under enormous pressure. But whenever we did see the children—when they would come into the dressing room, when she would play New York or get back to California—she was so natural with them. Joey was a little boy still, and he and Lorna and Liza were just embraced and loved . . . just the way her audience was [loved]. She just put her arms around everybody.

I thought I'd never seen such a natural mother as this; I thought she was sensational. She gave every-thing she had to anybody, and more than anything to her children, whom she adored.

—*Shana Alexander*

She just worshiped those three children—all equally. All she cared about was those three children . . . and she was so proud of them.

When she had to be away, she'd call them. And there were times—just at the moment she was supposed to be somewhere else—she'd need to call Lorna or Liza or Joe in New York or California. And we'd have to get a phone, and we'd have to find, somehow, where they were. She just needed to hear their voices, to talk to them.

—*Matthew West*, British publicist

Above: *Backstage with Lorna (age eight) and Joe (age five) after a concert in Manchester, England, December 4, 1960.*

Right: *At home with Liza (age fourteen), December 1960; the Lufts rented the London town house of Sir Carol Reed during their several months' residency in England and contemplated making the permanent move from America. By New Year's Eve, however, Judy and the children were back in the United States, and her annus mirabilis was at hand.*

Right: *On the set of* Judgment at Nuremberg *with producer/director Stanley Kramer, March 1961. He later reminisced, "Though she hadn't made a picture in seven years, Judy had lost none of her skills as an actress, and they were all wonderfully evident in this role. One need say no more than to note that, despite her fame, she was able to make herself eminently believable as an anonymous German hausfrau."*

Opposite: *With the incomparable Spencer Tracy, behind the scenes on* Judgment at Nuremberg *in Hollywood. The two had been friends since the late 1930s in Culver City, and the intervening twenty-five years had brought both of them to rarefied pinnacles of respect in their industry. (Or, as Judy would say of herself and another Metro star in 1963, "Not bad for a couple of M-G-M rejects!")*

*J*udy was very fearful. . . . She played a plain German hausfrau; she just had to sit in that witness box and testify—she couldn't move around at all; that's very difficult for an actress. She was very uncertain about it.

But the day after she'd finished the scene, she got a call from [producer/director] Stanley Kramer. They had just looked at the rushes; Spencer Tracy had been there, and Abby Mann, the writer. And [Richard] Widmark and some of the other actors. And when they looked at Judy's stuff, it was so tremendous that they all burst into applause in the little screening room. They stood and applauded.

She had such great respect for Tracy. And he for her.

—*Shana Alexander*

Above: *Stanley Kramer (left) pays the traditional last-day-of-shooting homage to a screen leading lady by gallantly, graciously making her a gift of her film wardrobe. In this case, it was cause for tongue-in-cheek laughter for both Judy and costar Maximilian Schell; her Nuremberg costumes pretty much consisted—per the press—of about "$1.98 in rags." Garland rose to the occasion and solemnly told onlookers that she would "treasure this as though Dior had done it."*

JUDY
AT CARNEGIE HALL

JUDY
IN PERSON

JUDY
GARLAND

RECORDED LIVE AND COMPLETE
AT CARNEGIE HALL
SUNDAY, APRIL 23 AT 8:30 P.M.
ORCHESTRA UNDER THE DIRECTION OF MORT LINDSEY

Opposite: *Garland's greatest recording success, taken from her most famous performance, April 23, 1961. She would later comically comment on the album art, "Every time I see this, I think of Cary Grant"—and she would then mimic the actor's famous delivery: "Ju-dy, Ju-dy, Ju-dy." Jokingly, Garland continued, "Someday, I'm going to make an album and call it 'Cary Cary Cary'!"*

Right and below: *Judy at Carnegie Hall. She made two standing-room-only appearances at the fabled auditorium: April 23 and May 21, 1961. It was the first of these shows that Capitol recorded; the album was released in June and spent ninety-five weeks on the charts altogether, thirteen of those weeks as the number one best-selling album in the country. (On May 29, 1962,* Judy at Carnegie Hall *was further honored with an unprecedented five Grammy Awards: album of the year, best solo vocal performance/female, best engineering contribution/popular recording, and best album cover; there was also a special "artists and repertoire" award for the album's producer, Andy Wiswell.) Alan Livingston remembers, "I was president of Capitol by this time, and I had to be concerned about profits and so forth. I didn't really know whether I wanted to spend the money that it would cost to record Judy 'live.' But I must give Freddie Fields credit, because he was on my back about it: 'Alan, you're crazy. You've got to do this.' I probably would have done it anyway, but Freddie pushed me into it. And this was a smash, smash hit—and very profitable for Capitol. But it was such a classic performance that it was more than a commercial success; it was really an artistic success."*

I was seated in the seventh row, my wife and I, one seat off the aisle. There was an empty seat, and I thought it was for a critic. And just before the overture started, this elegant man—double-breasted, chalk-striped suit, with a little waxed mustache and a boutonniere—walked in with a silver-headed cane . . . and it was Harold Arlen.

And he looked at me and said, "Have you seen Judy?" And I said, "No. I talked to her, but I haven't seen her." And I could see that he was concerned, because the last time we'd seen her, she'd been ill and quite large; she always had a weight problem.

Then she walked out. She was magnificent: svelte, beautifully dressed, perfectly made up. She sang, "When You're Smiling," and when she got to the second chorus . . . she started with that famous "pump" [walk]; when she went into that big sock finish, she used to kick that right foot.

And Harold Arlen turned to me and said, "I think we're in good shape tonight."

—*Alan King*

I really think she felt that she was most at home in front of an audience; she might have felt nervous, but she was still the most comfortable there—and she felt that she was getting the most out of life and giving the most.

Maybe it was her built-in vulnerability that kept an audience's interest. But she had a really good instrument, and if there were times when it wasn't quite what it could have been, she had a lot of audience-grabbing mechanisms that she did with her hands or her head or her body. And her orchestrations—by everybody—were just as spectacular as you could want. All the songs were very carefully thought out. Each one was a production; you didn't just do a number. You didn't modulate up the half step where everybody else did. Sometimes you'd modulate up a third, or instead, as you got to the last chorus, you slowed the tempo down, and suddenly you're into a completely different tempo. Sometimes it went double time. . . . [But] in the really spectacular songs, there was something that happened in that last chorus that got everybody going with her.

The shows themselves had a construction to them, like a beautiful building. It wasn't just hit-or-miss. The peaks were there, the climaxes were there where they were supposed to be. And she knew what she was doing on that stage. She knew how to use that audience.

I don't remember her ever vocalizing before a show, but I never started the overture until I could see her in the wings. She always stood stage left. And I couldn't watch her because I was busy with the orchestra. But as we got to the last part of "The Man That Got Away," I could see her starting to move and jump up and down and tap her foot. And she would walk out just as we finished the song—and that's how she warmed up to perform. She'd always watch the overture from the wings, and that would kind of get her up.

— *Mort Lindsey*, Orchestrator/Conductor

Reviewers were spoiled for choice in their scramble to describe the Carnegie Hall concerts, but Hollywood's Hedda Hopper was particularly declarative (and, attendant to this picture, especially evocative) when she wrote: "Judy Garland took a jam-packed crowd in Carnegie Hall into her arms, and they hugged her back—never saw the like in my life. She was sensational as she clowned, talked, danced a bit, and used the mike as though it were a trumpet."

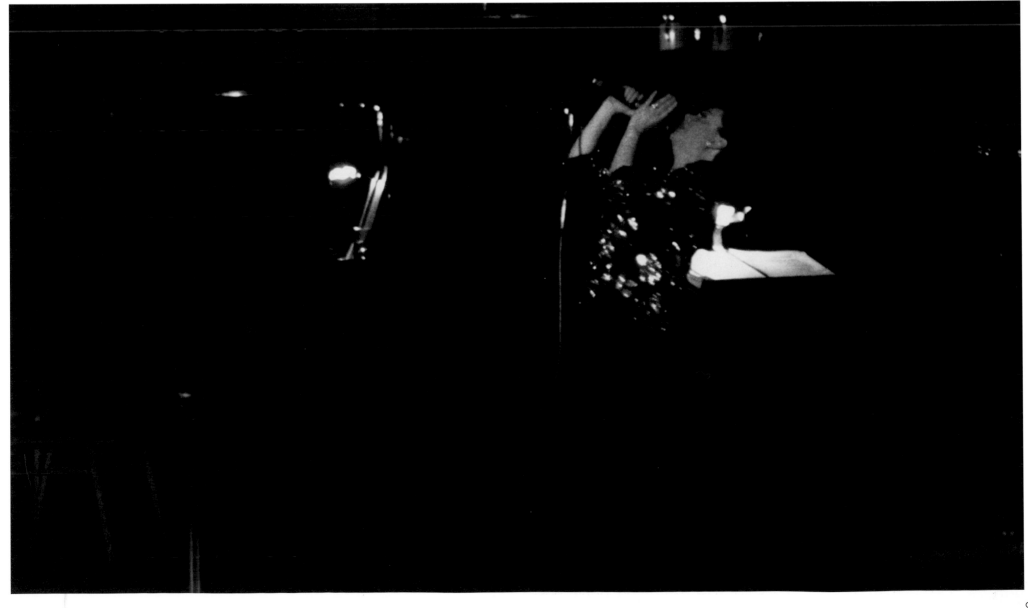

I was carried away by Judy. I had the most wonderful time, the most terrific fun. And I was lifted up by these concerts. She worked harder than any other entertainer I've ever seen to please the audience. She said, "I want to give blood!" And she would have if that would have pleased. Offstage, in her private life, she also gave everything to the encounter: she was so giving of herself . . . so outgoing and so much fun to be with. She was frisky; it was kind of like being with a pony in a way.

On the tour, we had Mort Lindsey as the conductor. And there was a drummer and a trumpeter—and then they picked up the rest of the musicians, whoever they needed, in each city. (I think there was a bass player, too, but we lost him in Atlanta; he met some lady and never got back on the train!)

Mort had a wonderful overture, which built up in tremendous excitement; you could hear the trolleys clanging and "Over the Rainbow" and all these very familiar tunes. And it just built, and it got bigger and bigger. And by that time Judy was standing backstage, and she would grab the curtain. And as the drums were going, she would yell at the audience, "Fuck 'em! Fuck 'em! Fuck 'em!" And she seemed to sort of blow up like a balloon in a Macy's Thanksgiving Day parade; she would inflate! And then at the last explosion of the [musical] chords, she would just sail out onto the stage; it was like she was a pull toy—she was on a string, and she would glide out. And you would hear roars of applause.

Then the audience was so keyed up by the end of the show that they would storm her dressing room. And sometimes it was frightening, because there was no way to get out; we didn't have a lot of security [guards] in those days; there weren't people making way for us. And Judy was a little, small woman— and so am I. So she'd say to me, "All right, Shana: hold my hand—I'll go first." And we were in these huge stadiums, having to make our way through mobs of fans. And she said [to me], "Walk very slowly, smile at everybody, shake every third hand, and just keep going." She knew how to do it!

—Shana Alexander

Opposite: *A Monday matinee at the Newport Jazz Festival, July 3, 1961. Perched—outdoors—with Lindsey and Orchestra*
on a tall, tiny platform in front of a vast expanse of audience, Judy could only joke, "For an ending, I fall off the stand!"
A fan later described one particular moment in the second act when "the sky had clouded over during [the song]
'Stormy Weather.' Just as Judy raised her head, extended her arms, and sang, 'All I do is pray that the Lord above will let me /
Walk in the sun once more,' the clouds parted—and the sun came out and shone right in her face."

Below: *At the War Memorial in Rochester, New York, October 17, 1961. "In my memory," wrote critic Hamilton B. Allen*
in the local Times-Union, *"there's never been such a demonstration of hero worship in this staid old city.*
She earned and deserved every bit of it. [The songs] were belted out with more energy and power and sparkle
and glow than it seems possible for one singer to possess."

*N*ot only did she break the attendance record, but it rained. It was starting to pour rain, and no one left. No one left. As far as we could see, there were eighteen thousand people there at the beginning and eighteen thousand people there at the end. And they all sat in the rain.

The only thing Judy worried about was whether or not she was going to get electrocuted! There was a pool of water out in front of the stage, and she'd had a ramp built out over the water. But she then had to manipulate the microphone and the cord. So that was the only real concern.

— Mort Lindsey

Opposite and above: *Judy at the Hollywood Bowl, September 16, 1961. She broke both attendance and box office records for a single performance, and despite weather that could be at best described as inclement, the crowd of 17,823 demanded that Garland sing "San Francisco" a second time to close the show.*

Right: *Rehearsing the score for Gay Purr-ee in Los Angeles, November 1961. Mort Lindsey was the conductor/orchestrator, Judy and Robert Goulet were the vocal stars (the latter on brief hiatus from his career-making role in Broadway's* Camelot*), and Judy's old friend Kay Thompson (just visible at right) was nearby as coach and cheerleader. The songs for the feature-length cartoon were written by composer Harold Arlen and lyricist E.Y. "Yip" Harburg, who had done* The Wizard of Oz; *Judy loved their work for* Gay Purr-ee, *and in autumn 1962, she briefly added "Little Drops of Rain" and "Paris Is a Lonely Town" to her concert and television repertoire.*

Below: *Half-sheet poster for the original release of* Gay Purr-ee, *November 1962. Referencing her character (a pussycat named Mewsette), Garland jibed, "Oh, I really look beautiful! I never looked this good in my heyday; from now on, I think they'll have to draw me in."*

These days—with so many jazzed-up versions of delivery—it's a wise composer who can recognize his own tune. It's a wiser composer who can get Judy to sing his melodies.

    She is a treasure, and one's musical creation could not be in better hands. She does a superb job and, while the rest of the cast and numbers come off excellently, she alone shines. Just give her a stage and a spotlight and get out of the way.

—*Harold Arlen*

Her voice, I think, was the greatest in the first part of the [twentieth] century; she went right through the bone and flesh into the heart. When Harold and I worked with her on the score for Gay Purr-ee, she sat down at the piano with him and began singing along. She was almost a line ahead of him! She is so attuned, has such an affinity for music and lyrics, you don't have to tell Judy anything.

—*E.Y. "Yip" Harburg*

I feel the picture is terribly important. I think it's important that my children see the clarification that Judgment at Nuremberg brings about. It's a "clearing" of certain issues. I also think it's one of the most adult pictures ever made; the issues have been presented correctly, [so] I say it's important from that viewpoint—from the viewpoint of young people learning from our errors.

—Judy Garland

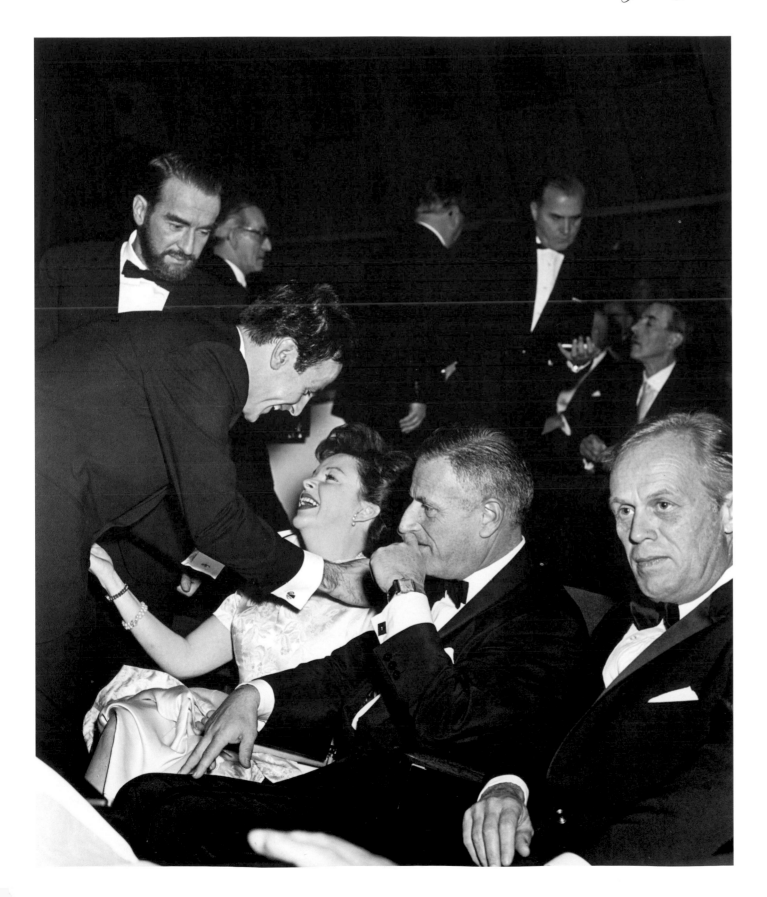

Left: *At the West Berlin premiere of* Judgment at Nuremberg, *December 14, 1961. From left, in foreground, Montgomery Clift, Maximilian Schell, Judy, Stanley Kramer, and Richard Widmark—all of them admittedly nervous about German reaction to the three-hour film about the Nazi crimes of World War II. But the majority of critical and popular consensus, at home and abroad, was genuinely admiring and laudatory.*

Above: *Italian poster for a later release of* Judgment at Nuremberg, *circa 1968.*

Kay Thompson, Judy, myself, and Mort Lindsey worked week after week trying to put together what we felt could be something dazzling for television. I knew I was dealing with the most powerful medium of communication in the world . . . and I knew I wanted this to be one hour that would just knock their socks off. And I wanted to capture Judy just once—she was like quicksilver—just once on video-tape on camera.

And we got Frank and Dean. And at the rehearsal, Judy was so feminine. She was so sexy with Frank. She was so flirtatious when she wanted to be; she became like a little girl. She flirted with Frank. She flattered Dean. She was bubbly; she was very inspiring that night. And Frank, all of a sudden, was very professional; he was contributing—I even got them up on their feet and had them working.

By the time we got on the air, it was a frenzy of pressure. This was a turning point in her career. This is what she'd worked for. This was going to be the culmination; America was waiting, we had the right time slot; everything was going for us. The last seventeen minutes of the show is Judy alone on a ramp, and I can honestly say that I think it's the best television I ever did.

In rehearsal, I had always been the camera. And I realized that to her, the camera was a friend. The camera became the personification of all those people she was singing to, and so I would play this camera with my hand. Whenever I knew I was going to dissolve or cut to another angle, I would do that with my hand. I'd run back, and I'd be wide. And then I'd come in. And she liked that, and she got so used to it that when we actually [taped] it all, she was there instinctively. This woman had such instinct. I've never seen a talent like that. Ever.

—Norman Jewison

Opposite: *Dean Martin, Judy, and Frank Sinatra, January 1962.* "It's like Carnegie Hall, the Hollywood Bowl, and opening night at the Palace all rolled into one. This is Judy at her singing and swinging best, and she deserves every adjective in the book." *So wrote Sinatra in a prepared letter for newspaper television editors all over the country, advising them of the forthcoming February 25, 1962 CBS telecast of* The Judy Garland Show. *The program was taped over three nights; the trio did their stuff on the first evening, and—except when time came for an actual "take," and all three old pros clicked into performance mode—the studio audience was treated to massive amounts of jokey byplay and teasing.* "The boys" *made continual reference to* "Crazy Legs Garland" *and* "Mrs. Norman Maine" *yet were basically content to step back and let their hostess shine.*

Below: *Rehearsing* "The Man That Got Away" *for her television show, January 1962. Norman Jewison plays "the camera," bottom right. The finished production created a sensation, winning CBS its highest rating for a special program to that date; the tape was repeated by popular demand a few months later and ultimately racked up four Emmy Award nominations: Program of the Year, Outstanding Variety or Music Program, Outstanding Performance in a Variety or Music Program or Series (for Judy), and Outstanding Art Direction and Scenic Design.*

$\mathcal{K}$ay wrote an elaborate arrangement on "You're Nobody 'Til Somebody Loves You." And I looked at it, and I said, "Gee, you've got Frank Sinatra singing harmony, and Dean Martin singing harmony. I don't think they're going to like that; first of all, they're not going to want to learn it." So what we did, I had all the music put in folders with spiral binding, and I had their names in gold letters on their individual books. And the one piece I didn't put in the spiral binder was "You're Nobody"; I just left it in there loose.

And Frank came in around seven in the evening, and he said, "You guys have got me for three hours." Then he looked at the spiral binder: "Ohhh. This is nice. Look at this, Dean." And we started going over the music. Now, I knew from experience that an artist has gotta find something he doesn't like; they'll say, "Well, I think this could be better." And Frank comes across the one loose piece of music: "What's this?" And I said, "It's a nice arrangement, Frank." He said, "I don't want to do this, [but] I've got a great arrangement on 'You're Nobody'; Nelson Riddle did it." I said, "Gee, that sounds terrific." So he sent out his pianist Bill Miller, who went and got it, and I thought, "Now we're home free; we'll sing his arrangement."

And then about three o'clock in the morning, we couldn't get rid of Frank Sinatra. He was still there rehearsing and talking with Judy and Dean; we won him over with a little three-dollar investment in spiral binding.

— $\mathcal{M}$ort $\mathcal{L}$indsey

Opposite: *Judy and Dean (at left), Mort Lindsey (seated at piano), Frank (in hat), and Norman Jewison (far right) in rehearsal for the CBS special.*

Left: *Between takes, January 1962. As Judy herself gleefully recalled, "Dean made everybody laugh; I've never seen Frank laugh so hard in his life. Frank is always giving orders, you know, and he was telling Dean in one number, 'When you come to the note of D, really try to hit it.' Dean nodded, walked down the stage singing, and at the note of D, he just fell right down on his back. 'When you tell me to try,' he said to Frank, 'I don't fool around.'"*

Above: *In rehearsal for Stanley Kramer's* A Child Is Waiting, *1962; actresses June Walker and Gloria McGehee stand to Judy's left. Garland's role as a music teacher in a school for the mentally retarded was especially meaningful to her. The children at a nearby Boston hospital had been maximally beneficial in their contributions to her recovery from a 1949 breakdown: "I spent a lot of time with those children, thinking that I was helping them in some way . . . [but] they cured me." Young residents from Pacific State Hospital "played them- selves," in effect, in* A Child Is Waiting; *they were augmented by several expert child actors, including Bruce Ritchey and Billy Mumy.*

Right: *Garland—as Jean Hansen—stops outside her dressing room for a costume test reference photo.*

*R*etarded children are realists. They know what
it is to be rejected, because they have been rejected
many times. As one woman worker [at the hospital]
explained to me, it isn't a bad thing to learn. Most
people reach their middle years before they have to
face the reality of being rejected and having to stand
alone.

These children want affection, yes. But most of
all, they need to be accepted as human beings. They
need to feel useful.

People don't want to face such things. Human
beings hate things that are mysterious to them. But I
think shining a spotlight on such things can make
people understand and want to help.

— *Judy Garland*

Above: *In conference with director John Cassavetes
on the set of* A Child Is Waiting.

Left: *Bundled up against the cold between takes of
the film's picnic sequence. Garland's costar, Burt
Lancaster, played the school administrator whose more
stringent rules for (and demands upon) the children
clash with the emotional involvement to which her
character falls prey; she gradually comes around to
his approach. In December 1962,* A Child Is Waiting
*was given a dignified Washington, D.C. send-off by
the Joseph P. Kennedy Foundation, which specialized
in work on behalf of mental retardation. The picture
won mostly compassionate reviews, although the
"truths" of its telling were only minimally palatable
to the masses.*

Opposite and below: *At a Manhattan Center midnight recording session in New York, April 26, 1962.* Judy Takes Broadway *was intended as the Capitol follow-up to the Carnegie Hall album: Garland—in concert—singing thirteen show tunes, with all but two of them new to her repertoire. If an excellent concept, it was a poor idea: the evening was arranged as an invitational "event," and Judy was torn between her attempts to entertain the jubilant crowd and to read lyric sheets and music for material with which she was at best unfamiliar. She was also battling the laryngitis that invariably occurred when she least needed it. Nonetheless, she completed nine tracks (a tenth was pieced together after the audience had gone), but the material lay fallow at Capitol until "rediscovered" and issued in 1989. Garland's verve and performance savvy, some expert editing, and Mort Lindsey's exemplary and exciting orchestration retrospectively overrode the difficulties of the original session.*

JUDY GARLAND   DIRK BOGARDE

"I COULD GO ON SINGING"

lighting up the lonely stage in the singing-acting role of her life!

IT'S JUDY!

co-starring JACK KLUGMAN   Screenplay by MAYO SIMON   Story by ROBERT DOZIER   Title Song by HAROLD ARLEN and E. Y. HARBURG   Directed by RONALD NEAME   Produced by LAWRENCE TURMAN   Executive Producer STUART MILLAR   Musical Supervisor SAUL CHAPLIN   Music by MORT LINDSEY

Filmed in EASTMAN COLOUR and PANAVISION®

Above: *A British poster for* I Could Go On Singing *(1963). Filmed on location in England, this somewhat autobiographical saga would prove to be the finale of Judy's motion picture career. She played Jenny Bowman, an international pop concert singer battling a traumatic personal life; the property was originally titled* The Lonely Stage. *If dismissed by critics for its sodden plot, the final product remains a valedictory for Garland's talents as actress and entertainer. Seldom has any screen performance garnered such raves—even when those writing struggled to comprehend their own enthusiasm. The reviewer for the* British Listener *wrote: "So often in the cinema you are reminded of how the medium is mechanical; you know you can see the film again and again, and it will never change. But the incandescent Miss Garland brings us the excitement of a first night in the theater. You find it hard to believe she can sustain the nervous tension, the complete vulnerability. . . . Surely this performance can never be repeated, surely it must burn up the celluloid. A dumpy hausfrau with tousled hair, [she] is an enchantress. She can get away with anything: mouthy sickly sentiment, sing trash, wear the most appalling dresses . . . and yet convince us that she is total perfection. I Could Go On Singing has no more than a competent script and competent direction, yet it turns out to be a memorable occasion."*

Opposite: *Two of the film's five songs actually were filmed at the London Palladium. Here, Jenny Bowman waits in the wings on her opening night, electrically charging herself with the overture being conducted to herald her entrance. Her manager, played by the correctly excitable Jack Klugman, urges her on.*

255

Right: *In a mock-up set of the interior of a limousine at Shepperton Studios.* I Could Go On Singing *gave Garland a raft of dramatic scenes with costar Dirk Bogarde, and whether bantering, baiting, romancing, or (as here) confrontational, the two—old friends in real life—played dynamically well together. With Judy's help, Bogarde reworked much of their dialogue; this was especially apparent in an eight-minute sequence late in the film wherein the slightly drunk Jenny Bowman refuses to keep her singing date at the Palladium. Garland's lines and delivery therein make up one of her most memorable performances, all done (as with so much of her finest film work) in an unbroken, single take.*

Opposite: *Belgian insert poster for* I Could Go On Singing. *Garland's image is redrawn from a still posed during her bravura eight-minute dramatic scene. Bogarde is apparently the silhouette behind her in his role (as Judy wryly described it) as "the man that got away."*

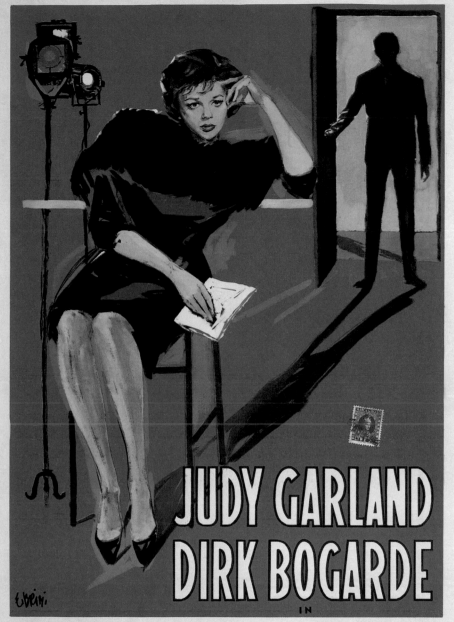

We had our up days and our down days. Our good days and our bad days. Our difficult days and easy days. Our happy days and sometimes our sad days. But we never had a dull day, and through it all . . . we loved Judy.

We filmed the last shooting day on the lawn behind Shepperton Studios. We did her last close-up and printed take two. I said, "It's finished, Judy. It's really finished." She looked at me, gave me a slight smile, then said quietly, "It's really finished. . . ."

She looked at the film unit standing around in the sunshine. Then she said, "You'll miss me when I'm gone."

Without another word, she left us. Some of the crew were in tears. And— my goodness—how we missed her!

—Ronald Neame, Director

Above: With actor Gregory Phillips and her son, Joey, on location for I Could Go On Singing. In a modest, self-effacing performance, Phillips played Garland's illegitimate son by Bogarde in the film, delighting in the chance to work with her: "I'd seen The Wizard of Oz, of course. Three times! But it wasn't until I actually met Judy that I realized this was a great artist and not just a famous name."

Opposite and above: *On a mock-up of the Palladium stage at Shepperton Studios, Judy films two sequences as "Jenny Bowman in Concert." At right, she sings the Howard Dietz/Arthur Schwartz ballad "By Myself." The song was worked into what critics would later term "a showpiece," reconstructed for* I Could Go On Singing *by Mort Lindsey's orchestration and Saul Chaplin's vocal arrangement. Garland would later term it her favorite "chart" and sing it on five television programs and in countless stage shows. In the song being photographed above, she offers the Kurt Weill/Maxwell Anderson "It Never Was You." But instead of prerecording the vocal and lip-synching to the track (as was the decades-old procedure for most motion picture musical numbers), she sang live, on camera, in one fluid take—from long shot to left profile close-up—with David Lee as her accompanist at the onstage piano. (Lee had played for Judy during a number of her 1960 concerts abroad.) "It Never Was You" was a personal favorite of Dirk Bogarde's; Judy had brought him onto the real Palladium stage to sing it to him at her premiere concert two years earlier.*

The finale of I Could Go On Singing *brings Jenny Bowman back to the Palladium, albeit an hour late for her performance and nursing a sprained ankle (which she brandishes in the picture opposite). In a dazzling display of humor and self-deprecation, she wins over an understandably irate crowd—although managing never to apologize for her tardy arrival—and launches into the film's title number. Though an Arlen/Harburg effort (and masterfully orchestrated by Lindsey), the song itself is unimpressive. What saves it is the gradual build from rubato to an all-stops-out delivery that allows Garland to caress the lyric, stride the stage, toss in flash imitations of James Cagney and Jimmy Durante, and wind-up (in best show business parlance) belting her heart out.*

Either you are or you aren't—a Judy Garland fan, that is. And if you aren't, forget about her new movie and leave the discussion to us devotees.

The very least Miss Garland's new and mediocre movie offers us is our pop-tune Pagliacci making four separate appearances on stage at the Palladium. And you'll see her in close-up as the very best seats in Carnegie Hall or the Palace or even your television set has not enabled you to, in beautiful, glowing Technicolor and striking staging, in a vibrant, vital performance that gets to the essence of her mystique as a superb entertainer. You'll wish that she had better songs to sing, or at least, more familiar standards . . . but the performance is there for the devout to revel in.

In the course of her sorrows and fleeting joys, Miss Garland is, as always, real, the voice throbbing, the eyes aglow, the delicate features yielding to the demands of the years, the legs still long and lovely. Certainly the role of a topnotch singer beset by the loneliness and emotional hungers of her personal life is not an alien one to her. . . .

—Judith Crist,
New York Herald Tribune

I have served as musical director for a number of artists. It would not be demeaning or belittling to them to state that Judy Garland was head and shoulders above them all. She was as warm and generous as she was talented. Her sense of humor was fantastic. In short, it was an honor, a vital experience, and a privilege to make music with her. In all the concerts, TV shows—no matter where or how often—I always felt the goose bumps when she sang.

She was truly one of kind. God bless her. We miss her.

— *Mort Lindsey*

Judy expresses her professional and personal gratitude and admiration to Mort Lindsey at the Sahara Hotel in Las Vegas, autumn 1962. The two had first worked together in February 1961, when he agreed to conduct a one-night concert she was presenting at the Concord Hotel in The Catskills. Within months, he was ensconced as her regular conductor; by June, he had begun to orchestrate new additions to her repertoire. Their association together would eventually tally two films, more than thirty hours of television, scores of arrangements—including many of the post-Carnegie Hall Garland classics—and more than one hundred live performances. Lindsey was arguably her finest orchestrator/conductor.

Left: *At the Sahara, autumn 1962. Garland's engagement was history-making on several levels. Booked at top dollar for three weeks, she was required to do only one sixty-minute show a night, "in concert;" all other Vegas headliners did at least two or three performances per evening. The rave notices and record-breaking crowds that she attracted led the management to extend her show for a fourth week. After that, with the Sahara's Congo Room prebooked for other acts, producer Stan Irwin implemented an innovative plan: Judy was signed to appear once a night at 2:30 A.M. for an additional two weeks. Even then, it was standing room only.*

Below: *In her Sahara dressing room, autumn 1962. Tanned, freckled, and more slender than she had been since the Metro days, Judy was—at this juncture in her career—the biggest name in entertainment. The Carnegie Hall record set was still on the bestseller charts, more than a year after its release. She was commanding top salries in Las Vegas and in concert, with every performance an in-advance sellout. Her television special had been the talk of the preceding season, and there were plans for the next. She'd been an Academy Award nominee that spring and had three feature films being readied for release. That workload had already been more physically and emotionally demanding and debilitating than most could imagine, but in terms of star power, Judy had never been brighter, more sought-after, or more acclaimed.*

Add one incandescent facet to the brilliance of Judy Garland, and credit Jack Paar for discovering it. We have known Miss Garland as a singer who can melt your heart and as a sensitive actress. Now we've met her as a personality who fizzes like a supercharged bottle of freshly opened soda pop. And what a joy it was to behold her thus, bursting into the sunlight . . .

Miss Garland's appearance confirmed the reports that she looks better than she has in years. Her features are sharp again, her eyes sparkle and, praise be, she was attractively dressed. She acted like a frisky cat. She revealed herself as a born storyteller [in] salty but innocuous tales out-of-school. . . . It was a quite wonderful hour. And please, Miss Garland, stay as you were Friday night, and come back again.

—Robert J. Williams, Philadelphia Bulletin, December 10, 1962

Below: Taping at NBC in New York, December 2, 1962. Telecast five days later, this edition of The Jack Paar Program *marked one of Judy's finest hours; the host presented her with simplicity: "I've learned in show business: the greater the talent, the smaller the introduction. . . . And if that be true, then Judy Garland needs no introduction at all—except to say that she's pure magic. So . . . abracadabra: Judy Garland." The entire studio audience rose in greeting and acclamation.*

Opposite: "Punchy and Judy" was Paar's self-description of his teaming with Garland; here they share the show's final moments with Robert Goulet.

𝒯o promote Gay Purr-ee, *we went to about four or five different movie theaters in New York; she said a few words, I said a few words. I don't even think we sang anything.*

But on Jack's show, we decided to sing one of the songs from the cartoon. And we didn't know the song by heart; the music had been right in front of us when we recorded for the movie. So I never memorized any of it, and neither had she.

Now these days, they have "crawls" underneath the television cameras, so that as people look at the camera, they can read at the same time. But back then, we had cue cards that were several feet high and several feet wide; they were right next to the camera. And we were singing, side by side, looking at this card—and I thought we were doing quite well! But Jack took the card and turned it upside down! Meanwhile, the music is still playing, but Judy and I don't know the words. But I looked at her: "Keep on going," and we just kept repeating and repeating and repeating, until we finished—both of us—with high notes.

Then we chased Jack around that studio; eventually, we just said good-bye. I picked up Judy, put her over my shoulder, and we walked off the set. That was a fun night.

—ℛobert 𝒢oulet

We rehearsed in Beverly Hills at Judy's house. And I remember being there for a full day with Phil [Silvers]. And no Judy. Now he knew her better than I did, and he was getting a little angry. And the next day, we were there again, going through all the material. And no Judy. And Phil is fuming.

Finally, she walks in, full of spunk: "Hi, guys!" And Phil is growling, "Where have you been?" He started to give her hell. And she said, "Oh, for goodness sakes, Phil, settle down. Relax. What are we doing here?" And she looked at the music at the piano: "What's this? What's this? Okay . . . Harmony here? Harmony there? Okay." She sang the harmony. She said, "And this over here? Okay. Fine. Did that." And then she said, "Is that it? See you later!" And she walked away; that was it for rehearsal! She did it; she was a pro. Don't worry about Judy!

Of course, we did worry about her, because she was working too hard. And she was a frail little thing; she wasn't a big robust lady. We wanted to hold her and say, "Take it easy."

—Robert Goulet

Opposite: *Judy tapes her 1963 CBS-TV special in Manhattan, January 1963. She is seen here in her second song, the appropriate Cole Porter anthem "I Happen to Like New York."*

Left: *The show was titled* Judy Garland and Her Guests Phil Silvers and Robert Goulet, *which left little room for conjecture about the cast. Taped over five nights, the three-person revue was a symbolic pilot for the next season's television series; it began to separate Judy from the trappings of nostalgic show business and ease her into a more youthful blend of music and comedy.*

Right: *Slamming out "Almost Like Being in Love" on* Sunday Night at the London Palladium, *March 10, 1963. While in England for the world premiere of* I Could Go On Singing, *Garland topped the bill on this British TV equivalent of* The Ed Sullivan Show. *She was terrified of live television, but—with Dirk Bogarde crouching in the orchestra pit for encouragement and Mort Lindsey next to him to wield the baton— Judy managed within her five-song segment to not only raise cheers from the theater audience but to debut to unforgettable effect Lindsey's orchestration of "Smile." Ed Sullivan actually excerpted that performance from the Palladium tape for his own show in the States a month later; it has since been run and rerun as a classic moment. One music historian has described Judy's "Smile" as "a master class in the delivery of a ballad: soulful but never sinking into the inherent trap of bathos. For all her 'tragic legend' reputation, Garland never lost sight of the fact that this was intrinsically a wise, consoling, and encouraging song."*

Opposite: *Judy sings at the SHARE benefit evening in Los Angeles, May 1963. Founded in 1953 to "raise money and organize programs to better the lives of the developmentally disabled," SHARE has remained a thriving Hollywood women's organization; their annual "Boomtown" party each spring offers all-star entertainment and an informal but oft-adhered-to western dress code. For her appearance, Judy soloed "San Francisco"; duetted with Sammy Davis, Jr. ("Shine On, Harvest Moon"), Gene Kelly ("For Me and My Gal"), and Johnny Mercer; and shared a table with John Wayne—a fellow former resident of Lancaster. (Judy always recalled Wayne's efforts to bolster her on a less happy occasion: "Judy, if you can live through Lancaster, you can live through anything!")*

*B*efore I got the job [as producer of The Judy Garland Show], I was fascinated by Judy's reputation. I had worked at Ciro's. I'd been an agent at MCA. And I'd heard about the reputations of people like Sophie Tucker, Maurice Chevalier, Pearl Bailey, Martin and Lewis. . . . And I've really gotten along well with them, because most of those people are not really difficult. They are exacting and demanding because they demand the same kind of perfection out of others that they expect out of themselves. Judy was the same way. She was great. She was An Event!

She was one of the most cooperative people I have ever worked with. She would try anything. She'd come out and kick the fire out of you; I don't think she said no to anything I've wanted to do.

I've worked with some very cooperative people. But Judy *worked*. And she *listened*. And she would try anything. And she didn't just try it—she committed. She went out there like a little bantamweight fighter.

—*George Schlatter*, Producer

Opposite: *Judy and Mickey reunited on the set of her TV series,* The Judy Garland Show, *CBS Television City, Los Angeles, June 1963. Rooney was Garland's personal choice as the ideal first guest; unfortunately, by the time the show debuted in September, network interference had already bumped that episode to later in the season. When this post-rehearsal picture was taken, however, all was optimistically well. George Schlatter is seated in shirt and tie on the edge of the stage, just to Judy's right.*

Left: *Schlatter's third episode, taped in July, marked the first "official" teaming of mother and eldest daughter. Liza Minnelli was then seventeen and had just made her first independent success off-Broadway in a revival of the Hugh Martin/Ralph Blane show,* Best Foot Forward. *Here, she and Mama tear through a family favorite, "Bob White." Vincente Minnelli himself attended the taping and afterward beamed at Schlatter: "You made Judy look like a star."*

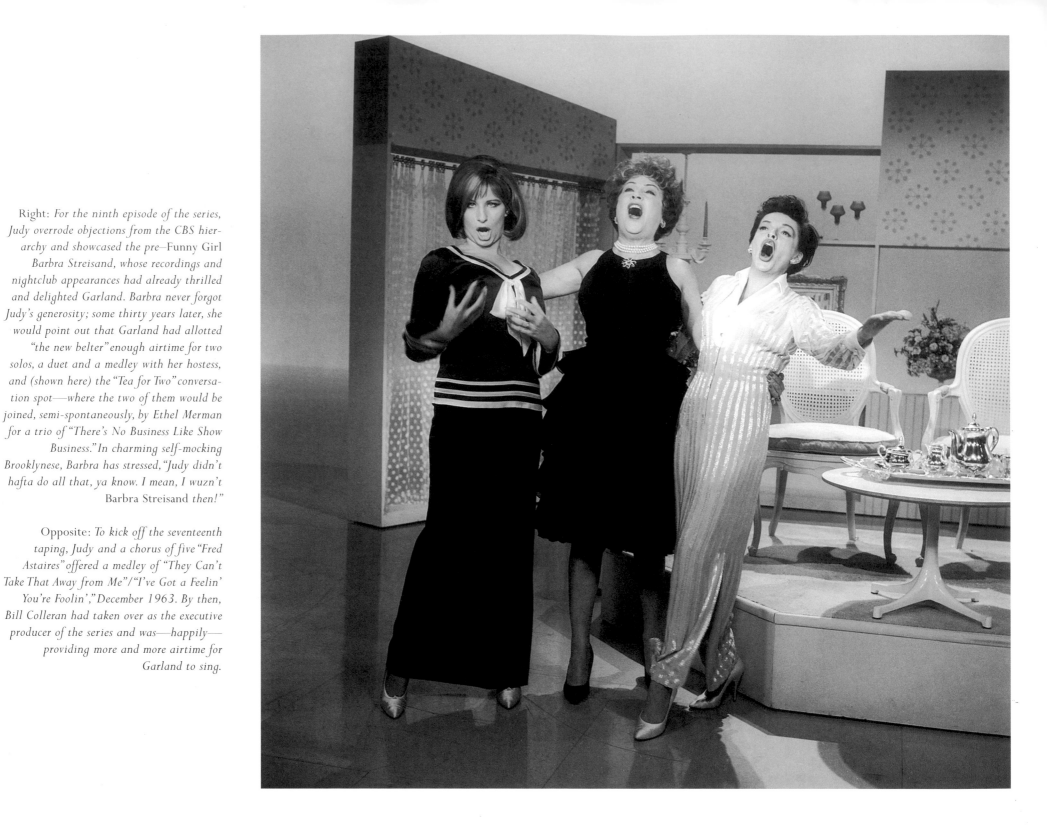

Right: *For the ninth episode of the series, Judy overrode objections from the CBS hierarchy and showcased the pre–Funny Girl Barbra Streisand, whose recordings and nightclub appearances had already thrilled and delighted Garland. Barbra never forgot Judy's generosity; some thirty years later, she would point out that Garland had allotted "the new belter" enough airtime for two solos, a duet and a medley with her hostess, and (shown here) the "Tea for Two" conversation spot—where the two of them would be joined, semi-spontaneously, by Ethel Merman for a trio of "There's No Business Like Show Business." In charming self-mocking Brooklynese, Barbra has stressed, "Judy didn't hafta do all that, ya know. I mean, I wuzn't Barbra Streisand then!"*

Opposite: *To kick off the seventeenth taping, Judy and a chorus of five "Fred Astaires" offered a medley of "They Can't Take That Away from Me"/"I've Got a Feelin' You're Foolin'," December 1963. By then, Bill Colleran had taken over as the executive producer of the series and was—happily—providing more and more airtime for Garland to sing.*

*J*udy had great respect for talent. She got very excited about people she liked or admired. So the first thing I did [when I took over as producer] was . . . book certain stars. We built numbers around them that didn't have anything to do with Judy, thereby lessening her load. Then we would have Judy do a number with a star, and then we would end up with Judy. And all of a sudden, we started to do some shows that were quite remarkable.

I remember the three belters: we got Streisand, and I got Ethel Merman to come out of the audience as a surprise. Judy, Streisand, and Ethel . . . oh God, I mean just capturing them—it was like a special again. It had moments of such brilliance. And Judy started to cook; when the red light went on, she was there.

[So] the failure of the television show was not Judy's fault. It was the network's fault, essentially, because they were in control. And it was Freddie and David and a lot of people around her who were very greedy and wanted to make a lot of money.

—*Norman Jewison*, Executive Producer

*O*nce I came on as the executive producer of her series, we would get together on Sundays at her house, where we'd spend the day planning the next show. And then we'd watch the previous show that night. She usually chose all her own songs; she'd decide how many choruses she wanted to do, or if she had any tricks she wanted the arrangement to do.

Her television shows—particularly the concerts—are terribly personal. When you saw them, she was working right to you, whoever you might be. And that very often didn't happen in the movies, because there was a character to play and a part to get progressed. But on TV, she was suddenly able to turn to you and sing for you and only for you . . . she made a personal statement to you in your home. And I think it's just so rare that one gets that from a great performer.

And you believed everything she said, right then and there. You believed it, and grabbed it to you. She could make you feel whatever she wanted you to feel—because she felt it so strongly. That's what made her special to me and to everybody: that incredible ability to tell you exactly what she meant and make you feel it.

—*B*ill *C*olleran, Executive Producer

Opposite: *All but four episodes of the TV series ended with Judy on her runway at "the trunk," signifying her vaudeville heritage. Her solo songs here each week were invariably a highlight of any given show—whether delivering such Garland-appropriate material as "As Long as He Needs Me," tackling the unexpected in "Ol' Man River," or presenting a solemn, unspoken dedication to the just-assassinated President John F. Kennedy in "The Battle Hymn of the Republic."*

Left: *Singing "Something's Coming" during a* West Side Story *medley on the seventeenth episode, December 1963.*

*J*udy would watch from the booth; Gary Smith was the producer at that point, and he had pressed my wife into service. She would run through the numbers with the orchestra, and Judy would watch from the booth and see where she was going to make her moves. And then she'd do the dress rehearsal. If there was something new [in the show] that she didn't know, then she naturally had to rehearse with the people . . . but that's about the amount of rehearsal that she did. She was very quick. I don't know what her IQ was but it seemed like it was way up there. She was very, very bright.

— *Mort Lindsey*

Opposite: *The finale of a musical comedy sketch on episode nineteen. As sirens, firefighters, and billows of fog raged on around her, Judy sang an absolutely straightfaced rendition of Jerome Kern's "Smoke Gets in Your Eyes." (She loved Kern, hated that number.) When asked to name her own favorite song, Garland's public, generic answer was inevitably "Over the Rainbow." Privately, however, she expressed even more affection for "By Myself," "If Love Were All," and— above all others—the Vincent Youmans / Edward Heyman ballad "Through the Years."*

Above: *With guest Diahann Carroll on episode twenty-one. Each woman sang the songs of the composer with whom she was most associated: Richard Rodgers for Diahann, Harold Arlen for Judy.*

The concert programs were the best of all—and I'm so glad I was able to contribute that, to give that [format] to Judy to do. And my favorite memories of all the time we spent together come from those shows. Because I'd be standing off-camera, offstage, just in back of the proscenium. And she'd come off after having done a spectacular number . . . I mean, like nobody in the world had ever done. And she'd come into my arms, and she'd look up to me, put her head on my chest, and say, "Okay? Was it okay, Bill?" It breaks me up now, years later—and I could barely take it then.

— Bill Colleran

Miss Garland's Gowns Designed by
RAY AGHAYAN

The Judy Garland Show   •   Sunday at 9   •   Channel 2

Opposite: *Judy in concert on episode twenty-four, February 1964.*

Left: *Judy in concert on episode twenty-five, March 1964.*

Above: *Trade paper ad sketched and taken by the master artisan who created the majority of Garland's wardrobe for the series and for several years afterward. Ray Aghayan did more for Judy than any other designer.*

*T*he Beatles may come and go, but the past week belongs to Judy Garland. There has never been a Stadium show like it. And there never will be again.

From the foot-stamping, cheering applause that broke out fully five minutes before the star made her entrance, until the last strains of "Over the Rainbow" died away, her Wednesday night concert was another triumph for Judy. In the eyes of the audience, she could do no wrong. Despite technical troubles with the sound equipment, forgotten lyrics, and a messy stage she described as "a minefield," the frail figure under the light conquered all.

When she stopped in mid-song to ask whether she could be heard clearly, a member of the audience spoke for everyone when he called in reply, "It's Judy Garland. That's enough."

And it was.

—*Sydney Sun Herald*,
Sydney, Australia, May 1964

Above: *After a week's vacation, Judy and traveling companion Mark Herron depart Honolulu for her concerts in Australia, May 1964.*

Right: *Onstage during her premiere concert at the Sydney Stadium, May 13, 1964. Garland's two ebullient performances in that venue won "the greatest audience ovations in Australian theatrical history" (*Variety*), as she reached out to impact on the crowd of ten thousand that surrounded her each night. Unfortunately, the fact that her essential medication had been impounded when she first arrived in the country eventually led to illness and laryngitis; she was consequently an hour late for a Melbourne appearance on May 19, and the evening deteriorated into disaster and a welter of international headlines.*

"*N*ight of A Hundred Stars" was a big charity show every year; everybody came out and did a bit. In 1964, my job was to hold all the fur coats: Gloria Swanson's, Zsa Zsa Gabor's—I looked like a hat rack. But this meant I was watching from the wings, only about eight feet away from all the activity.

In the second half, the stars were seated on stage at tables. Judy wasn't expected to do much, because she'd been in the hospital. But [when she was introduced] the audience went mad and stood up, screaming and yelling. And the stars on stage screamed and yelled. Shirley Bassey was in tears—it was all very exciting. And all Judy had done was walk on and sit down. Later, Richard Attenborough tried to close the show, and the yelling began again. And Judy finally had to get up and sing—and then I think the roof fell in! The most amazing thing was that the other stars all wanted Judy to be the most important person that night. There were some huge stars dotted about—The Beatles were there—but they all wanted Judy to be the main one.

—*Matthew West*

Left: After leaving Australia, Judy took a recuperative, nonperforming tour. She traveled to Hong Kong (where there was a near-fatal overdose), Tokyo, and Copenhagen; in late June, she and Mark Herron arrived in London for a five-month stay. Her first real appearance came at the July 23 midnight Palladium benefit, "Night of A Hundred Stars."

*J*udy was my date when Oliver! opened on Broadway in January 1963. She knew the show very well; she'd brought her kids to see it in London again and again. At the end, I was brought up onstage; the audience wanted a word from the author. All I could think of to say was "Thank you." Judy turned to someone else in our party and said, "Good speech, but it needs tightening."

In 1964, she recorded songs from another show of mine, Maggie May. And it was quite amazing because she wanted me to coach her. She said, "Look, you've got to show me how to phrase them." Then when we got to Abbey Road, she turned up with four enormous hampers full of caviar and champagne. She did everything in one take, but the orchestra got trashed!

—*Lionel Bart*

Right: With (from left) composer Lionel Bart, actor Kenneth Haigh, librettist Alun Owen, and Mark Herron at the Liverpool opening of Bart's musical Maggie May, August 1964. She and Bart were close and supportive friends.

Backstage at the London Palladium, November 15, 1964. The highlights of Judy's British sojourn that year were the two concerts she gave with Liza: an 8 P.M. show on Sunday, November 8 and a midnight matinee a week later. Even before they could be advertised, the performances were sold out; Capitol recorded both nights for use on an album, and the midnight program was also videotaped for a television special. Perhaps understandably—with no previews or tryouts out of town—the actual concerts were musically uneven and laced with vocal problems, forgotten lyrics, and missed cues among the orchestra. None of it mattered, however; the audiences came to the Palladium to revel in Garland—whose showmanship was wonderfully intact—and to discover a fledgling new star in Minnelli.

Daughter and mother acknowledge the cheers after their first duet of the evening. Jerry Herman's original lyric for "Hello, Dolly!" needed only slight revision to bring down the house: "Hello, Liza . . .," sang Judy as she sauntered on from the wings; "You're lookin' swell, Mama . . .," sang Liza a few moments later—and the audience roared in concurrence.

Below: *Judy and Mark Herron at the premiere of* Lord Jim, *spring 1965. They had remained a duo for most of the preceding fifteen months and would marry in Las Vegas on November 14.*

Above: *Judy introduces The Allen Brothers to an American television audience, February 5, 1965. Though not really brothers, Peter Allen (center) and Chris Bell had performed as a duo throughout their native Australia and were working in Hong Kong in June 1964 when Judy heard them sing. She delighted in their youthful approach to traditional show business and asked them to tour with her as an opening act. The boys first joined her in London later that year, and they'd been in town only a few weeks when Peter and Liza Minnelli became engaged. Their initial stage shows with Judy were promoted on the CBS-TV* On Broadway Tonight, *a prime-time "talent scout" hour in which the trio (above) sang "I Wish You Love." Though the boys' act would later break up, as would the eventual Minnelli / Allen marriage, Peter's career as a song-writer and music hall entertainer would flourish; he always credited Judy with his "discovery," noting that she early on and instinctively had recognized his potential and talent. He repaid the favor in 1974 by writing (with Carole Bayer Sager) "Quiet, Please, There's a Lady Onstage." Though initially inspired by cabaret entertainer Julie Wilson, the song evolved into a celebration of any legendary female performer— and paramount among all of those was Judy Garland.*

At the Arie Crown Theatre, McCormick Place, Chicago, May 7, 1965. Judy gave more than fifty concerts in 1965, most of them easy and happy successes. But there were also several cancellations or evenings of strained vocal performance; this Chicago appearance fell into the latter category. Constricted by medication, Garland's voice caused her so much trouble and worry that she tripped over the lyrics to half a dozen songs during the first part of the night. Yet, with her uncanny ability to rise to the occasion, her voice gradually shook loose, and she soared through the climactic, big-belting, final moments of her songbook during the second half of the show. The clincher came at the very end. Vocally drained, she found it impossible to sustain the quiet singing required for "Over the Rainbow"; after attempting the first eight bars, she said apologetically, "I'll have to talk it." With Mort Lindsey conducting a twenty-eight-piece orchestra in underscoring, Judy spoke the words to her theme, summoning up a recitation that aligned acting ability, decades of performance experience, and an uncanny knack of underplaying an emotional moment. When she reached the last eight bars of the song, she tentatively began to sing again. Every note emerged and when she sustained the final phrase, it was as if all 4,500 seats in the theater had been wired. The audience was on its feet as one, and as an eyewitness tried later to explain: "They offered up this roar . . . this wall of sound. . . . It was acceptance, approval, gratitude."

*L*orna and Joe played a very important part in her psychological structure at that time; I don't think she could have made it without them, because she had nobody else to run to her when she came home at night, to say good-bye to her when she left for rehearsal.

When they were at rehearsals or at the tapings, it always had a profound effect on Judy. She was much easier to get to, because she was so aware of them being there. Therefore, she was happier, it was easier, she took better care of herself—because she had two people there who loved her. Besides me!

But she loved kids so much in the first place. I remember the first time she met my daughter, Kate, who was then about three or four years old. Judy saw some drawings that Kate had done of the characters from The Wizard of Oz, and she loved them; she started to cry: "I've got to see her." I said, "She's asleep," so we went in quietly, and Judy sat down on Kate's bed. Kate rolled over and opened one eye, and Judy said, "Kate. It's Dorothy." And Kate said, "What?!" And we all just laughed and laughed.

—*B*ill *C*olleran

*S*he was the most loving mother I have ever seen. She just worshipped the three children—even more than you would expect of a mother. Maybe it's because she never felt that, as a child, she had that kind of love.

And so, whatever they wanted, whatever they needed. Whatever the kids would do was just the greatest. And when they weren't with us, she was on the phone with them, all the time.

—*A*lan *K*ing

Above and right: *At home in the pool with Lorna and Joe, spring 1965.*

Opposite: *From a series of publicity photos taken on the grounds of her home in Brentwood, 1965.*

Right: *At the Thunderbird in Las Vegas, June 15, 1965. After two hospitalizations in the preceding two weeks and convulsions (brought on by medication withdrawal) in the hotel elevator during the afternoon, Judy opened her two-week engagement that evening as scheduled.* The Las Vegas Review Journal *offered: "She bounced onstage just as if she hadn't spent a miserable weekend in the hospital. Members of her cult, some of them in tears, gave her a standing ovation. . . . The star look[ed] in the best of health, smiling radiantly. . . . With an air of confidence with which she seemed to want to reassure her fans, she grabbed the mike and, in the distinctive Garland tones hoped for, socked across a memorable 'Whole World in His Hands.' It was as if she had hit a home run with the bases loaded."*

Opposite: *During a live telecast of* The Ed Sullivan Show, *October 3, 1965. Sullivan introduced Judy as "one of the all-time greatest"; after her three-song segment, she bowed to cheers and left the stage as rehearsed. But the applause continued, and the delighted host could only concur with the studio audience: "I don't blame you."*

*P*eople always expect me to be funny. I was never funny; the writers were funny!

Do you know who was really funny? Judy Garland. Judy Garland was naturally funny . . . the funniest lady in Hollywood.

She made me look like a mortician.

—*L*ucille *B*all

Above: *Judy and Lucille Ball at a "Town & Gown" evening, hosted by the University of Southern California Cinema Department (Delta Kappa Alpha/National Honorary Cinema Fraternity), January 1966. Ball was one of the evening's honorees, as were Gregory Peck, Hal Wallis, Frances Marion, and Sol Lesser.*

Right: *Just prior to taping the NBC-TV program, Perry Como's* Kraft Music Hall, *February 1966. Friends since the 1940s, Como and Garland had worked together on radio, but this was their only television show as a team. Enthused the* New York Daily News, *"We guess all Judy Garland ever needed was a real guy like Perry Como to take her by the hand and make her feel at home on TV. Although the show had some ragged ends, the Judy/Perry duet was cozy Como at his best—and Judy at hers." Along with a stint as hostess of ABC's* The Hollywood Palace *in November 1965, this was one of the best post-series Garland television outings.*

Opposite: *Dress rehearsal for the Como show. Judy sings "What Now, My Love?" which she'd first added to her repertoire at the Palladium in 1964. It became a concert staple.*

With Sammy Davis, Jr., on his NBC-TV variety
series, March 18, 1966. Davis encountered many of
the same difficulties with his weekly hour that Judy
had experienced a couple of seasons earlier: network
pressure, low ratings, and a poor time slot. As an old
friend, however, he was delighted to have her on the
program; in fact, at Davis's invitation, Garland was
a guest twice in two weeks. They concluded the first
show in tramp costumes, singing a blithely arranged
medley of Judy's film hits. On the second, they
dressed as minstrels and did a vaudeville/show biz
montage. Unfortunately, however, Judy was saddled
with laryngitis for both appearances; the programs
thus became an interesting study of how her stage-
craft and technique were used to work around (and
draw attention away from) some of the vocal pitfalls.
For his part, Davis remained a rabid admirer; he had
rejoiced in Judy's 1961 renaissance and offered
appreciatively, "It's the same thing that happened
when Frank Sinatra came back after he seemed to be
down for the count. People like to see the champ get
off the floor and score a knockout."

Van: We clowned around at M-G-M . . .
Judy: Ages ago!
Van: I don't see all my movies on "The Late, Late Show."
Judy: Well, how 'bout Thirty Seconds Over Toh-keee-yoh?!

— *"Mr. and Mrs. Clown," The Hollywood Palace, ABC-TV, Telecast May 7, 1966*

The Metro-Goldwyn-Mayer alumni association, circa spring 1966. Judy taped her second stint as hostess of The Hollywood Palace
in early April; one of her guests was Van Johnson, costar of In the Good Old Summertime *(1949). Their number together paid
special material reference to the old days on the lot.*

She had such devoted fans—and possibly more deservedly than any other performer. It was such a spectrum of ages, from seven- and eight-year-olds to grandparents. There was something in her that reached everyone. You felt it. You knew it. And you were rooting for her: this brilliant creature has got to win!

I must say the audiences at the Palace screamed so much. Now, they've done that for the Beatles and others. But for Judy, it was a kind of roar that I don't think I've ever heard anyplace else. So personal. Each individual seemed to be receiving her and appreciating her—and you felt the love going back and forth.

There was this little person up there on the stage, just so full.

—Betty Comden and Adolph Green

Opposite: *Mother of the bride, March 3, 1967. Peter Allen and Liza Minnelli (center) are flanked by Judy on their left and maid of honor Pamela Rhinehart on their right, immediately following a private wedding ceremony at the New York apartment of Stevie Phillips Friedberg, Liza's theatrical manager. At her request, Judy was escorted to the festivities by Vincente Minnelli; Sid Luft and Lorna and Joey were in attendance as well—and Joey caught the bridal bouquet when Liza tossed it into the crowd.*

Above and right: *After months of inactivity and another spate of unpleasant headlines over her dismissal from* Valley of the Dolls, *Judy suddenly soared into action again in June 1967. Sid Luft booked her on the East Coast summer stock circuit, where she triumphantly worked in the round at the Westbury Music Fair (on Long Island), the Storrowton Theater (in Massachusetts), and the Camden County Music Fair (in New Jersey). Draped in a beaded and sequined Travilla pant suit designed for* Valley of the Dolls, *Garland performed with dedication and élan; her success enabled Luft to book her back into the Palace on Broadway for the third time, starting July 31.*

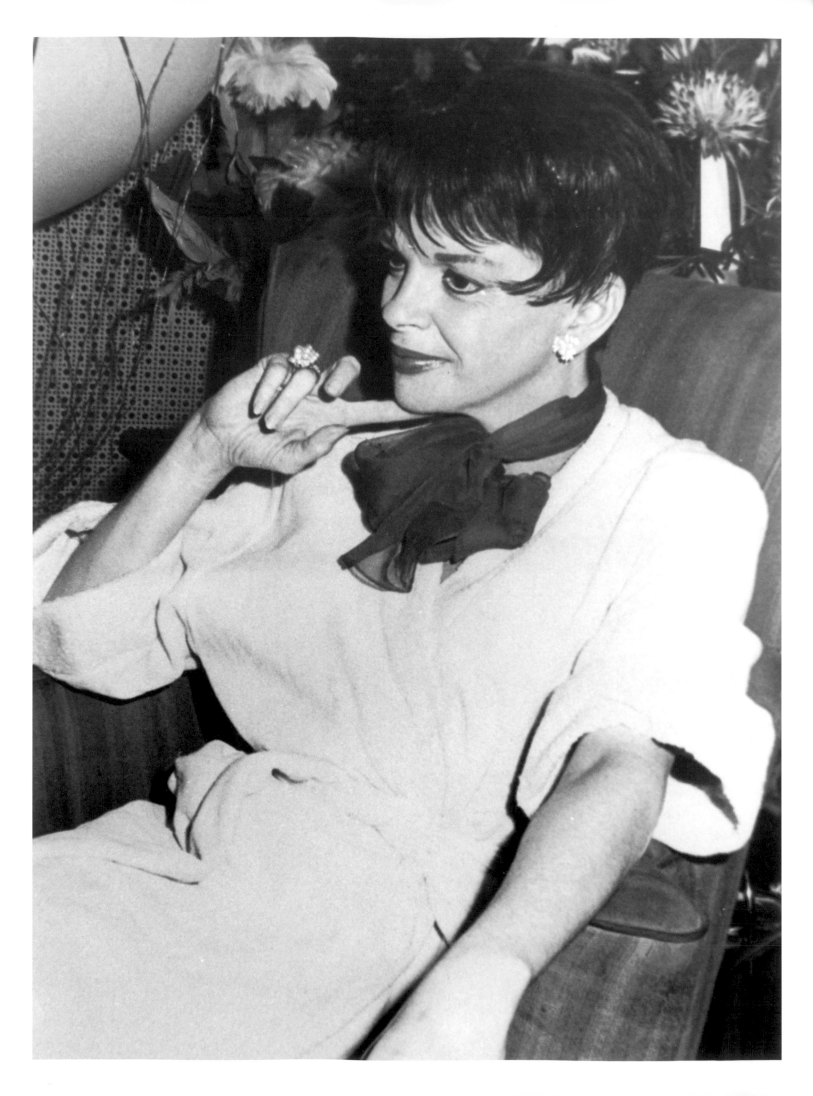

I'd like to explain myself a little. So much of the past that has been written about me has been so completely just authored. Not even correct. I think the nicest thing to say is that I enjoy my work, that I'm a very happy woman, a very healthy woman, and that I look forward to my shows every night and am having a marvelous life. I've had press agents that I've paid to whom I've said, why don't they put that in a magazine? And they've said, no, they're not interested in that. That's not news. You have to do something terrible. Well, I don't believe that you do. I think it might be awfully smashing news for people to find out that I'm a very contented, happy, healthy woman.

—*Judy Garland*

Backstage, "At Home at the Palace," July 1967. In many ways, it was a no-win situation: to attempt a triumphant return to Broadway, to reappear at the scene of such early and major successes, to try to publicly recover from being (yet again) written off, to commit to singing night after night when fully aware that one's voice is a fragile and already overtaxed instrument. Yet, in a consolidation of style and courage, and in the words of Jerry Tallmer in his review in the New York Post: "Judy for the thousand and first time has come all the way back."

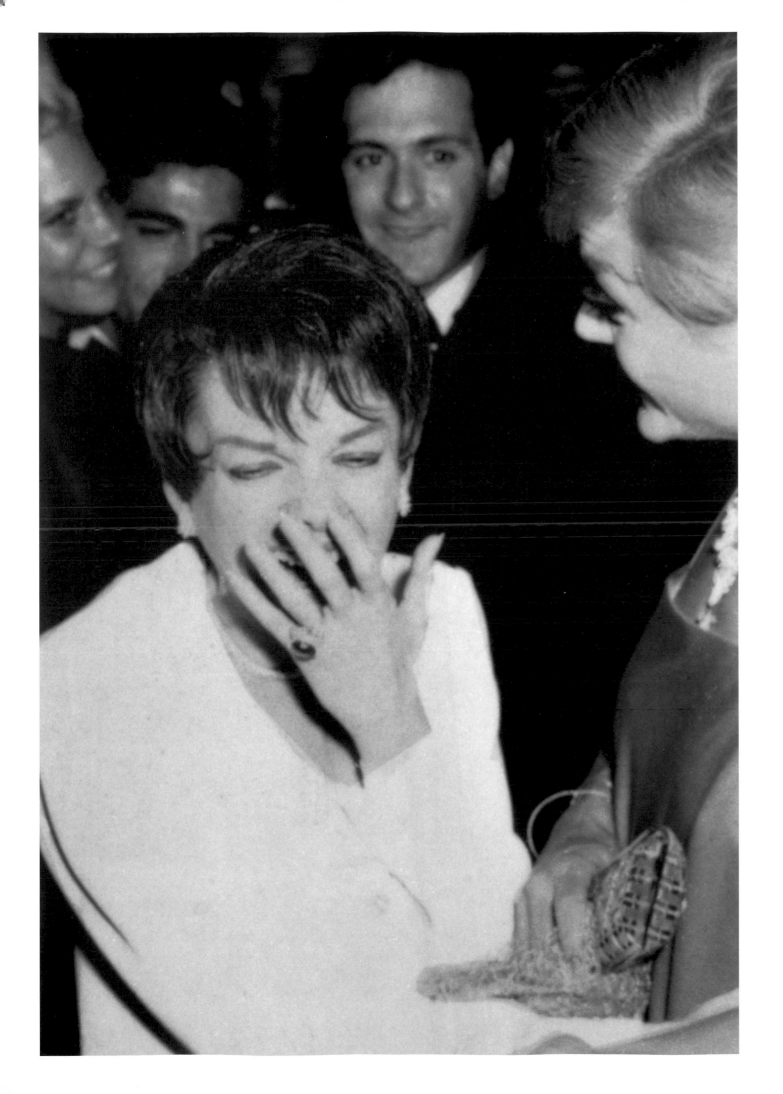

Above: *En route to her opening night party at El Morocco, July 31, 1967. Judy sang every night for four weeks at the Palace—and every night she left the theater through the front of the house, down under the marquee, and out onto Broadway, where hundreds waited to see and cheer and adulate. (A longtime fan remembers that the crowds seldom got out of hand; on the rare occasion when the surge forward was suddenly too much, "All Judy had to do was stop, stand still, smile, and raise her index finger. Instantly, peace would be restored, a path would be cleared, and she would walk slowly to the car, speaking briefly, sometimes shaking hands, giving everyone a chance to say hello. But I'll never forget that all it took for her to control the crush was a smile and her index finger.")*

Left: *Laughing with delight—and Angela Lansbury—at the opening-night party. For all the excitement of Garland's performance triumph, Judy's treasured friend John Carlyle remembers another touching and magical moment of the evening. Bert Lahr and his wife were thrilled by the show and had come along to the party; when the music began at El Morocco, Bert asked Judy to dance, and they joined the other guests on the floor. Suddenly, their fellow dancers realized what they were seeing . . . and as if on cue, everyone else moved off the floor to leave just Dorothy, circling the parquet in the arms of the Cowardly Lion.*

Every night was celebrity night during Garland's Palace engagement. One evening, in a lull between ovations, a voice caroled up to Judy from a front orchestra seat, "You have the most splendid talent." Judy did a take, beamed, and asked permission to introduce the speaker: "Ladies and gentlemen, Miss Joan Crawford." On closing night, Roger Edens flew in as a surprise to Judy, whose thrilled reaction was plainly apparent when she found him in the audience. Also present the final two evenings of the engagement was Liza, just back from appearances abroad. ("How was Australia?" Judy pointedly queried and grinned, "You know I want to hear about that!")

I don't know if I was still in diapers that first time, but my mom brought me up onstage. I must have been about two years old. And from then on, at certain concerts, I would join her out there every now and then. Then, when she did the TV series, we went to the tapings just about every week; we sat right in the front row. And the first time we all really performed together on television would have been the Christmas show at CBS.

But the stage work was the most fun—when we played the music fairs in Camden and Springfield and then went into the Palace and on tour. In the Palace show, I did a drum solo onstage for about three minutes; then I played the bongos while Lorna and my mom sang "Together Wherever We Go." And the three of us did a dance act called "Me and My Shadow" with John Bubbles; Richard Barstow did the choreography for it. First John Bubbles would come on and do the song, make an exit, and when he came back on again doing a second chorus, my mom was right behind him as his shadow. Then they would go off; when the third chorus started, Lorna was behind my mom. The fourth chorus was when I came out, and we all danced together.

—*Joe Luft*

Mother and son on the post-Palace tour, prior to opening the show in Chicago, September 13, 1967. It was Joe and Lorna's last weekend as part of the regular act; they returned to New York four days later to start the school term.

What a beautiful show that night. She had three ramps, in the tradition of Al Jolson: on each side and one straight out, so she communicated with everybody. Yet it was very intimate; I thought it was so intelligent of her to create that.

Shortly thereafter, I was the mystery guest on What's My Line? *And I said to somebody in the control room, "I just saw Judy Garland at the Garden," and he said, "Well, she has a claque." I asked what he meant. He said, "Well, it's a claque. You know . . . just a certain group of people that follow her around." And I said, "Well, it was Madison Square Garden; it was filled up. How much of a claque can there be?!"*

There was a lot of envy; she intimidated people, too, just because she was Judy Garland. Everybody was walking around with big egos at these cocktail parties, and Judy walked in and . . . the egos go right down.

—*Tony Bennett*

Above: *At the new Felt Forum of Madison Square Garden, December 25, 1967. On opening night, she dragooned Tony Bennett out of the audience (he always returned the favor when she attended his shows) and he sang a chorus of "The Christmas Song."*

Right: *At Seton Hall in New Jersey, November 1967.*

A warm, vibrant Judy Garland bewitched an audience of about 4,000 persons at the Garden State Arts Center last night, and before it was over, she had them swarming in the aisles. The young, the middle-aged, and the oldsters left their seats midway through her performance and surged around the footlights as she sang the old Garland favorites to an audience whose craving couldn't be satisfied.

She started singing at 10 P.M. and she didn't stop until it was nearly midnight. At several points during the concert, the crowd gave her a standing ovation. . . . For her premiere night, it was a rousing success, magnificently performed by the Judy Garland who had not in the least lost her magic touch to captivate an audience.

—Joseph Carragher
Newark Star-Ledger, June 26, 1968

At the Garden State Arts Center in New Jersey, June 1968. This engagement was indicative of the dichotomy of Judy's last year. The second and third nights, she was in very poor form. The fifth night, she collapsed on stage. The first and fourth nights, she gave fine performances, singing well and performing with vigor and bazazz.

Judy's last United States concert, John F. Kennedy Stadium, Philadelphia, July 20, 1968. Having completed another stint at Peter Bent Brigham Hospital in Boston, Garland was in fine shape, vocally and otherwise, for this show; she was backed by the Count Basie Orchestra. It was somehow fitting that the performance occur in Philadelphia, as it had been the locale of her first concert as well, at the Robin Hood Dell some twenty-five years earlier. In another happy coincidence, the 1968 show was reviewed by one of the same critics—Samuel L. Singer—who wrote: "A warmly affectionate Judy Garland was her old self at the Philadelphia Music Festival on Saturday night—which means that she held the audience in the palm of her hand from her first entrance. The crowd of nearly 20,000 gave her a standing tribute on her entrance and an ovation at the close of her program. Her voice had that distinctive throb and resonance and she sang with her practiced ease. Only on an occasional high note was there any tightness of tone. It was a love affair from first to last between Judy and her audience."

The only time I worked with her was on The Merv Griffin Show. Merv was on vacation, and she took over the program. She had Margaret Hamilton and Van Johnson and me. And she was extremely nervous; she was not skilled at being the hostess of a talk show.

But she did quite well. And she really, actually tried to interview me; she did a professional job of trying to be Barbara Walters. And even though she was frightened to death, she just brought out the best in me because she was so warm. And she was so human.

What I saw was a real professional, trying to do her best, even when she was out of her league; yet she did a really nice job—we had quite a lot of fun.

—Rex Reed

Judy's last United States television appear-ance, as hostess of The Merv Griffin Show, December 1968. In addition to working with Mort Lindsey—who had the house band on the Griffin program—Garland was surprised on her entrance by a brief reunion with Margaret Hamilton, the eternal Wicked Witch of the West. There was only time for a quick exchange; Hamilton was due at rehearsals for a Broadway musical, Come Summer (starring fellow Ozian Ray Bolger). But as she prepared to depart, she was implored by Judy, "Laugh! Just do that wicked mean laugh!" Maggie threw back her head and cackled at full throttle; it brought down the house.

The morning she maried Mickey, there was a huge crowd on the street, because it was Saturday. And King's Road was at that time the big thing— "swinging London." And the whole of King's Road was there, because word had spread: hundreds of people. And then she arrived and as she came through this huge crowd with Mickey Deans and Johnny Ray, she talked on both sides to everyone who spoke to her; it was an enormously gracious thing.

When she came out after the wedding, they all started to sing "Hey, Jude"—the big Beatles song. She couldn't quite hear what they were singing because of all the chaos; I remember she asked me— because I was standing at the top of the stairs of the registry office. And when I told her, she really loved that: hundreds of people on the King's Road singing "Hey, Jude"... that's quite exciting! So she stood on the steps and gave them all a wave.

—Matthew West

Above: *During her usually triumphant / sometimes controversial five-week engagement at the Talk of the Town in London, Judy also made her last television appearance, once more topping the bill for the Sunday Night at the London Palladium TV series, January 19, 1969. She is seen here after the show, her stage costume billowing in her lap.*

Right: *Three days after their March 15 wedding, Mickey Deans and Judy were off to Stockholm for what would be her final series of concerts.*

Opposite: *On her last tour, with Johnny Ray at the piano. He served as the opening act and joined Judy during the second half of the show for a couple of duets. The duo played in Stockholm, Malmo, and Copenhagen, where, on March 25, Judy gave her last formal performance.*

All I can say is that, even at the very end of her career [despite all the illness and problems], Judy was still the ultimate professional. Out there on the stage, she was magic! Alert and alive, as much a part of the orchestra as she was a part of the audience, she never missed a cue and she never hit an unmusical note. Even at her very last concert, Judy Garland was still quite simply the Greatest. We got on so well that I was really thrilled at the prospect of a long association with Judy. Sadly, it was not to be, but those are three concerts that I will never forget.

—*Tony Osborne,*
Muscial Conductor

*W*e loved our mother very much, and it was a love we shared with millions of people. The only thing that comforts us now is the thought that nothing can destroy that love or the legend she created. To us, that was and always will be a beautiful thing.

—*Liza Minnelli, Lorna Luft, Joseph Luft,*
June 22, 1969

*W*herever she's gone, she'll get in.

—*Earl Wilson,*
Columnist, *New York Post*, June 23, 1969

*S*he was a lady who gave so much and richly both to the vast audience whom she entertained and to the friends around her whom she loved that there was no currency in which to repay her.

—*James Mason,*
In his Eulogy, June 27, 1969

*I*t is now a year to the day that I walked out into the sunshine of a New York street, preceding the yellow-rosed coffin of Judy Garland, leaving behind the voices singing *"The Battle Hymn of the Republic"* in the cool of the chapel and into the most touching event of those tense three days.

For as Judy made her last journey through a city she had been acclaimed in with tumultuous ovations at the Palace and Carnegie Hall, suddenly the thousands of people who lined the streets dropped their voices into silence. And as I looked at the faces peering from windows and lamp-posts at every level, I realized that these were people who had lost a friend. This was a personal loss for them—not simply the enigma of the star, not an explosive talent, not a tragic figure.

But the loss of someone who truly could be called a friend.

—*The Reverend Peter Delaney,*
Judy Garland Memorial Service,
St. Marleybone Parish Church,
London, June 27, 1970

The concluding moments of Judy Garland's funeral service, outside
The Frank E. Campbell Chapel on East 81st Street in New York City, June 27, 1969.

$\mathscr{E}ncore$

"How characteristic, how incredible, how hilarious it is that—six years after her death—Judy Garland is making yet another comeback. How she would have loved it!" So wrote pop culture historian Richard Christiansen upon publication of the first spate of Garland biographies, five of which almost simultaneously hit the stands in 1975. His words reflected both an understanding of Judy's own power of self-perception as well as a wry appreciation for the many legendary "returns" to prominence she made during the last couple of decades of her life. But if his statement was indeed spot-on, it could have actually been coined at least a year earlier and adjusted for the passage of time and reprinted on a semiannual basis ever since.

There is no question that Garland's image and reputation were at very low ebb in the years just prior to her passing. As lifelong admirer Sonny Gallagher pointed out in 1969, the mass public had by then reached a saturation point with Judy: they couldn't bear to hear more about the sad things that were happening to her, to see her reach again and again for a stability she somehow never attained, or to watch her (on some occasions) scramble to perform against overwhelming odds. Unfortunately, there was no way then for people to know or understand the reasons for her struggles—or why she had been left worn and appallingly in debt after more than thirty years of hard work. But even the public's self-distancing was in its own way an indication of the real and genuine gratitude that millions felt for Garland; a radio commentator in June 1969 said that most of the time a mass audience couldn't have cared less whether or not a star was happy. And even at her passing, *Variety* took pleasure in reporting that Judy was someone not pitied but loved.

What has grown out of that love and the thirty-plus years of work is an ongoing victory. As noted earlier, her talent and spirit seem to be rediscovered on a regular basis, and there has been a legitimate Garland "comeback" every few seasons. She is thus not only regarded as a high-water mark of entertainment history but—over and over—as a thrilling matter of the present.

The litany of Garland's triumphs since 1969 can be traced on both artistic and popular levels. The first noteworthy "return" came with the 1974 theatrical release of *That's Entertainment!*, a compilation film that celebrated thirty years of the M-G-M musical. The studio's age-old, self-promotional slogan—"More Stars Than There Are in the Heavens"—was impeccably supported by the performance power intrinsic to this assemblage; amidst it all, Garland came out on top, with only Astaire and Kelly her immediate company. *That's Entertainment, Part 2* (1976) and *That's Entertainment! III* (1994) didn't enjoy the same box office bonanza, but their moments of Judy in action won the greatest attention and response. This was particularly true when the third film showcased a masterful, deluxe Garland routine that had been filmed for (but deleted from) *Easter Parade*. Chuck Walters's staging of Irving Berlin's

"Mister Monotony" offered Judy at her sophisticated, soigné and tongue-in-cheek best.

Meanwhile, after months in the Warner Bros. vaults, archivist Ron Haver managed in 1983 to achieve a restoration of *A Star Is Born*. Although tracking only fragments of the deleted dialogue scenes, he retrieved all three of the Garland musical numbers that had been dropped from the film in the preposterous post-premiere purge. With the virtually complete soundtrack intact and stills to cover moments for which no footage could be found, *Star* sold out New York's Radio City Music Hall at benefit prices and sparked additional jam-packed benefit showings across the country. *That's Entertainment!* provided proof positive of Garland's early glory; the visibility of a nearly intact *Star* did the same for the middle period of her career.

Finally, all the foregoing effort was capped by *Judy Garland: The Concert Years* (1985), an eighty-eight-minute retrospective of Judy's television and stage work assembled as part of the PBS-TV "Great Performances" series. With most of its performance footage drawn from the 1951–67 period, *The Concert Years* offered stunning evidence that Garland provided joy, music, emotional truth, and inspiration to virtually the end of her career. The cumulative impact of the M-G-M, Warners, and PBS product resulted in a healthy reassessment of the Garland legend; when examining her lifelong productivity and the quality thereof, historian James Fisher spoke for many in 1992 when he succinctly observed, "Few popular entertainers have dominated so many areas of entertainment as Garland, and even fewer have been regarded as artists. Her body of work would have to be considered extraordinary by any standards."

Since the mid-1980s, Garland-related events and programming have only increased; the corresponding audience has kept pace as well. There have been widely attended exhibitions of Judy-related memorabilia at the New York Public Library for the Performing Arts at Lincoln Center (1992) and London's Museum of the Moving Image (1993). "Live" celebrations of Garland and her songs packed Carnegie Hall in 1998 and the London Palladium in 1999; equally well received has been the touring presentation *Songs My Mother Taught Me*, in which daughter Lorna Luft uses film clips, stills, and original musical arrangements to sing a heartfelt tribute to her parent's musical legacy.

An even larger-scale indication of the public passion for Garland was exhibited when a four-hour ABC-TV adaptation of Luft's 1998 memoir, *Me and*

Opposite: *Judy was in the first group of "legends" asked to pose for the Blackglama mink campaign in 1968. (The other four were Lauren Bacall, Bette Davis, Melina Mercouri, and Barbra Streisand.) In 1985, Andy Warhol added his own touch to Garland's picture; this is one of a series of varicolored lithographs.*

and actresses of the screen. She ranked eighth among the women and—as on virtually every one of the many other tallies in which she appeared—she was the only star whose career encompassed outstanding success in every media, not just motion pictures. (It's worth noting that as of 2001, four of Judy's films had been selected by the Library of Congress for protection and preservation under the National Film Registry: *The Wizard of Oz*, *Meet Me in St. Louis*, *A Star Is Born*, and *Love Finds Andy Hardy*.) All her feature films have now appeared on videotape and laser disc; they are being slowly restored and issued on DVD, as has been the complete 1963–64 television series.

Musically, much of Garland's recorded work has been assembled from random vaults for compact disc—most notably in a superior MCA box set of her Decca output; a series of exciting Rhino soundtracks of her Metro work; and a bestselling Capitol remastering of the complete Carnegie Hall concert. Her original recording of "Over the Rainbow" and the Carnegie Hall album were inducted into the Grammy Hall of Fame in 1981 and 1998 respectively. Judy herself was posthumously honored by the Grammy Lifetime Achievement Award in 1997.

Finally, the star has also become a vibrant feature of the Internet via a proliferation of websites, a "Judy List," and individual chat exchanges—most of them beautifully assembled and maintained. Additionally, her omnipresence in auctions provides day-to-day proof of the collectible mania for Garland material.

The cornerstone for the all-ages awareness of Judy Garland stems, of course, from the ceaseless popularity of *The Wizard of Oz*. Passion for the film continues to cut across every generation, and celebratory festivals across the United States have flourished since the mid-1980s. Tens of thousands of *Oz* fans are annually drawn to Chittenango, New York (birthplace of original *Oz* author Frank Baum), Aberdeen, South Dakota (one of Baum's later hometowns), Grand Rapids, Minnesota (Garland's birthplace), and Chesterton, Indiana (which draws the largest crowds of any of the venues). The omnipresence of *Oz* on home video ensures its ongoing familiarity, but its unique fame grew first and best from the nearly annual national teleshowings of the film beginning in 1956. Even before Judy died, her appearance in the once-a-year *Oz* telecast was already humorously but accurately acknowledged—along with birthdays and the December holidays—as one of the three most important events of the year for any child. Garland herself was genuinely grateful for and aware of the power of the film and her character, refusing ever to spoof or exploit Dorothy or Dorothy's song. Her sincerity paid off, even retroactively: in 2001, Judy's rendition of "Over the Rainbow" was voted the number one "Song of the Century" in a poll conducted by the National Endowment for the Arts and the Recording Industry Association of America.

The real Judy Garland—as both human being and entertainer—has long since proved capable of (in her own phrase) "rising above" the morass strewn by many of her biographers. The exhilaration and purity of what she offered and left behind is something very few entertainers have been able to touch, let alone sustain. The memories and quotes from those who knew her best and loved her most continue to provide both leavening and perspective to her legend; what is apparent is how much they themselves wish to correct some of the misreported history. All of them acknowledge her share of trouble, unhappiness, and difficulty. But for them and her audience of millions, Judy Garland was and unwaveringly remains much more a person they deeply cherish and an entertainer whom they joyously venerate.

My Shadows, drew extraordinary advance interest, astronomical ratings, and ultimately garnered a dozen major awards. *Life with Judy Garland* (2001) was critically praised on every level but especially for the manner in which it "brought humanity back to a legend." Four years earlier, a two-hour Garland documentary had been presented with equal success as the anniversary highlight of the Arts and Entertainment cable channel "Biography" series; *Judy/Beyond the Rainbow* won the second-largest audience in that program's ten-year history as well as the 1997 Emmy Award for "outstanding informational series."

Naturally, the new millennium brought scores of reflective listings attendant to twentieth-century achievement. Garland's name turned up again and again, most notably in the American Film Institute poll to determine the finest actors

It's difficult to think of anyone more multitalented. Because she could move. She could dance. She could sing. She could act. She was larger than life.

She was a star—a real star—and, I think, the most important, talented star I've worked with. I've worked with a lot of actors, and I've done a lot of films. But nobody comes close to her.

—*Norman Jewison*

I learned something from watching Judy Garland. She knew the secret: a performer is a mirror. And as much as you feed the audience, that's how much you're going to get back. And when she came out on that stage, wherever it was, she loved the audience so much . . . and that's how much intensity came back to her.

And that's where I learned that a performer is nothing but a reflection of the audience. You give to the audience, and that's what an audience will give back. Judy did that better than anyone else.

—*Tony Bennett*

There was a lot of singing around my house; I come from a long line of singers. And I can recall hearing Judy from about the age of five, I guess. And before I understood what she was singing about, I was just attracted to quality of sound—the timbre of somebody's voice . . . feeling moved or relaxed when you listened to somebody. And those are the qualities I recall hearing when I would listen to her. Later on, I realized it was her own inner life that she was allowing us to share. . . .

And when you heard a concert of hers that went on for two hours. . . . That's physical work. It's emotional, it takes a lot of endurance and memorization, and it takes years to just get relaxed enough . . . to do it with such control—and take from the audience what she needed and take from the orchestra what she needed. And she gave it back. Fiftyfold. We were all lucky to be in the neighborhood at the time.

—*Melissa Manchester*

Who was like her? Who made the impression she made? Name the top ten, the top five—you couldn't leave out Judy Garland. Talk about The Wizard of Oz; talk about A Star Is Born. There hasn't been anyone like her in my estimation; you can't compare her to anybody. It's just such a shame that she's not here at this age—nine months older than me—to be able to enjoy looking back on what she accomplished and what she did.

—*Jackie Cooper*

She was generous in spirit. She was warm . . . a wonderful human being doing her very best, anytime she was called on to perform. She didn't have the talent to be unpleasant; everything she did was true—she was a genuine, genuine performer, and that's the best compliment you could pay anybody.

There was a naturalness: "This is her." She wasn't imitating her; she was her. No matter what she did, [it] was true. And when she sang a song, every song came true. That's why she was so winning. Everything that I'd seen when she was twelve years old stayed with her through her whole career. And the audiences were hysterical with pleasure. Always. It was jubilant.

—*Burton Lane*

It would be very difficult to imitate her. And anybody who tried to imitate her is unfortunate. She set a standard for this intensity of participation in what she was doing that is a hard one to live up to. There aren't too many popular performers who do concerts the way she did that had the kind of intensity and joy and freshness and spontaneity that she brought to them, no matter how tired or bored she might have been until she got up onstage.

I'd put her way up high in the annals of American popular entertainment. For the reasons I mention above. The extraordinary voice. The way with a song to make it a complete dramatic experience. The improvisatory quality. The acting ability. The first-time quality of everything. The joy of it.

I think anybody who is involved in the arts of communication or has any sensitivity at all—anybody who experienced her—was bound to have been profoundly affected by what she did. The people I've talked to whose opinions I respect and who were able to objectively examine what she brought to [her] performances (almost to a person) are fulsome in their praise.

On a scale of one to ten, I'd give her a ten-plus. Because in everything she did from the time she started as a little schoolgirl type to A Star Is Born, she runs the whole gamut: comedy, dancing, singing, and acting. There wasn't anything she couldn't do.

—*Edward Albee*

In Chicago, March 1938.

She's every writer's dream of the perfect musical comedy heroine. Every book writer and every songwriter. I still think of Judy when I write a song, and she's been gone a long time. But she's still here!

The heart and soul of Judy, to me, was the way she was ready always to forgive, always to look for the best in people, always to trust people—which, on occasion, was her downfall, trusting the wrong people. But she was a pure, beautiful treasure that I'll remember and dream about as long as I live.

Mickey Rooney made a statement in an interview back in 1994 or so. He said, "Judy is probably the greatest talent of this century and maybe the next." And I don't think it's hyperbole. I think she is. She did everything better than anybody else.

—*Hugh Martin*

Judy was to me the great talent of the twentieth century. I was fortunate enough to work with many people; I worked with both Fred Astaire and Gene Kelly. Judy had the greatest talent of anyone I ever worked with: natural talent. But not only the great talent—a wonderful person. Loving. A lot of laughter. And she loved everyone, reached out to everyone. . . .

—*Dorothy Tuttle Nitch*

She's certainly at the top of the list for me. And in watching her and working with her and getting to know her and see her talents, I think she could do it again today. I don't think the public can ever forget Judy Garland . . . and it was the greatest experience I could have had in my career as a dancer to have worked with her. I just don't know the words to describe what an honor it was. And I have that to remember the rest of my life.

—*Dorothy Gilmore Raye*

Judy was a part of every life in America, really. . . . And the important thing to remember now is that she was here, she was adored—and we were lucky enough to have her.

—*Marcella Rabwin*

She was honest. Honest. There was nothing phony about her. If she was having a breakdown, she made sure you had a breakdown, too, right along with her. If she was happy, there was no way you were not going to feel her happiness.

The camera cannot lie. It can telegraph completely fabricated emotions, but it cannot lie when the honesty is already there. With Judy, you never saw a dishonest moment. Everything she did was so real that you don't believe you're watching an actress; you knew that you were seeing something that went beyond acting, greater than acting. It was reality.

And she could take one song and give you a two-hour M-G-M movie between the first and last bars. And I've never seen anyone else do that. And then, of course, there was that incredible instrument; I've never heard a voice like that, either. In the world of popular music, she was what Joan Sutherland is to opera; she was what Joe DiMaggio was to baseball.

—*Rex Reed*

Opposite: *The laughter of Judy Garland remains among her best-remembered personal hallmarks; she seems to have been caught in the act—spontaneously—in this 1941 rotogravure portrait.*

Below: *A peaceful moment on location for* A Child Is Waiting *in spring 1962.*

I'd rank her certainly in the top five, top three. She could even be ranked number one. I think of her with great empathy, with great sympathy, and with great, tremendous admiration for her wonderful talent. She's special; there's nobody I can think of in the history of the entertainment business that is anything close to her in that regard.

—*Alan Livingston*

She was a great reader. Very intelligent, brilliant; she knew all about everything—a great sort of knowledge of things that you wouldn't expect her to have. You'd see (or perhaps you'd be surprised to see) The Bible over there on the shelf.

And she's only the greatest: song, dance, acting—everything she touched. Nobody's been anywhere near her. I've seen the big stars, but I've never been more excited than sitting in an audience watching a concert by Judy.

I just thought she was the hottest little firecracker of a woman. She lived forty-seven years and spent forty-five of them on stage being in show business. She never wasted one minute of her life. Some people we all know are eighty years old and still lurching around, trying to put on some show—and never come near the energy and talent she had. Because she lived every day and used it and worked at it—and she was amazing.

—*Matthew West*

313

I love a lot of entertainers: I can put on a Fred Astaire record, and it brings back wonderful visual things of this terrific dancer and a dear man. And Ethel Merman. But Judy? Number one. I never get tired of hearing her. Never. She's fresh all the time; she's outlasted all of them.

— *Leonard Gershe*

I happened to love Judy. Dearly. A platonic love, of course. But I loved her for her and for her talent. You have to rank Judy way, way up there amongst the gods and goddesses. She had a talent that transcended anything else. No one else came close to her . . . because she was so vulnerable.

— *Robert Goulet*

No one in the world ever sang with the warmth and the beauty and the quality that she had. She'd look at you with those beautiful eyes of hers, and she'd sing . . . and she'd break your heart, because she meant it.

I remember her laugh. I remember her warmth. I remember her singing. I remember her crazy sense of humor, and then I stop and think: what a great performer. What a great artist.

— *Margaret Whiting*

I rate her number one as an actress. I admired Lunt and Fontanne, who could keep talking onstage and what they were saying was completely different. But they blended into each other, and you'd still be able to hear both of them and understand what was going on. In Summer Stock, I overlapped Judy a couple times to see what would happen. And she would come in and top it! She was a thinking actress; everything was subtle and real and honest. No one in this world that I know of—I've never heard anybody tell me that they did not like Judy. Because love came out of this young lady. It captured me. And I'm sure it captures everybody else. It was her eyes, her thinking, her warmth. It was exuberant, it was just wonderful.

She was the best. Number One Entertainer of All Time. Can we go higher?

— *Eddie Bracken*

I think she's the greatest entertainer of the twentieth century. Number one. Everybody talks about Al Jolson; I don't know Al Jolson, but I can't conceive of anybody being better than Judy. There's not too many people that can hold an audience for two hours, just by themselves. She danced, she moved, she sang, she acted. I just feel there's nothing, anything, anywhere near her.

— *Mort Lindsey*

Her whole life was a series of ups and downs: a roller-coaster life. I don't see how she survived it for as long as she did. She was a woman of enormous strength. And she used to say that about herself: "I'm very strong!"

— *Shana Alexander*

Judy was so fragile. Some people thought she was really a tough lady and could [handle] it. She wasn't. She was very soft. And I have to use the word "fragile"—almost afraid she would break. And she broke many times.

But I think she was the most loyal person and the greatest entertainer in the world. And the first thing you think of is the great warmth of Judy, the great, giving, little person that she was. Her heart was bigger than all of her put together.

She was just one great big heart.

— *June Allyson*

There was nothing tragic about coming to watch her. There was great elation and joy and stomping and flowers thrown at her—and she'd only been out there two minutes! And you can't be as good as [she was] without being smart and bright. She knew a lot. She read newspapers, books; she had many literary friends. Of course, everybody flocked to be in Judy's presence. But she was knowing and a very bright, very bright woman.

I've been in show business more than fifty-five years. And I've been watching show business from the age of five when my father took me to see my first movies. Some people always say Al Jolson: the world's greatest entertainer. I was privileged to see Al Jolson. He would have had to open the show for Judy Garland.

Let me put it a nicer way. Caruso would never follow Jolson at any benefit show. On a Sunday night at the Winter Garden, Enrico Caruso would come from the Met and say, "I go on in front of Jolson. Not after Jolson."

Judy could go on after Jolson.

And today, when anyone says, "Judy Garland," to me, it's as if it was a knee-jerk reaction or a Rorschach test. My favorite line in Guys and Dolls was when a cop walks into the mission and looks at Sister Sarah and says to her, "Were these men here all day?"—because he's trying to get them for shooting craps. And prim Sister Sarah says, "I've never seen these gentlemen before, and they've been here all afternoon." And Big Jule in the back says, "That's a right broad."

Judy was a good, solid, right broad.

Dynamite lady.

— *Alan King*

Opposite: *In London at the Dominion Theatre, 1957. When Carnegie Hall celebrated the music of Judy Garland with two concerts in 1998, Broadway's Jerry Herman was one of the few people asked to speak or perform on both evenings. His musical scores include (among others) Hello, Dolly!, Mame, La Cage Aux Folles, Mack and Mabel, Dear World, and Mrs. Santa Claus; Jerry Herman is the only American composer-lyricist in history to have had three shows play more than fifteen hundred performances each on Broadway. At Carnegie Hall, he announced, "I have a confession to make. All these years writing musicals, whenever I had a real hit-'em-in-the-gut show tune to write, I would picture it in the voice of Judy Garland. And invariably the work that came out of me was much more exciting, just because of this little trick that I used. So I've come here tonight, not only to honor the greatest entertainer of the century, but to thank Judy for all the years that she has been my secret muse." Then Herman went to the piano and played and sang his own version of the Howard Dietz / Arthur Schwartz standard "That's Entertainment." His lyric, reprinted in full on the facing page, speaks for millions.*

A note that is really a note
Makes the song that the songwriter wrote
Seem sublime when it comes from the throat
Of Judy Garland.

And how we loved watching her grow
When she had Mickey Rooney in tow,
And she'd say, "We could put on a show!"
That's Judy Garland.

She sang on a trolley and danced with Astaire.
And Judy and Gene made a helluva pair.
But then she topped it, I swear,
When she played a girl named Esther
Who turned into Vicki Lester.

And then there's a night I recall
When she proved she was queen of them all,
And the roof shook at Carnegie Hall.
And nobody will
Compare to the thrill
Of Judy Garland.

For years, there's a debt that I've owed
To the girl from the Yellow Brick Road
Who could make my emotions explode.
So, thanks to the gods above
For letting me fall in love
With Judy Garland.

—Jerry Herman

End Credits

PHOTO CREDITS

Judy Garland fans and collectors are legion and often extraordinarily selfless in their desire to contribute and cooperate; such generosity and dedication is especially apparent in both the illustrations and information presented herein. When a book is composed of as many individual elements as is this one, the credit for any quality it might possess belongs to a multitude of people:

Fred McFadden's dedication to archiving the Garland career is second to none; that passion is equaled by his capacity to care and share, and much of any beauty this volume may possess is due to his generosity.

Bill Chapman spent similar decades amassing an extraordinary collection; this has now passed into other hands. However, Bill's efforts in gathering and preserving so much remarkable history warrant specific recognition here.

Max Preeo has been a friend for forty years, and his early publication, *The Garland News*, remains the best United States-based reference guide for several years of Judy's career. As a result, his files contain much unique material.

Steve Sanders wrote one of the few nonpareil Garland books to date; *Rainbow's End* (William Morrow and Company, Inc., 1990) deals with the corporate machinations that helped sink her television series. But our association pre-dates that volume, as does his enthusiasm attendant to any projects that have been undertaken on Judy's behalf. His interview transcripts, photographs, and counsel remain (as always) invaluable.

Christian Matzanke has shared a Garland and personal bond since 1967, and his belief, support, and generosity have never wavered. Matthew Ryan is a comparatively new friend, but he offered immediate encouragement and contribution when he learned this book was in the offing. Further valued information, research, and/or illustrations were shared by: Maggie Adams, Capitol Records, Denis de Wulf, William Patrick Dunne, Kim Lundgreen, and Laura Pilot.

No one anywhere associated with the film industry works with more diligence and care than the indefatigable Roger Mayer or the incomparable George Feltenstein, both of the Turner Entertainment Company. There is no compromising their dedication to the standards of excellence associated with the best of Hollywood, and their assistance has been adroit and appreciated. It is through the courtesy of the Turner Entertainment Co. that original Metro-Goldwyn-Mayer material appears here: ad art, publicity pictures, stills, and production materials.

Additional acknowledgment is due to: Bernie Abramson/MPTV.net: page 269; Nancy Barr: pages 285, 287 (both), 292 (left), 295 (right); The Willard Carroll Collection: page 65; Frank DeGregorio: page 298; Ernst Haas/Getty Images: page 13; Hulton Archive/Getty Images: page 202 (left); MPTV.net: page 73 (both); Nicholas Muray/George Eastman House/Getty Images: page 130 (right); John Perri, page 25; Gabi Rona/MPTV.net: page 206; Bob Willoughby/MPTV.net: pages 8, 246; and Malcolm Woolfson, page 233 (left). *Ads: Blackglama (Judy Garland), 1985* (page 308) © 2003 Andy Warhol Foundation for the Visual Arts / Artists Rights Society (ARS), New York / © 2003 Ronald Feldman Fine Arts, New York. BLACKGLAMA® and WHAT BECOMES A LEGEND MOST® with its pictorial representation are trademarked and copyrighted by the Great Lakes Mink Association.

Supplementary photography was handled with the expertise, good will, and mastery of Jellybean Photographics & Imaging in New York (Steve Regina, Geri Bauer and their compatriots George Hernandez, Ron Koenig, Louie Laureano, Dennis Lyn, Felix Moreau, Eileen Munson, and Linda Tutauer) and Richard Glenn in Los Angeles.

Opposite: On the set of The Judy Garland Show *television series, January 1964.*

SELECTED BIBLIOGRAPHY

The vast majority of anecdotes that accompany this text have been drawn from interviews conducted by the author. Additional material has been excerpted from contemporary media sources, including newspapers, magazines, radio, television, and from the following:

Books:

Gruen, John. *Close-Up*. New York: The Viking Press, 1968.

Haley, Jack (edited by Mitchell Cohen). *Heart of The Tin Man*. Los Angeles: R. J.Communications, 2000.

Hepburn, Katharine. *Me*. New York: Alfred A. Knopf, 1991.

Hope, Bob (and Bob Thomas). *The Road to Hollywood*. Garden City, NY: Doubleday & Company, Inc., 1977.

Kobal, John. *Gotta Sing, Gotta Dance*. London: Spring Books, 1983.

Kramer, Stanley (with Thomas M. Coffey). *A Mad, Mad, Mad, Mad World*. New York: Harcourt Brace & Company, 1997.

Meyer, John. *Heartbreaker*. Garden City, NY: Doubleday & Company, Inc., 1983.

Murphy, George (with Victor Lasky). *Say . . . Didn't You Used to Be George Murphy?* New York: Bartholomew House, Ltd., 1970.

Rooney, Mickey Rooney. *Life Is Too Short*. New York: Villard Books, 1991.

St. Johns, Adela Rogers. *Some Are Born Great*. Garden City, NY: Doubleday & Company, Inc., 1974.

Steen, Mike. *Hollywood Speaks*. New York: G. P. Putnam's Sons, 1974.

Periodicals:

Rainbow Review (1963 to the present), *The Garland News* (1964–1968), and *The Garland Gazette* (1955–1966)

Web Sites:

Judy Garland Database (www.zianet.com/jjohnson/)

Judy Garland Live! (http://users.deltacomm.com/rainbowz/hotjudynews.html)

Lorna Luft Online (www.lornaluftonline.com)

For further information about the Judy Garland Club, please write Ronnie Smith, 39 Boscombe Road, Worcester Park, Surrey KT4 8PJ, United Kingdom; or visit their Web site at www.judygarlandclub.org.

Acknowledgements

I'd first like to extend happy gratitude to the many Garland fan/friends whose company, memories, and/or work on Judy's behalf have warmed and informed my life—and this project: Woolsey Ackerman, Marcus Bagshaw and Craig Johnson, Kenny Berube, Roger Blunck, John Carlyle, Roger Cogar, Dana Correll Dial, Al DiOrio, Thomas Duncan, Robert Finkelstein and The Judy Garland Heirs Trust, John Michael Flate, Neva Foley, Joe Fonseca, Bill Franklin, Angie Fucci, Peter Gannaway, Brian Glanville, John Gordon, Scott Horgan, Gary Horrocks, Mike Isaacson, Mitchell Ivers, Joseph Janangelo, Steve Jarrett, Jim Johnson, Timm Johnson, Robert Kerr, Michael Killinger, Anthony and Ruth Landini, David Layton, Kathryn Leach, Sue LeBeau and The Parrys of Pasadena, Richard Leslie, Peter Levy, Pat Losiewicz, Stephen Lynch, Peter Mac, Sara Maraffino and Kevin Willis, Hugh Martin, Bert May, Gary Moon, Stephen Noonan and John Rowe, Ron O'Brien, Amanda Osborne, Les Perkins, Gwen Potter, Gonzalo Rodriguez, Shane Rosamonda and Rene Reyes, Jill Santoriello, Ken Sephton, Michael Siewert, Lorna Smith, Ronnie J. Smith, James H. Spearo, Ian Stahlhut, Zeke Steffens, Charlotte Stevenson, Jonathan Summers, Anne Suter, Eric Tasker, Judy Thompson, David Torresen, Charles Triplett, Bobby Waters, Jerry Waters, Norman Webster, and Pam Wulk. (And a quieter but no less heartfelt tribute to those fans who have now—in Judy's words—"joined the choir" but whose preservation of materials regarding her life and times during their own lives continues to enrich and enlighten: Richard Connolly, Bobby Cook, Sonny Gallagher, Mark Harris, Don Koll, Wayne Martin, Pat McMath, James Squires, and Betty Welch.)

My thanks as well to many professional cohorts from over the years, with whom Garland toil has manifested not only fine product but ongoing pleasure and laughter: Joan Kramer and David Heeley, Allan Fisch, David Engel, Bradley Flanagan, Peter Jones, Andy Tilles, Genevieve Halili, Larry Blank, Ken and Mitzie Welch, Richard Allan Ackerman, Dona Granata, Lynda Sheldon, Rick Amon, and especially Marilee Bradford.

For their friendship, support, and extended personal and professional kindness, I thank: Russell Adams and Kurt Gardner, Dr. Daniel Brook, John Burke, Paul Brownstein, Barry Alden Clark, Dennis Cleveland, George Dalzell, Eric Decker, Jim Deliman and Kenn Gaither, Sean Dickson, Amy Dickson-Tong, Mitch Douglas, Barbara and Robert Evans and Family, Michael Feinstein, Karl Greengrove, Elaine and Fred Harrison, Greg Henry and Bill Stewart, Marc Hulett, Jon Jankowsky, Jim Jensen, Richard Jordan and Billy Barnes, Sean Kelley, Daniel Kinske, David Kitto, Steve Kmetko, Jim Kowal, Barry Manilow, Patrick McCarty, Tom O'Neil, Robert Osborne, The Reverend David Peters, David Rebella and Jim Downs, Ned Price, Omar Prince, David Rambo and Ted Heyck, Josh Reynolds, Mitchell Rose, Dr. Ira Rubenstein, Dr. John Schaefer, Carla Sellers, Mark Sendroff, Daniel Shenman, Robert Sixsmith, Richard Skipper and Dan Sherman, Anthony B. Sloman, Donald F. Smith, Josh Smith, Seth Stuhl, Dr. Justin Sturge, Ryan Sucher, Ben Wetchler, Walter Willison, and Eric Zollinger.

It was the unfailing kindness of Donald Stannard that brought about a renewed association for me with Marc Rosen, which in turn led to the agency representation and extended friendship of Parker Ladd. All professional arrangements attendant to this project were executed with his customary sheen and class.

At Bulfinch Press, there are many who deserve commendation. Publisher Jill Cohen is first among these, for her professional and personal glow and sincerity. I also thank Adrienne Moucheraud, Matthew Ballast, Cassandra Reynolds, Daniel Krugman, and, paramount among them all, our editor, Karyn Gerhard, whose belief in this project withstood delays and madness and, in turn, never failed to send forth the all-important waves of encouragement, faith, and joy.

For special, ongoing, and essential counsel (both journalistic and emotional) I thank Richard Coombs, Frank DeGregorio, Scott Roberts, Haydn Slomack, Rick Skye, John Walther, The Reverend Raymond Wood, and—especially and always—Brent Phillips and Patty Fricke.

Singular and special gratitude go to the late Christopher O'Brien, with both ongoing and retroactive love and recognition; to my mother, Dorothy Fricke, who will (I hope) love this book; to my father, Walter Fricke, who would have loved it; to Jerry Herman for the honor and delight inherent in presenting his heartfelt declaration-in-lyric, and to his mainstay Sheila Mack for the ebullient enthusiasm that paved the way for Jerry's participation; to Lorna Luft for her time, trust, and friendship over many years and for her willingness to support and participate in this project; to her husband Colin Freeman for both his music and his excellent, bemused-by-it-all camaraderie; and to her children, Jesse and Vanessa, in the hopes that they will find some measure of their grandmother's magic in these pages.

Finally, my appreciation and affection go to Ranse Ransone, who championed, cosseted, commandeered, and never compromised in his contributions to the dreams and plans for these pages. His ability and eye, his sensitivity and knowledge, and his insistence on quality made immeasurable contribution to any of the worth, glory, and excitement they might possess.

—John Fricke

My own involvement in this project would never have come about without the able assistance of many extraordinary people. Incalculable thanks to James Stirling and Dorothy Pietrewicz, whose unsurpassed skill and unwavering dedication kept me (almost) on deadline and (nearly) sane. I never could have done it without them. Thanks, as well, to Karyn Gerhard, Pamela Schechter, Alyn Evans, and Denise LaCongo at Bulfinch Press for their unflappable patience and professionalism in making it all come together; to Glenn Completa for the midnight-hour assist; to Steve Regina and the Jellybean crew for the beautiful work; and—for the wonderful images—to Lisa Dubisz and company at The Motion Picture & Television Photo Archive (MPTV.net), to Timothy McCarthy at Art Resource, to Laura Muggeo at Ronald Feldman Fine Arts, to Rona Richter at Artists Rights Society, and to Valerie Zars and Nick Webb at Getty Images.

A tip of the hat to my mentors and colleagues for their personal and professional guidance through the years—particularly, Dorothy Barnett, Fabien Baron, Kitty Sue Booze, Dot Carson, Helen Coffee, Audrey Cusson, Alison Donalty, Leslie Gallagher, Daisy Kline, Harriet Little, Deborah Morse, Katie Prown, Annie Ransone, Joan Rosen, Betty Rodgers, Lucille Schneider, Nancy Schoenberger, Carlos Spellman, Lauren Stein, Liz Tilberis, and Erik White.

My deepest appreciation and love to my sprawling Southern family and to the many friends who might as well be family—but especially, to Patrick Price, for getting me here; to Richard Brooks, Craig Burke, Jason Imfeld, and Carter Vonasek, for making it worth it; to Johnathan Cedano, for understanding; and to Ken Salby, for always.

For their unwavering love, support, and encouragement in this and every endeavor, my eternal gratitude to: my parents, Babe and Barbara Ransone—I couldn't have been blessed with any greater gift than the two of you; to my sister and sister-in-law, Cindy Thomas and Janis Keim—whose devotion and love (personal and otherwise) continue to teach me so very much; and to my grandparents, Murphy and Beatrice Thomas—who first nurtured my ever-growing imagination.

Finally, my heart to the two extraordinary women who've inspired my contributions to these pages: Judy Garland, whom I hope would be pleased; and Margaret Ransone Hall, my cherished "favorite aunt," who started me down my own yellow brick road so many years ago.

—Ranse Ransone

In Los Angeles, circa 1940.

Index

Following page: *Onstage at the London Palladium during the filming of* I Could Go On Singing, *May 1962. Mort Lindsey smiles from the orchestra pit.*